WHY IS THE TEACHER'S BUTT SO BIG?

PLUS **111** OTHER MYSTERIES OF PUBLIC EDUCATION

WHY IS THE TEACHER'S BUTT SO BIG?

PLUS **111** OTHER MYSTERIES OF PUBLIC EDUCATION

Debra Craig

A.T. Publishing • New York

Craig, Debra
Why Is the Teacher's Butt So Big? Plus 111 Other Mysteries of Public Education.

ISBN 0-9740534-1-4
Library of Congress Control Number 2005929441

Requests for interviews or permissions should be addressed to Debra Craig. Email: Debracraig@hotmail.com

Editing: Nina Bouska and Mark Bredt
Interior Design: Fiona Raven
Cover Design: Cathi Stevenson, Book Covers Express
Photography: Joe Lyman, Glamour Shots

First printing September 2005
Manufactured in the United States of America

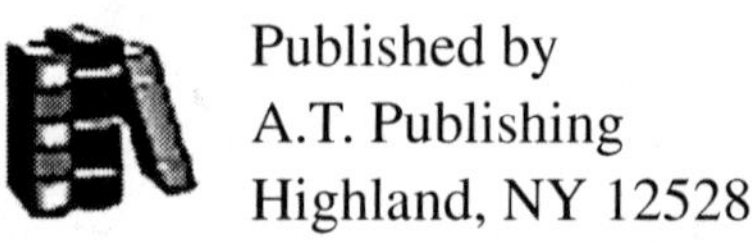

Published by
A.T. Publishing
Highland, NY 12528

*To my husband, Gary,
who kept encouraging me to write.*

*To my children, Jenna and Matthew,
who stayed home for many vacation breaks
while I wrote the book;
and to my stepson Jonathan,
whose support was always there
even though he lived many miles away.*

*To Tony, who came into my life
at just the right time
and for just the right reason.*

Acknowledgments

There are many people to give thanks to who either inspired me or helped me in the process of writing and eventually getting this book published.

In the inspiration department, this book never would have happened if it were not for my principal at Hendrick Ranch Elementary School, Robert Gordon. He had the insight (or was it desperation) to suggest that I teach fifth grade. I don't know how he did it, but he did the impossible and convinced me to leave the comfort zone of teaching kindergarten. If it were not for his salesmanship skills, I never would have known about another side of teaching that includes things like homework and test scores. Then I never would have been so perplexed about why we do the things we do in education and been so motivated to write this book.

Of course, I still might be singing kindergarten songs if I had ignored my urge to attend church one Sunday and missed the sermon on "Leaving Your Comfort Zone." I thank Pastor Bill Martin, of Palm Canyon Community Church, in Moreno Valley, CA, whose inspirational words that morning convinced me that, yes, "God does have better things in store for me if I just take a chance."

I also thank Debra Alexander, a fellow fifth grade teacher, for reminding me to dream big.

There are even more people to thank when it came to actually turning my writing into a published book. My dear publisher, Anthony Prizzia, was there from Day One. He was my teacher, friend, and often voice of reason when I needed help in making decisions about my book.

I was also fortunate to have found a talented production crew who transformed my manuscript into a book I am proud to show off. I give many thanks to Nina Bouska, who had the strength and courage to edit my book twice. Cathi Stevenson was the talented artist who was able to turn my very wordy title into an inspired and colorful cover. Fiona Raven was a creative genius who actually turned a "blossoming" manuscript into pages of easily readable text. I thank all of them for their hard work and for enduring my long emails.

Also deserving thanks is my photographer, Joe Lyman, at Glamour Shots. His photographs captured a me I had never seen before, one that looked good in pictures. Of course, part of the credit also goes to Dorothy Stoll, at Glamour Shots, who did my makeup and hair for the shoot. I also want to thank Maryanne Altieri for a great hairstyle which made me look and feel ten years younger.

I am also very grateful to the publication "The California Educator," which gave me permission to use information and quotes from its September 2004 issue.

I also want to thank the editorial department at the Riverside Press-Enterprise who gave me a forum to air my views on being a school teacher prior to embarking on this career as an author.

In conclusion, what would a book about education be without thanking all of the many teachers who work and thrive as public school teachers all across America? Finally, I am grateful to all of the parents who, despite the negativity, still have enough faith to send their children to public schools.

Contents

Contents

Students & Parents 99

Kindergarten: Has California, and all states, learned everything they need to know about kindergarten?   157

Miscellaneous Mysteries   165

No Child Left Behind Act, No Child Left Untested   185

TIME: It's all about time   215

Contents

The Educational "Bill of Rights": Helping your child, Helping our public schools   223

Are our public schools really that bad?: How would I fix the schools?   235

Could I be wrong? Could it really be "all about the teachers"?   243

Introduction:

Confessions from a teacher who "left behind" students

> What nobler employment,
> or more valuable to the state,
> than that of the man who instructs
> the rising generation?

Cicero, a famous orator, philosopher, and politician during the fall of the Roman Empire, spoke these most famous words between the years 106–43 B.C. Isn't it amazing how these words ring true even today in the 21st century, thousands of years later? Is there a more noble profession or one more valuable to the state than that of being a teacher?

I think not. And I should know because I am that noble person who is valuable to the state: I am a teacher. I'm not just a school teacher, but a *public school* teacher. By most teaching standards, I am really still just a "babe in the woods" when it comes to teaching since I have only been one for a mere seven years. The first five years I was a kindergarten teacher and for the past two years I have been teaching fifth grade in Moreno Valley, California, a community 60 miles east of Los Angeles.

For the record, I am not a teacher who inspired her inner-city low-achieving high school students to do so well on an Advance Placement test that the administrators thought they had all cheated on it. Nor am I teacher who was a former Marine sergeant who was able to control an uncontrollable group of hoodlums in a high-risk neighborhood. Unfortunately, I'm afraid my story is one that probably no one would want to make a movie of.

I am just a teacher. A regular elementary school teacher in the trenches, who tries very hard to get her students to learn. The school I work at is a nice, quiet school. It is also a "Title I" school, or a low socio-economic school. At least 75 percent of our students have qualified for the reduced or free lunch program. Sixty percent of our students are Hispanic, 30 percent are African-American, and 10 percent are Caucasian or some other ethnicity. Every student, 100 percent, is in need of a great education. That's where I come in. I'm a cop. I mean, I'm a teacher and my job is to make certain that no child is left behind.

Are teachers respected?

Results from a 2005 Harris Poll found that teachers ranked behind only scientists and doctors as being the most respected professions. Actually, teachers are tied for third place with firefighters as the professions "with the greatest prestige." Over a 27-year period, the Harris Poll also showed that "those who see teachers as having 'very great' prestige has risen 19 points from 29 percent to 48 percent."

As a teacher, I was very surprised by this. I get the impression that today most people think public schools are in need of help. Private schools are thriving and home schooling has become a very popular alternative to public schools. I've heard comments like, "I would never send my child to a public school." (And some of those comments were from public school teachers.)

In researching this book, I went to the internet to see what else I could find about teachers being "respected." I came across a newspaper column written by Bill Maxwell of the *St. Petersburg Times*, in St. Petersburg, Florida. In August 2002, he wrote a column stating, among other things, "Teachers, especially those in Florida, which has one of the nation's fastest-growing school populations, deserve higher salaries." He couldn't believe the "avalanche of angry—no, hostile—mail arguing that teachers deserved their low salaries because they are part-time workers and because they have failed their communities." His colleagues were also surprised at the negative reaction.

Mr. Maxwell wondered why teachers have gone from "being heroes to being pariahs." His theory was that it is the fault of "powerful politicians, including several governors, who have an anti-public school agenda." He felt our government officials were portraying public schools and teachers as the enemy.

Thankfully, Mr. Maxwell thinks this is an unfair portrayal. He, like the majority of us, is the product of public schools. Do we really want to think that we turned out so bad? Why do many think the quality of public schools has changed for the students of the 21st century? Have teachers and teaching declined so much that we now need to enact legislation like the No Child Left Behind Act? Mr. Maxwell summed it when he said, "While everything else in society has changed, we expect our schools and teachers to perform the same miracles of old."

I found it also interesting that a lack of respect for teachers apparently isn't just a problem unique to the United States. People responding to a question presented by the British Broadcasting Company about their educational system resulted in letters from readers saying, "The problem is a total lack of respect for teachers these days," to one woman who felt, "Teacher training has a long way to go to address this (showing respect to students) and standards have gone down; it is 'bums on seats' or 'teachers in the classroom,' not quality." Ouch.

I also found a report that Education International (EI) "decries the declining level of respect and appreciation for teachers on the occasion of World Teachers' Day on October 5, 2004." Even in China, the land where Confucius is a paragon of all teachers, there was a writer who was bemoaning the fact that "teachers are afraid of their students" and that their country's teachers have had low self-esteem since the dreaded years of 1966 to 1976. He goes on to state that "most normal (public) school graduates don't even dream of teaching; they want to be business people."

As Mr. Maxwell ended his column "Frankly, I am amazed—but thankful—that so many people still choose teaching as a profession." Not only do some people want to become teachers, some are really darn good at it as well.

Meet a teacher

He teaches students to be respectful by requiring them to respond to adults with a "Yes, sir" or "No, ma'am." He explains to students how to keep their books and papers organized. He even shows them the best way to wash their hands after using the bathroom.

More importantly, this teacher motivates all students so that they not only finish homework every night, but actually look forward to receiving homework. He also arranges the fundraising so that his students can go on as many as 30 field trips a year, some to large urban cities, others as brief as going to the local bowling alley. He has the knack for turning a simple field trip to a bowling alley into an important math lesson on fractions. He turned a class of misfits and school behavior problems from Harlem into a high-achieving group of inspired learners who were accepted into one of the most prestigious middle schools in New York. The teacher's proudest accomplishment is that he lifts all children up to a level they have never achieved before.

Am I that teacher? Obviously not. But I had the opportunity to meet and listen to this great teacher speak. His name is Ron Clark and he beat out 70,000 other teachers to receive Disney's most prestigious "Teacher of the Year" award.

He also has written a book, *The Essential 55*, which is not only a must for teachers, but for parents, because it's a book really more about good parenting than good teaching. He is truly my hero. However, though I might try, I will never be Ron Clark.

Now meet another teacher
(Confession is good for the soul, isn't it?)

It might not surprise you to know that I am not, nor ever have been a "Teacher of the Year" winner. That's right, not only have I not won it for Disney, I haven't won for my school either. In fact, according to our government, I might even be a teacher who "left behind" students from her fifth grade class. There I said it! Yes, it's true and please don't hate me or regret buying this book! I think it's only fair to hear my side of the story.

Contrary to what our politicians might want parents to believe, I didn't intentionally leave students behind. I also don't think I'm a bad teacher. In fact my class's test scores even improved over last year's test scores. Yet sadly, many of my 33 students didn't perform at the "proficient" level or better on our state assessment. I want you to know that my lower-than-acceptable scores weren't because I didn't try!

On the contrary, I actually worked very, very hard at helping my students so they too would become what every politician dreams for them, students who have reached that "proficient" level. Nothing was more important for me than knowing my students could exit fifth grade knowing their success in life was now more likely because they had become "proficient" or even "advanced" on the state standardized tests—tests that were probably created by a bunch of excessively educated, ivory tower people who don't have the foggiest clue about what children, all children, can really accomplish.

Seriously, I can't believe I "failed" in the eyes of the government despite my good intentions and hard work. I thought I was doing everything right. I did the things I was taught in my credential classes and school in-services. I taught to the core curriculum and to our state's academic standards. I tried my best to give creative lessons and worked many hours beyond my workday. I gave homework. I required that my students read every night. I gave tests on the curriculum and even gave tests to help prepare them for our state academic tests.

It is true, I probably didn't give it the Herculean effort that Ron Clark did, but I also have a husband and two school-age children to raise, which I don't think Ron Clark had at the time he was doing all of these magnificent deeds for his students. I'm not trying to make excuses, this is "just the facts, ma'am and sir."

I thought my co-workers also gave it their all. But alas, whatever we did, I guess it wasn't enough. My school didn't make the necessary growth and is now in the first year of being an "underperforming" school as mandated by the 2002 No Child Left Behind Act.

What is the "No Child Left Behind" Act?

Even if you don't have children in the public school system, it would be hard to miss the uproar in the media about how our public schools are not doing enough to educate our next generation. According to the government, children, mainly minority children, are being "left behind" while supposedly white Caucasian students are succeeding. Colleges are also reporting that many students entering college, regardless of race, have terrible math and writing skills. The conclusion: obviously, our public schools, i.e. teachers, aren't doing the job they are getting paid to do. We are failing to educate all students.

So concerned was our President and Congress about this lapse in our public schools all across America that they felt it necessary to enact the No Child Left Behind (NCLB) legislation in 2002. Their goal is that ALL students, regardless of race or background, reach a proficiency level in math and language arts. Thus the name, No Child Left Behind. I go into greater depth on the NCLB Act in Chapter 8.

So how does the government expect to achieve this worthy goal that 100% of all students will be successful? They believe that the only difference between a successful school whose students achieve higher on test scores and a school that doesn't can be attributed to mainly one thing: the teacher. Good teachers must teach at smart schools and bad teachers must teach at failing schools. Therefore, the government must find a way to give all students "qualified" teachers. It's just that simple for them.

As a teacher in the trenches, whose students are not succeeding, I respectfully disagree with their premise. It's not that simple. According to the government, I am a "qualified" teacher, and I think I work very hard at teaching, so what then am I doing differently? What are all of the teachers at my school doing wrong? Could there be more to a student's achievement beyond who their classroom teacher is?

It makes sense that if the successful teacher has all of the answers about how to make students successful, then the "unsuccessful" teacher should have all of the questions about why she didn't succeed. And fortunately I do have 111 questions, or what I call mysteries of education, about not only things related to being a teacher, but about our public school system. Some of my mysteries go beyond just things I don't know answers to, and include many things I consider absurdities of education. By definition, if something is "absurd," it is contrary to reason or in other words, illogical.

What are these mysteries and absurdities that I speak about?

You don't have to be a teacher to wonder why teachers and schools do things the way they do. But because I work at a school 180 days a year, I have had more reason to ponder not just things I don't understand, but things I question when it comes to schools and teachers. I also wonder if some of these absurdities of education, and not just the teachers, are preventing schools from being more successful than they are.

There are many other things that have me perplexed, bedazzled, and beguiled as a teacher. Here are some of my favorite mysteries and absurdities.

- Why is homework considered so important? Students at underperforming schools get homework, but still do poorly on tests.

Does that mean their teachers give them inferior homework? Why do teachers base grades on completion of homework and not just how well the student knows the information?

- Why do teachers have children fill out reading logs? Do teachers really believe that children actually read all of the books they list on a reading log? Do reading logs really help a child comprehend what they have read?

- Why do we give state assessment tests six weeks before the end of the school year? Doesn't it make more sense to give students their state assessment tests the last week of the school year when the teacher has had the opportunity to use most of the school year for instruction?

- Why do schools think it's important that kindergartners should be able to write phonetically correct sentences? Will this help them become better writers in high school?

- Why has the number of days in a school year basically stayed the same for the last eight decades despite our complaints about how poorly students do and the fact that academic standards require that students actually have more to learn?

- Why do children in more affluent areas seem to outscore children in poorer neighborhoods? Is it really that the teachers are worse, or is something else going on?

- Why, even in states like California where public education (including colleges/universities) gets almost get 50% of the state's budget, do people in education and teachers' unions say this isn't enough? Will schools ever get the funding they say they need? Private schools, historically, have taught children in America without spending as much money per student and they seem to produce well-educated students. Could motivated students and involved parents be a more important ingredient in successful schools than money is?

- Of course, the one which was the motivation for writing this book, "Why don't President Bush and other politicians put any responsibility on parents and students for their academic success, always assuming the problems in education are the teacher's fault?

- Finally, could solving any of these mysteries or absurdities actually lead to answers that will make schools and/or students more successful?

For the record, I'm not clueless about everything when it comes to our educational system. Believe it or not, I understand why we give students standardized tests. Some people might foolishly think that we give them to see how much students have learned by the end of the school year. (I'm sorry, I mean how much they have learned four to six weeks before the end of the school year.)

No, no, no. That's what they want people to think. The real reason we have standardized testing is so that politicians have some way to find out how well teachers are teaching. How else are they going to know which teachers are "leaving children behind?"

The truth is, contrary to what politicians think, I (like most teachers) do not want children to be "left behind" either. However, one of the "mysteries" about this very powerful legislation is why politicians expect that *every child, regardless of background and biological issues,* should be able to achieve academic success, not only at the same rate but under different circumstances.

Aren't the 18 students in my sister's fifth grade class in Texas more likely to succeed than the 33 fifth graders I have in my class just because they get more individualized attention? Yet we both are held accountable to the same standard. Or are we?

Texas gives a completely different standardized test than California does. Their test is a criterion-based test, which means the students are tested only on specific information they are taught. California uses a norm-referenced test based on information the students may or may not have been taught. Are these tests similar enough to compare results or is it like comparing apples with oranges? With the No Child Left Behind Act there is no standard test that all states use, yet our growth goals remain the same. While the politicians' hearts might have been in the right place when they created this act, I will share with you some of its major flaws in Chapter 8.

My own personal mystery: What should I title this book?

Personally, the biggest mystery I had to solve was, "What do I title this book?" I agonized about this for months (ask my family, co-workers, and publisher), even at the very end when I was working with a designer on the book cover. Some of my choices were "Leaving Children Behind: Confessions from a 'Bad' Teacher," "Why Is It Always the Teacher's Fault?" and "Everything You Wanted To Know About Public Schools, But, Well Honestly, Don't Really Want to Know." My own personal favorite was, "Why Is the Teacher's Butt So Big? Plus 111 Other Mysteries of Public Education."

Why did I finally choose "Why is the Teacher's Butt So Big?" besides the fact it was my personal favorite? Am I insinuating that most teachers have big behinds? No, no, no!!! Most teachers don't have big butts because they are constantly working their asses off.

Besides being an absurd title (like much of the thinking that happens in public education), there is actually a story behind the title. I was hired as a kindergarten teacher. I was so happy because it was the grade level I wanted to teach. On the very first day I taught, even though my pupils were only four and five years old, I still worried about making a good first impression. Does my hair look okay? Is my outfit nice? Have I chosen a good book to read?

Despite my careful planning, I didn't really know what concerns a kindergartner, even though my son was also in kindergarten at the time. I just never would have predicted what one particular kinder-gartener was thinking on my first day of teaching.

I was passing out gummy bears to the students who were sitting quietly in a semi-circle on the rug waiting for me to read a story. As I walked past this little boy named Joseph, I heard him ask the boy sitting next to him, "Why is the teacher's butt so big?"

The student sitting next to Joseph replied, "I don't know."

I had something in common with that kindergartner. I didn't know why either. "Why is the teacher's butt so big?"

I have often thought about that innocent question and how it relates to my teaching career. I liked the title because I felt it is an example of what my career as a teacher has been like. I realized that, from the very first day I taught until the day I dismiss a class for the last time, as a school teacher I'd find out that everyone's a critic! There will always be students, or parents, or administrators, or other teachers, or politicians, and even yourself, who will always think that I could have done a better job, that I could be a better teacher, or that I should have a smaller derrière.

Is there much difference between a five-year-old wondering why his teacher's physical appearance isn't perfect and includes a big be-hind vs. a politician wondering why my students aren't perfect and have only "basic" test scores? (Well, okay, maybe there is a slight difference, but you get my point.) Don't we secretly really expect and want our teachers to be perfect, or at least "very good"?

Recently, a fifth grader gave me an idea for another title. One day the weather was unseasonably warm. I decided to wear a short-sleeved polo-type shirt, which I seldom do. Once the class had settled down in their seats, a student raised her hand to ask a question.

"Mrs. Craig, do you really go to the gym every morning at 4:30 in the morning to work-out?"

"Yes, I really do," I replied and was curious where this was leading.

She then said, "Then why are your arms so flabby?"

Let's see, "Why Are the Teacher's Arms So Flabby?" It would

work. Some days you just can't win. I decided that since I didn't know the answer to this question or "Why is the teacher's butt so big?" these could be my first "mysteries" about teaching. For the record, they are not included with the other 111 mysteries. (Besides, I attribute the size of my gluteus maximus to genetics and my flabby arms to my age.)

Which mystery is the one that I would really love an answer to? That of course is "Why aren't my students achieving the way I want them to achieve?" I have had the same teacher training as other teachers—is there something I'm doing differently? Students think teachers should have all the answers. Yet after seven years of teaching, I am amazed how much I don't know about teaching and public schools. Maybe this book will reach someone who does. Solving even one mystery would be great.

What's the real purpose of this book?

While it is true that I do have lots of questions about public schools, I do have a hidden agenda for writing this book. Besides finding answers to my mysteries, when I first started writing this book my main goal was to let the American public know that, in the end, it's not all about the teachers. The reason some public schools aren't succeeding isn't necessarily because the "teachers aren't qualified" or that the "teachers need more training." This might be hard for some politicians to believe, but we just can't blame the teachers for failing schools or for students who graduate the public school system uneducated.

During the second year I was working on my book, my son had the misfortune to have a teacher who was unyielding and uncompromising in the way she taught. This teacher was a "highly qualified" teacher, yet the thing my son learned most that year was how to hate school. Then it occurred to me that we teachers, even highly qualified ones, might be culpable and public schools do have problems. I realized I had to write this book also from the vantage point of a parent who has a child in the public school system. I now had a second mission: not only to help parents understand how public schools work, but to give them advice on how to deal with the system. I also want parents to know that despite claims of low test scores, leaving children behind, and the misfortune of getting a bad teacher now and then, I genuinely believe most public schools do a very good job of educating our future generation. Parents shouldn't think that only private schools give students the best education.

Do you have a mystery or absurdity about public education?

I recognize that every teacher has his or her own unique perspective when it comes to teaching. Whether you are a teacher or a parent, do you have a mystery or absurdity about public education that I haven't listed? I would love to know what it is. Please send me your mysteries, thoughts, views, or personal stories about teaching, teachers, and public schools, to this address:

Debra Craig
P.O. Box 1226
Moreno Valley, CA 92556 or
Debracraig@hotmail.com

1

Teachers 101:

The good, bad, and the unappreciated

Mystery #1: What could be so hard about being a teacher?

After being interviewed by the school administration, the eager teaching prospect said, "Let me see if I've got this right?"

"You want me to go into that room with all those kids, and fill their every waking moment with a love for learning."

"And I'm supposed to instill a sense of pride in their ethnicity, modify their disruptive behavior, observe them for signs of abuse and even censor their t-shirt messages and dress habits."

"You want me to wage a war on drugs and sexually transmitted diseases, check their backpacks for weapons of mass destruction, and raise their self-esteem."

"You want me to teach them patriotism, good citizenship, sportsmanship, fair play, how to register to vote, how to balance a checkbook, and how to apply for a job."

"I am to check their heads for lice, maintain a safe environment, with colorful, creative, print-rich materials on the walls, recognize signs of anti-social behavior, offer advice, write letters of recommendation for student employment and scholarships, encourage

respect for the cultural diversity of others, and oh, make sure that I give the girls in my class fifty percent of my attention."

"My contract requires me to work on my own time after school, evenings and weekends grading papers. Also, I must spend my summer vacation or off-time, at my own expense, working toward advance certification and a master's degree."

"And on my own time you want me to attend committee and faculty meetings, PTA meetings, and participate in staff development training. I am to be a paragon of virtue, larger than life, such that my very presence will awe my students into being obedient and respectful of authority."

"You want me to incorporate technology into the learning experience, monitor web sites, and relate personally with each student. That includes deciding who might be potentially dangerous and/or liable to commit a crime in school."

"I am to make sure all students not merely pass, but excel at the mandatory state exams, even those who don't come to school regularly or complete any of their assignments."

"Plus I am to make sure that all of the students with handicaps get an equal education regardless of the extent of their mental or physical handicap."

"And I am to communicate regularly with the parents by letter, telephone, home visit, newsletter and report card as well twice yearly conferences."

"All of this I am to do with just a dry erase marker, a computer, lots of textbooks, a big smile AND on a starting salary that qualifies my family for food stamps."

"You want me to do all of this and yet you expect me NOT TO PRAY?"

I wish I knew whom to give credit for this now famous-in-teacher-circles "job description." My wonderful mother-in-law, Beverly Craig, sent me this version, but I have read others very similar. In fact, I think my local teachers' union even printed one in their monthly newsletters.

Contrary to the last sentence, this chapter is not devoted to putting prayer back into our classrooms. In fact, I would argue, prayer has never left the classroom. I know teachers who pray every day and ask God to help them make it through another day.

Okay, maybe teaching isn't that bad. (Well, substitute teaching is, but that's a subject for another day.) Back to our "job description." Ask most teachers and I would say this pretty much captures what we do. It is a lot of work! It's more than just standing in front of a bunch of kids and presenting a lesson.

I also don't want to come off as being an ingrate about teaching. I know lots of people who have harder jobs, more dangerous jobs, or even no job. In addition, despite the long hours there are lots of rewards for being a teacher, especially knowing you made a difference in a child's life.

I myself, contrary to my whininess, do not have an aversion to work. In fact, I pride myself on having a great work ethic. So my problem isn't about the nature of the job and all it entails, but just the amount of work that some days seems never-ending. However, the frustrating thing is that despite all of our work, in the end, it still isn't good enough.

Mystery #2: Do most teachers like being a teacher?

When I was in high school,
I felt like I wanted to be somewhere else.
Little did I realize that
teachers felt that way too.

— *Mr. Holland's Opus*

This isn't my quote, but Richard Dreyfus's character's quote in the movie, "Mr. Holland's Opus." Actually, I don't think this is exactly what he said, but it's pretty close. If you haven't seen "Mr. Holland's Opus," it is about a teacher who would rather be composing music, but finds out his calling really was in education.

How many teachers out there are Mr. Hollands and have this frustration about the fact they would really rather be doing something else? Am I a Mr. Holland? Yes, I probably am.

Or is it just the natural progression of the job? In the beginning it's new and exciting. But are the annoyances harder to deal with after teaching 20 years? Maybe it's after only seven years.

You might be thinking that I am in the wrong profession. Am I alone? In March 2004, a Harris Poll of 1017 public school teachers was published and the proportion of public school teachers who reported that they were "very satisfied with teaching as a career" rose to 57%, the highest level they have ever recorded!! Imagine that!!!! (We know Ron Clark is in this category.)

Of course you know what that means? It means that 43% of teachers "aren't satisfied" that they chose teaching as a career either. How can 43% of teachers not understand Cicero's concept: *"What nobler employment, or more valuable to the state, than that of the man who instructs the rising generation?"*

We all assume it is very rewarding to see children learn and gain knowledge that they might use their entire life. Obviously, it's not everything.

Or is it that teachers actually love teaching, but sometimes even loving what you do is overshadowed by the political climate of maligning teachers. "They," meaning politicians and others, say our schools are failing, our students aren't learning, and that children are being "left behind."

Of course, as we keep hearing, we know why. It is the teachers' fault. Most teachers become teachers for the noble goal of helping children learn; it's ironic then that anyone could think that they are the ones letting students down.

No one should wonder why more teachers aren't more satisfied with their job.

Mystery #3: Will politicians ever think teachers are smart enough to teach kids or why do they think teachers always need more training?

It is remarkable how much you have to know before you realize how little you know.

— James S. Hewett

I should have been cued in from the beginning.

It should have been obvious to me when I entered my first required credential class. But I didn't see it until I had been a teacher for a few years.

The fact is, a person who becomes a teacher really has to like school. I don't mean just because they are going to work in one, but because throughout your whole career you not only will be a teacher, you will also be a student. Whether it is through school in-service trainings or going back to school to get a master's degree, or the educational conferences we are encouraged to attend, it seems there is always something more to learn when you become a teacher.

For the record, I am a proponent that everyone should be a lifelong learner. Education is good. Remember, I am a teacher.

Will there, however, be a time during my teaching profession when I don't hear that the reason kids aren't learning is because teachers need more training?

When does the law say a person has become a credentialed teacher? There is not a standard across the country; it varies from state to state. Until the early 1990s, in most states all you needed to do was to graduate from college as an education major. But things started to change in the mid-90s. By 1993, 40 states changed their requirements so that a person could have a degree in anything, but then you had to supplement your degree with certain required teaching courses. This was done because there was a shortage of teachers and it was hoped fresh blood would enter the field.

I did not have a degree in education, but it didn't matter because I was one of those non-traditional applicants who needed to get a California teaching credential just like education majors. To get a California credential, I had to take about six more classes on learning methods and teaching strategies. I also had to pass two basic knowledge tests. One was called the CBST and the other one was specifically for teachers who were going to teach in elementary schools called the MSAT (both I believe have been replaced by different tests). I was also supposed to do 20 weeks of student teaching at two different grade levels, but because I got hired on an "emergency credential," I had a professor evaluate me while I taught in my classroom and was given "student teaching credit" based upon a successful evaluation from my professor.

An "emergency credential" did not mean I could teach in an emergency room, but is given to a teacher when he or she hasn't finished the requirements for the preliminary credential. I also had to pass a reading comprehension instruction test and a U.S. government test.

My preliminary credential was only good for five years. Within that five-year period, I then had to take three more classes. One was a technology class, another was on teaching a health class, and the third was a class on Special Education. I also needed to get my first-aid and CPR card. Once I had jumped through those hoops, only now would I have the coveted CLEAR credential.

But I wasn't done. At the point I received my preliminary credential, the state legislated that teachers also had to earn a CLAD certificate. CLAD stands for Cross-Cultural Language Arts Development. I think we were supposed to learn how to teach English Language Learners, which of course in California there are many.

These days, the CLAD is built into the Preliminary Credential. To get my CLAD I had to take three more classes as well as have two college semesters of a foreign language.

I thought when I earned my multiple-subjects teaching credential, which meant I was qualified to teach kindergarten to sixth grade, I was finished with classes. And legally I am. However, every five years I also have to complete 150 hours of continuing education courses commonly referred to as "professional growth" hours, in order to keep my credential.

If I were teaching a single subject like math or English, I would need a Single Subject Credential. The major difference between the two is I would need to pass a proficiency test in the field I would be teaching in instead of taking one of the general knowledge tests.

With the advent of the No Child Left Behind (NCLB) Act, all of this just isn't good enough. The buzz words here are "highly qualified." The law outlines a list of minimum requirements related to content knowledge and teaching skills that a "highly qualified" teacher would meet.

Thank goodness the federal government is doing this. How awful it was that we let colleges, universities, and state governments decide what a teacher needed to be "qualified." Obviously, they were wrong because our children are being left behind.

Wait, I jumped the gun. NCLB "does recognize the importance of state and local control of education and therefore provides the opportunity for each state to develop a definition of 'highly qualified' that is consistent with NCLB as well as the unique needs of the state."

How I became a "highly qualified" teacher

According to "A Toolkit for Teachers," a publication found on a Department of Education website:

"In general, under No Child Left Behind a highly qualified teacher must have:
- A bachelor's degree
- Full state certification, as defined by the state
- Demonstrated competency, as defined by the state, in each core academic subject he or she teaches."

I'm confused? I already have all of that. (Okay, some might argue a case against the "demonstrated competency.") It even adds that *"Elementary school teachers who are new to the profession must demonstrate competency by passing a rigorous state test on subject knowledge and teaching skills in reading and language arts, writing, math and other areas of the basic elementary school curriculum."*

Fortunately, I do have everything the No Child Left Behind Act requires, as do most of the teachers I work with at my school. So are we now and always have been "highly qualified?" I think so. In fact, recently I received a piece of paper proclaiming that, by the No Child Left Behind standards, I am a "highly qualified" teacher. So, I guess I'm not the reason kids are failing.

The No Child Left Behind Act wants to eliminate teachers, like me, who were hired by school districts with an "emergency credential." The government is now saying that at least Title I schools, the schools in low socio-economic areas, can't hire a person unless he or she has jumped through all of the hoops mentioned above. Also, every state has its own requirements for teachers. In New York, I believe, teachers also need to get a master's degree within five years.

The government is also cracking down on school districts that feel they can hire any person to teach single subjects like algebra or chemistry. That's why NCLB is demanding that new middle and high school teachers qualify either by passing a "rigorous state test in each subject they teach, or by completing an academic major or coursework equivalent to an academic major, an advance degree or advance certification or credentials."

This does not seem like an unreasonable request. Even though teachers with experience must meet the requirements for new teachers, NCLB is also allowing them to become a "qualified teacher" by "demonstrating competency based on a system designed by each state."

My husband, who is a firefighter/paramedic, knows a firefighter whose wife is a high school librarian and has earned two master's degrees. Besides her regular librarian duties, her school district decided they also wanted her to teach an English class. Even though she had two master's degrees in the language arts area, that didn't qualify her to go back into the classroom and teach. She had to take additional college courses. (I see, despite twenty years in education and two master's degrees, maybe then she'll be smart enough to teach.)

How could I possibly have a problem with any of this? Even though I don't like the fact that there is not just one standard set of requirements to be used by all states, I can live with that. What I have a problem with is equating that if the teacher is highly educated, then he or she is going to be a better teacher.

Mystery #4: Why do public schools demand more education from their teachers than private schools do, yet private schools are just as successful, if not even more successful, than public schools?

The mother of my daughter's friend was working at a small, private Christian school as a teacher's assistant. She was telling me how some teachers at her school don't even have a bachelor's of arts degree. I was aghast! "How can they teach children without a four-year college education?" I protested. "I mean, five years of college under their belt!" Actually, I didn't protest. They teach students just fine, thank you, and I'm not certain whether or not their students take the state assessment tests, but if they did, my bet is that those kids probably do quite well on them. Or should I say, they do as well as if they went to a public school and were taught by a "highly qualified" teacher.

I find it so ironic that the government requires so much education and training for public school teachers while many students enrolled in private schools all across America are getting an equally good, and in some cases, maybe even a better education by teachers who don't have college degrees.

What about all of the students who are being home schooled by parents? Some of the most successful college students come from home schooling and I bet many of those parents don't have college degrees.

It is absurd to think that teaching kids is all about how much education a teacher has. Haven't our so-called leaders figured out yet that maybe a successful school involves more than having "highly-qualified" teachers on its staff?

Mystery #5: Why do politicians think the more education a teacher has in a subject, the better the teacher will be?

I will admit there are subjects in school, particularly at the high school level, that do require a high level of knowledge or expertise from the teacher in order to successfully explain it to students. The government is right in cracking down on school districts that feel they can hire any person to teach single subjects like algebra or chemistry. How can a person teach others, if they don't know the information that well themselves?

NCLB wants "highly qualified" teachers. However, you can require the highest academic standards, but it doesn't mean that you will get a "good" teacher just because the person aces math and science classes. In some cases, I think being very good in a subject can even hinder a person's ability to teach it to others who don't understand it at all. Case in point: I love fifth grade math. I loved fifth grade math even when I was in fifth grade. So does that mean I'm the best math teacher at my school?

Probably not, in fact the opposite might be true. I have a hard time explaining things to students who are just clueless. I don't understand how to make it any simpler. I also get very frustrated that they can't get it. I have students who have even admitted to me that they are afraid to tell me they still don't get it after several explanations because they think I will be mad. That's pretty sad but now I try really hard to be more patient.

Good teaching is really more than just knowing the information. That's why the government can require teachers to take more classes, more training, and get more years on the job, but hopefully someday the powers that be will realize that these things aren't the things that make a teacher "highly qualified."

Mystery #6: Why do experts assume that experienced teachers are automatically better than the inexperienced teachers?

"Experts" make all sorts of assumptions in order to figure out why all schools aren't succeeding like those in affluent areas. One of the common beliefs is that most affluent/successful schools have teachers who have the most experience. They figured this out by taking the average amount of experience teachers have at each school site and comparing the results

What they noticed was, and yes it is true, that affluent/successful schools seem to have teachers with more experience. The conclusion is, "Oh, that's why these schools are so successful!"

It doesn't take a rocket scientist to figure out why affluent/successful schools have teachers with more experience. What teacher is going to leave a school where the majority of students come prepared to learn, have no gaps in their learning, and whose parents are an integral part of their child's education?

With so much pressure for students to succeed on test scores, I'm sure not many teachers are saying to themselves, "Gee, wouldn't it be great to teach at a school where students are scoring in the bottom 30 percentile of test scores, whose parents aren't involved, and where education isn't a focus of the family." Granted, there are some teachers out there, like Ron Clark, who are up to the challenge, but I think it would be safe to say most are not.

I speak from experience when I say it's tough wanting to stay at an underperforming school where you are scrutinized on why your students aren't succeeding. As I have said many times, I don't understand why they aren't succeeding. I don't know what I'm doing wrong. Even though I like my school and I like my principal and staff, I did try to leave for a non-Title I school they were building not that far from my school. I didn't make the cut and thus decided it wasn't meant to be. Besides, contrary what you might think, I really like my Title I kids and feel they need good teachers too. (It's just that lately I don't feel like a "good" teacher.)

But I have digressed. Let's go back to why I think it's wrong that inexperienced teachers get a bad rap. I will be the first to admit that the first year of teaching is tough and I don't know if any credential class can prepare you for the reality of teaching. There are a lot of things, like classroom management skills, that are best learned after years on the job. It makes sense that the more a person learns and the longer one does something, it should result in becoming better at it, if for no other reason than trial and error. A teacher gets to see firsthand what works and what doesn't work.

However, five years experience as a kindergarten teacher did not prepare me for the challenges of teaching fifth grade. I did have the advantage of understanding how the school system works but, in essence, my first year of teaching fifth grade wasn't much different than a person coming in brand new to teaching.

Is this why I think that inexperienced teachers get a bad rap, because even "experienced" teachers can be challenged when switching grades or subjects? No. New teachers get a bad rap because even though that first year of teaching can be tough, there is something inexperienced teachers have that's almost as valuable as experience. Many times new teachers bring an enthusiasm to the job and a willingness to try new things. They are also very open to suggestions and put in very long hours. Enthusiasm and a positive attitude can go a long way in a field where experienced teachers are often burned-out and don't feel like putting in 110% effort anymore. That's why students can still be successful under the helm of a new teacher.

Mystery #7: What then is a good teacher?

A great teacher never strives to explain his vision—he simply invites you to stand beside him and see for yourself.

— *Rev. R. Inman*

We hear so much about schools needing "good, qualified teachers." I've explained what the government says a teacher needs to be "qualified," but what makes a good teacher?

I'm sure the government's definition of a good teacher is a person who is able to get every child in their classroom up to that "proficient" level. That's really the bottom line for them. Personally, I think a good teacher is more than just having students be successful on assessment tests. I decided to go to a man I think is the ultimate authority on being a good teacher. He calls them "effective teachers." His name is Harry Wong, and he is not only an author and lecturer, but a former teacher himself. In his book, "How to Be an Effective Teacher: The First Days of School," he describes the three characteristics a good or "effective" teacher has.

He says an "effective teacher":

1. has positive expectations for student success.
2. is an extremely good classroom manager.
3. knows how to design lessons for student mastery.

While I agree these things are essential, I think the most important attribute a good teacher needs is patience. Good teachers understand that children, even high school students, need things repeated several times, lose things, are disorganized, and some days just don't care about school. A good teacher will not expect adult behavior and skills from children who are literally just learning these things. I also think a good teacher should be a nice person who thinks about the best interests of the student. A good teacher needs to have that right balance of toughness and inspiration, and the ability to get more from students than they think possible. A good teacher also communicates with parents and lets them know how they can help their children. Despite being tired of the routine of teaching, a good teacher musters up the energy to give it his or her best shot every day they enter that classroom to teach. I will speak from personal experience—sometimes this isn't an easy thing to do.

Mystery #8: Who are these bad teachers messing up our schools?

Or teachers who work in glass schools (or write books), shouldn't throw stones?

I do not think of myself as a good teacher. I hate giving homework and I'm much too lenient with the students. However, I really don't want to think of myself as a bad one either. (Of course, what teacher does?) I fall somewhere in-between, like many teachers, hopefully closer to the good end of the spectrum. What I lack in talent and ability, I hope I make up in compassion and hard work.

I have a problem with my categorizing of teachers into two groups, either good or bad. The problem is, to paraphrase an old expression, sometimes determining who a bad teacher is in the eye of the beholder, or parent. Much of my opinion on what classifies a bad teacher is not based on my experience as a teacher, but my experience as a parent. Yet I also understand that some teachers, whom I have thought were horrible are loved by other parents.

That's why it's important to differentiate whether or not a teacher is "bad" or is just a teacher you hate. Often, the reasons I have not liked particular teachers my children have had is because I don't agree with how they teach or their policies. Does that really make them bad? Probably not, although in some cases it could.

We need to keep in perspective that even "good" teachers aren't perfect, and sometimes bad teachers have something good about how they do their job. Most teachers have their good points and their bad points, regardless of whether the teacher is a "newbie" or a "veteran."

The reality is bad teachers do exist out there. This shouldn't come as a surprise since in every profession, there are people who just shouldn't be doing what they are doing. In education, however, bad teaching comes at the expense of children.

I often wonder how politicians define a bad teacher. Our governor is very vocal about "all students deserve a good teacher." I agree. So who does he think a bad teacher is? Someone who can't get higher test scores? I think not. In part, politicians must think bad teachers happen when they aren't trained properly, when they don't have the right educational background, or I guess when they don't know how to present lessons. That's why they think it's all about "more training." Surely they don't really think it's that simple, do they?

Even I have a hard time defining what a bad teacher is. Some might say a bad teacher is someone who is horrible at explaining lessons. Others might think a teacher is bad if they have no control over their classroom. However, I think there are two kinds of really bad teachers. One quits caring about the job and the other puts policies over the best interests of the child and helping that child get an education. I will explain both kinds of bad teacher.

Bad Teacher #1: The apathetic teacher

I find it fascinating that politicians and educational experts have a total reverence towards the experienced teachers, yet I bet that some of the so-called "bad" teachers that politicians hate are teachers with lots of experience. These are the teachers suffering from job burnout and tired of putting endless hours into a job. At some point, the teacher begins thinking that he or she cares more about the student's success than the student himself. The teacher soon feels, "Why am I killing myself if the students don't care?" These teachers are at risk of becoming what I call the apathetic bad teacher.

Burned-out teachers may have been teaching for 15 or 20 years, or maybe even less, and are just plain tired of teaching. They are tired of rowdy kids, planning lessons, grading work, and the unrealistic expectations that are put upon teachers. So what do they do? They quit caring and are just hanging on until retirement. Some are lucky if they can make even make it to school on time because they have forgotten the importance of what their job means.

Maybe some of you have personally experienced a burned-out teacher. Most of the time they do the minimal requirement the job needs and thus the students do the minimal requirement they need to pass. A really burned-out teacher might not even do the minimal requirements. They know how to "work the system." They also hide under the protection of a tenure system, knowing many administrators aren't up to the task of firing an experience teacher who hasn't committed some horrible act. They know how to fly low and avoid the radar.

I don't want my fellow teachers to think that I'm saying experienced/burned-out teachers are the only kind of bad teachers. That isn't the case. Bad teaching can happen regardless of how much time a person has on the job. There are new teachers, teachers with five years, and teachers with fifteen years worth of experience who really don't know what they are doing in the classroom, or do the minimum only because they are lazy. The saddest part about these teachers is often they are clueless to that fact.

Bad teacher #2:
The "bad teacher in sheep's clothing."

Often parents are clueless to what kind of teacher their child has. Many parents assume their child's teacher is going to be competent. Others might think a teacher is brilliant because of comments from other parents. But don't let one parent's opinion close your eyes to what's happening in the classroom. What kind of teacher you think your child has isn't necessarily the kind of teacher your child is getting. This brings us up to the other kind of "bad" teacher out there, one who lurks around campuses, often unrecognized as a bad teacher by peers and parents.

I call this the "bad teacher in sheep's clothing." On the surface, this teacher does everything right. She teaches the curriculum, she's involved in the school, and she tackles extra projects. She is also, according to the government, "highly qualified." So what could possibly make her bad?

It is the way she treats certain students and her general attitude towards learning. To teachers of this kind, teaching is a power trip where they revel in the fact it is their rules, and their ways, regardless of how negatively it impacts the learning of a student. This kind of teacher usually favors the best and brilliant in the class and has little patience for those who struggle. Ironically, this teacher honestly feels this is the best way to teach all students. She equates toughness with excellence, and while I agree teachers must have high standards, it has to be done without alienating the child away from school.

My son, Matthew, had a "bad teacher in sheep's clothing" which resulted in a long and difficult school year. She had very strict and rigid policies about schoolwork, and she didn't waver or give students any leeway at all. Some parents might like that, but her style wasn't conducive to learning for my son. She wants children, even ten-year-olds, to be perfect like her and has no compassion if they aren't.

She proudly proclaimed that she goes very fast in math and if students don't get it, it's up to the parents to get them caught up. At least she was honest. I spent many nights and vacations tutoring my son in math. She also never found time to teach social studies until the last three weeks of school. Then she crammed all of this work and projects down them, which should have taken months.

His teacher had tough standards. At the end of the school year when the class was learning their states and capitals, parents had to give their child a practice test. My son had only misspelled one state. The next day when he came home from school he told me "Mom, my teacher said I missed seven other states." I told him, "No, you didn't Matthew. I checked them all. How could that be?" He replied, "Mom, I forgot the commas between the capital and the state, so she counted it wrong." I understood it as being only a "spelling test"; however, she's right, commas need to separate the city and state.

This teacher had a pet project happening at the school that occupied a great deal of her attention. This project seemed to take priority over teaching other subjects in science. In fact, it put the class behind in science and, prior to state testing, she told the parents they needed to go over the science book with their child. There's nothing wrong with that, but wasn't that her job?

She also was very negative about the school district and even expressed to a parent in the class how she was not going to let her children go to any high school in the city because it "will just turn their brain in mush." What kind of comment is that to make to a parent who is sending her children to a high school in the city?

But the biggest problem I had was with her zero tolerance policy of no late work, which I found out about the hard way.

My son has the misfortune of inheriting my trait of being disorganized. This came to light when I would find his papers scattered all through his backpack. Often, on nights I spent helping him with homework, I would also find unchecked work from a couple of days earlier still in his book. When I asked why, he said, "She never asked for it until later in the week and then I thought I had lost it." Oftentimes, it wasn't that he lost his homework, but that he actually didn't do it.

It became a huge source of frustration keeping up with his many missing assignments, especially after I had viewed his first progress report. I did what any involved parent would do, made Matthew use his weekend for redoing this work he should have turned in.

The whole time he was working on it, he kept telling me, "Mom, I'm not going to get credit on this."

I thought this was his way of getting out of doing it. I told him, "Of course you're going to get credit for this. You might not get full credit, but at least its better than the "0%" that's on your progress report.

"Mom, she doesn't take ANY LATE WORK!!!!"

"Matthew, I just can't believe it," and I made him keep working on it.

Then I got his next progress report and guess what? Matthew was right. He still had "0%" in the spots where he had finally turned in those missing assignments. I was shocked. I couldn't believe it. So I emailed her a letter.

She told me that she explained her policy at Back to School Night and that I even signed acknowledging these rules. Actually, she was wrong. While she had given me the information at Back to School Night, I hadn't actually read it. I found the original copy in my nightstand. (Tip for all parents out there: Read what the teacher sends home.) She explained to me that this is her way of getting them ready for middle school.

I know I should have been grateful for "wanting him to be ready for middle school" by having this tough policy. However, I wanted her to get him ready for middle school by making sure he knew his math skills.

Most parents probably agree with her strict policy, but seriously what would have been the big deal if she had given him some credit for turning it in late?

Did she accomplish her goal of impressing on my son the need to turn in work on time? No, because despite spending money for folders and organizers, the missing work continued to be a problem the whole school year and he got "Ds" and "Fs".

I know that these grades are my fault as a parent, not her fault. I needed to become a more "involved parent." However, and I know this is bad, I wasn't motivated to have him make up the work on weekends if he wasn't going to get any credit for it. I know he probably lost out in the end, but still it didn't make sense to me. Doing the work on weekends also might have been the motivation to be extra careful that he turned everything in. But why didn't she collect the work the next day or why couldn't she have a place they could turn it in before she was ready to collect it? I truly believe it wasn't just Matthew's fault.

I think the thing that really got me about this problem was, as I teacher, I would never have such a rigid policy. I know the hassles of collecting work that is past due, but I would still have my students do the work later rather than never. I also would have been thrilled if one of my student's parents offered to give up her weekends to get her child caught up. But this teacher was so rigid and unyielding. I do not understand what she had to gain by this.

The other thing that bothered me about not accepting late work was it skewed his grades. Even though she weighted her grades so that tests were worth more than homework, those "0"s in the grade book really brought his grades down. It wasn't a true reflection of how well he knew the standards.

I eventually complained to the principal, but I knew he wouldn't and didn't do anything about it. That was her policy and I guess she has the right to have that policy just like I have the right to tell you about it in my book.

I understand I'm probably not getting much sympathy from teachers or parents out there who think I'm just making excuses for my son. But seriously, I wasn't asking for much. What would have been so horrible to allow late work for half the credit? He was in elementary school, not high school. Wasn't it in my son's best interest academically to have him turn in late work instead of no work? Isn't that what a "good" teacher would do? Help all students, despite their flaws, to learn?

In reading back my list of complaints about this teacher, I know much of this probably seems very minor and maybe even petty. Are these accusations egregious enough to warrant the label of "bad teacher?" Maybe, not but I'm just telling you I couldn't wait until the end of the school year. Was I the only parent who felt this way about this teacher? No, not at all, in fact I know one parent who removed her daughter after two months in this teacher's class, and enrolled her into a private school for a year. Another parent switched her daughter to another school at the end of the second trimester because she couldn't understand why her straight "A" child was now getting Ds and Fs. When I ran into this mother at the supermarket at the end of the school year, she was so happy she made the decision to do this because at the new school, her daughter was once again getting straight "As" and loved going to school.

While most classes at that grade level are packed with 33 students, at the magnet school where this teacher works, she only had 24. I knew parents who were switching tracks just so their child wouldn't have her as a teacher. Because of teachers like this, I understand why public schools get a bad rap and why home schooling seems like a good idea.

I use my own experience as an example to prove that sometimes a teacher will be vilified by parents for unpopular policies she has in her class. However, parents need to be open-minded when a new school year starts and give their child's teacher a chance to prove what kind of teacher he or she really are before automatically assuming the worst.

We may know why a teacher is bad, or "ineffective" as author Harry Wong would say, but there is no single way to identify a bad teacher. You can't do it by looking at him or her, nor can you do it by the number of years they have been working, nor can you rely solely on other parents' comments, even though that usually is a good indicator.

A parent should always be on the lookout for a "bad" teacher and hope his or her child never has to have one.

Mystery #9: What should you do if you suspect your child has a bad teacher?

There is a teacher at one of the middle schools in town who has a reputation of being a terrible teacher. What makes him terrible? He does the least amount of work possible.

Supposedly, his classes watch video movies like "Clueless." It would be a stretch to tie-in a movie about a rich, spoiled Beverly Hills kid, who tries to do good, with ancient history, which is the state's social studies standard for seventh grade. His classes also spend time playing games like "Uno." Granted, these types of activities don't happen every day, but from what I hear, it happens enough that valuable classroom time is wasted.

At the school's "Back To School" night, this very teacher stood up in front of the parents and said, "I have really nothing to say, so feel free to leave for your child's next classroom." He has "nothing to say?" Couldn't he have told them what the students are going to be learning, or how he grades, or what kind of work he gives? This should have been a warning flag right then.

In addition, a friend told me that when her daughter had this teacher for language arts two years earlier, she went out and bought a whole bunch of reading and writing books to basically home school her daughter so she wouldn't miss out on language arts education that year.

Why don't parents revolt and get him out of there? Isn't that what involved parents would do? According to this mom, she and other parents tried, but to no avail. Teachers like this are why the teachers' tenure program gets a deservedly bad rap. Or are we being too harsh? As I explain later, maybe he's just teaching in his "survivor mode."

There was another teacher, at the same school, who dinged a student because she had a broken leg and couldn't do physical education. This student had to do an exorbitant amount of essays for not being able to participate in P.E., with a doctor's note and cast on her leg, and the teacher still gave her a "D." Is that fair? I guess it is to this teacher.

If you have a problem with a teacher, or are confused about what is going on in your child's class, it is your duty to check it out. First, make an appointment to see the teacher or at least try phoning him or her to share your concerns. As a teacher, I will be the first to admit that I hate getting phone calls from parents. But I'd rather be the first to know about a problem in my classroom than hear it from another teacher or worse yet, from the principal.

If you feel you don't want to discuss it in person, then take the route I usually take. That's right, I write letters, or more recently email. Three out of six of my son's teachers have received "Debra Craig" letters or emails from me, those lucky teachers. That is 50% of the teachers he has had. So maybe I could think my son might be the problem? I do recognize he isn't the best student, but he has never been a behavior problem. Teachers have to be able to justify their practices and policies to parents.

The key here is communication, communication, and communication!

As a parent, you must find answers to those questions you have about your child's education. You must speak out if there is something that bothers you.

My son has a friend whose mother and I have become good friends since our children were kindergarten classmates. She and her husband also have other children who are in high school. She was telling me one day about how her son is constantly complaining about his Honors English teacher. We use that term loosely, since it seems this Honors English teacher thinks it's educational for her students to play the game "Hangman." Her son, a straight "A" student, tells his mom that he isn't learning anything.

Unless you plan on auditioning for the television game show "Wheel of Fortune," there is only so much you can learn by playing "Hangman." I told this mom they need to find the time to meet with the teacher if for no other reason than to corroborate her son's story. If the story is true, it's unfair for that child to lose a valuable year of English instruction because he has a teacher who doesn't teach. This is when it is the parents' duty to get involved and go to the school's administration with concerns or complaints.

"If it doesn't fit, you must acquit."

Before taking it to the administration, make certain you have the facts right if you do want to complain about a teacher. Also, before going to the school, bounce your complaint off friends, relatives, or other parents. Why do this? You want to make certain you aren't overreacting.

For instance, I had a problem with the way a teacher was teaching reading comprehension. I spoke with two other parents in the class, one was even a teacher, and they didn't think there was anything wrong with it. So even though I was unhappy, I concluded that I was overreacting. Maybe my son was just being lazy, which of course he was. In this case, I never did speak to the teacher about my concerns and left it at that.

However, even if other parents don't agree with your stance, that doesn't automatically mean you need to be quiet. If something is bothering you about a class, a teacher, or the school, don't be afraid to speak up.

Tips for speaking with a teacher

1. **Do speak with the teacher first before taking it to an administrator.** Even if you think the teacher will not do anything about the problem, at least give the teacher an opportunity to explain in person his or her stance. Exception to this rule: I would go directly to an administrator if the issue is about a teacher who doesn't seem to be doing his or her job or if it's an issue of ethics and/or morality.

2. **Call first and arrange a time to talk.** If you see your child's teacher on campus, don't go up and start airing your problem. A teacher hates nothing worse than being blind-sided by a parent with a complaint. It is okay to approach the teacher and ask when is the best time to call for an appointment, but leave it at that unless the teacher tells you now would be a good time to meet.

3. **Don't start in "attack mode."** No matter how nice or diplomatic you are when first meeting with a teacher, chances are, the teacher is still going to be on the defensive side. That's just the way it is. So don't make it even worse by being accusatory and saying things like, "Why don't you like my child?" (Which of course any teacher will deny, but could still be true.) Teachers know from past experience that parents wanting to talk with us

usually means trouble. If you do come off as combative, that just exasperates the situation even more and does nothing but break down the communication between you and that teacher. Try your best to be nice and reassuring that you are there for the facts about a problem and a workable solution.

4. **Ask before you complain.** Instead of just assuming that what your child told you about the class is true, get the facts straight from the beginning. Ask "What is your policy on late work?" Or "How do you collect student work?" if your child insists he or she is turning papers in. If your child says the teacher doesn't explain something, ask the teacher how he or she presents a lesson. Does a teacher have much time to help a student individually? Did the teacher ever see your child ask for help?

5. **Don't expect a teacher or administrator to change a grade.** Many teachers want to tell parents that they don't "give" grades, your child "earns" them; but that isn't always necessarily true. Unless it's in math, often grades are very subjective. Ask, and listen to the teacher explain about her grading policy. As I will explain in greater depth, don't get too stressed out about grades. In the big scheme of life, a lower grade than usual isn't going to ruin the future of your child.

6. **Don't assume that because your child has done well in a subject during previous years of school it means the child should always do well in the same subject.** In my case, I think fifth grade math is much more complicated than fourth grade math. My daughter's pre-algebra is much more difficult than her sixth grade math. So it goes in all subjects. Also, each teacher brings to a class his or her own technique of teaching and, yes, some may be better at explaining things than other teachers.

7. **Ask how you can help your child.** Teachers have lots of students and while it's okay to ask if the teacher can tutor your

child after school, don't think it's his or her obligation to do so. A better thing would be to ask the teacher if he or she knows of a tutor or if there is anything else you can work on at home to get the student up to par.

8. **Be realistic about what kind of student your child really is academically.** It's hard for me, as a former straight "A" student who was totally self-motivated to get good grades and do everything right, to accept that I have a son who isn't like me except in being disorganized. He is somewhat lazy, not motivated by As, and doesn't care if his grades aren't the best in the class. While I still want to instill in him why I think he should be more like me, in reality it probably isn't going to happen, and that's okay too.

9. **Quit rescuing your child or making excuses for a child who really is at fault for either poor grades or bad behavior.** The child needs to be responsible and suffer the consequences for his or her action or lack of action. I know this is not as easy as it sounds.

10. **If you aren't happy with an outcome of a conference, it is okay to go request a conference with an administrator.** Do have the courtesy to let the teacher know beforehand this is your intention.

11. **Be prepared for the fact that, despite all of your efforts, nothing will change.** I hate to be so negative but, from my experience, I'm just being honest. I seldom got the results or action I wanted. You then just have to make the best of a bad situation or do something drastic and pull your child from the class or even that school.

Speaking as a parent, if you have a problem with a teacher or the school, you must speak out and not worry about offending teachers. Lord knows, I have done my share of complaining with my own children's teachers. I try to do it civilly and work hard at not being "bitchy," but I'm not always very good at it. You can see a sample of a typical letter in my next mystery.

Mystery #10: Why do some teachers forget that their job is to help students learn, even if it means giving more than one chance to succeed?

**Character consists of what you do
on the third and fourth tries.**

— James Michener

This mystery is, of course, dedicated to my son's teacher whom I spoke about earlier. Here is a letter I wrote to the principal of the school, when he wrote back in response to a letter I had written to him, complaining about the lack of help from the school in my problem with his teacher. It pretty much explains what I mean about this mystery.

Dear Mr. Xxxxx:

Thank you so much for your letter.

I guess the only thing I feel I need to address in response to your letter is the part why you don't understand my frustration with the school this year. As a teacher, I understood that you weren't going to have Mrs. Xxxxx change any of Matthew's grades. For the record, I was never asking for that.

However, I am curious, how or what did Mrs. Xxxxx and the school do to help find, I mean, really find a way to salvage

Matthew's academic year? Besides, the planner idea, that was about it. Nothing else was offered.

What did I want, or maybe I should put it, what did we need? The only thing I wanted from Mrs. Xxxxx, the only thing I wanted from you and the school was the ability to let Matthew turn some assignments in late for a lesser grade for at least some credit. Maybe that wouldn't have been fair, maybe that wouldn't have helped his lack of responsibility, but it would have helped him academically. And isn't this the bottom line in education?

What would have been so terrible about this? That it wouldn't prepare him for middle school? Well, I think we should worry about middle school when it happens. Do I think this year prepared him for middle school? Absolutely not. In fact, it did far worse damage because he absolutely hates school. And that to me, is really sad when a teacher, through her rigid, unyielding expectations, makes a child hate school. Is that what Mrs. Xxxxx wanted to accomplish this year? Well, she succeeded far beyond her imagination.

I'm sure Mrs. Xxxxx's system works great for self-motivated kids, and disciplined kids, or kids who have parents on top of things. But if any one component is missing, then what? It is the child who ultimately loses out.

Wouldn't it have been in Matthew's best interest to have at least late work coming instead of no work? I am sorry but, yes, as a teacher, I will NEVER understand her warped philosophy on education. In the end, was it is really too much to ask for in order to help a mom and a child who struggled with the system in place to let late assignments come in? Funny, I don't remember learning in my credential classes that accepting late work is such a crime, especially when we're talking about students who are only in the fifth grade.

Without offering Matthew that option, that's why I felt the school failed us and why he consequently failed school.

Again, I really appreciate the time and thought you put into your letter and many points were well made. Sometimes I think this struggle with Matthew and his school was sort of "meant to be." It gave me a very unique perspective when writing my book about parents and public schools that I never would have had before. It is the silver lining in this very dark cloud. Maybe I can help other parents who are facing this same sort of difficult situation.

No further correspondence is necessary. I hear your message loud and clear.

Sincerely,
Debra Craig

Matthew's teacher isn't alone in education when it comes to thinking that a student should only get one chance at homework, one chance on a test, and one chance to do well. In the case of a test, the idea is they need to study hard the night before to improve their chances of doing well. That sometimes seems to be the unwritten rule for teaching.

But what if a student did the math right when multiplying two digit decimals, but forgot or didn't put the decimal points in the right place? Obviously, that child failed the test. In reviewing the test, let's say he wants to try it again. What's wrong with giving him a new test after he realizes his mistake? Isn't it more important that he understand the concept even if it took an additional test to prove it? Also, often times I throw out the grade for a test if most of the students did poorly. I know teachers who are aghast over my policy. They feel if a test is given, those scores must stay in the grade book. But why be so unyielding?

I give the option to every student to improve his or her score.

Sometimes I give the whole class a second chance, other times a student needs to make the effort and tell me he or she wants a second chance. I want to encourage students to keep trying. What a wonderful thing it is when the desire to do well, and the belief in the ability to do well, comes from within the student and not just because the teacher or parent wants to see good grades. If a student can prove to me that he or she now knows a concept really well, he or she deserves that "A" just as much as the student who was lucky enough to grasp the concept the first time it was tested.

My son's teacher believed in giving second chances on tests. But we shared different philosophies on the grading of the retakes. Like many teachers, she believed all scores stayed in the grade book. If a student took a retake, not only did she keep the first bad score, but also the second grade even if it was lower. Granted, there's nothing wrong with this, but I don't understand why not just keep the higher grade? Why is she penalizing slow learners? Isn't it a celebration that the child kept trying and got it on the second or third try?

As I see it, my job is to teach these kids the standards that the State of California says they need to know. I am not here to play this game of "you only get once chance to learn it or else you're going to get penalized." Not all students learn at the same rate and pick up concepts quickly. I try not to have a "me vs. them" mentality; my goal is to have a "we're all in this together" attitude. I want students to take the test again if they think they just need more time to learn a concept. I want to reward them for their extra effort even if it took them two or three chances to "get it."

Teachers shouldn't be so strict in their policies and instead put the interests of the child's education first. What's that old saying, "Rules are made to be broken"?

Mystery #11: Why do they think that all a bad teacher needs to become a good teacher is more training?

I really don't know the answer to this mystery. My guess is they have to come up with some reason explaining why students are still not doing well in class despite having this highly educated teacher in the classroom. The answer they conclude is, "Oh, the teacher must need even more training."

The ironic thing with this thinking is that I have heard of teachers who go to every in-service and all the staff training they can attend. They have their master's degree and are the first to attend conferences during the school day. Are they the best teachers at the school? On the contrary, many go because it gets them out of the classroom and away from teaching.

Just because you make teachers learn all of this stuff, it doesn't mean it's automatically going to make them better teachers. Don't people realize that bad teachers can go to staff development meetings like the good teachers, but does it make them care more about their job?

Maybe in many cases teachers do need help with techniques on teaching. I have a personal example of this. Thanks to an in-service training I received, I can finally teach fifth graders how to write. I knew I needed help and luckily I got the help I needed.

From my experience, the majority of bad teachers are the ones who just don't care. They also want to do the least amount of work. As I have explained, a teacher has a lot of work to do and for those wanting to cut corners, sometimes it is at the expense of students' learning.

I don't know of any class or training that will help teachers who are bad or lazy become teachers who suddenly care.

Mystery #12: What should a teacher do if he or she sees signs that they are becoming a "bad" teacher?

Tip: Think about writing a book.

What are the signs that a teacher is in danger of being "burned-out?"

Forgetting to bring work home to check? No, not caring that you forgot the work to bring home and check.

A week's worth of papers not graded? No, a semester of papers not graded.

Not knowing what you're going to teach when you walk into the classroom? No, not caring that you don't know what you're going to teach when you walk into the classroom.

Counting the hours until the end of the day? No, counting the days until you retire.

These are some signs for teachers that they are in jeopardy of becoming a "bad" teacher.

It might be too late to help some really burned-out teachers, but as a society, the most important thing we need to do is prevent any more good teachers from becoming burned-out teachers.

Even if a person is not considered a truly talented teacher, I don't think people enter the profession wanting to be a "bad" teacher. (But then again, I could be wrong.) As I found out, teaching is a very tough job and it isn't for everyone. This is why 50% of new teachers quit within the first five years.

Those are the lucky ones who find out early that it's not for them. They leave before they get caught up in the familiarity of the job, the regular paychecks, and those very nice three-month vacations.

For other people it takes longer and by the time they realize they hate their job, they are trapped in the comfort of working at a job that will provide them a decent retirement.

Most teachers think they can handle the constant workload of the job, until one day they ask themselves, "What is the point? Why am I killing myself when it doesn't even seem to make a difference and they just want more?" Or worse, "Does anybody even care what I'm going through?"

How do we prevent good teachers from reaching their breaking point? Stopping some of the insanity that this book talks about would be a good start. Testing and accountability can be good things, but administrators and politicians have to recognize that there is truly only so much pressure a teacher can put up with to raise test scores. Despite trying to be everything for everyone, we are, after all, just mere mortals. There's got to be some way to determine when teachers are trying their best, without putting all this pressure on them for better test scores or making that Annual Yearly Progress score.

Teachers do bear the burden of responsibility for recognizing when they are feeling overwhelmed or frustrated with the job. Maybe all they need to do is speak to another teacher or confide in an administrator they feel comfortable talking with. Realistically, I know that's easier said than done.

The reality of teaching: Putting it into survivor mode

As a teacher who has often felt overwhelmed with the work involved with teaching, I have finally discovered what most veteran teachers know. While I paint the picture that teaching is a job that requires many hours beyond the school day, the reality is, teaching, like many professions, can be as hard or as easy as a person makes it to be. The truly dedicated teacher wouldn't even think of taking short cuts or skimping on the number of hours they put in, even if it is at the cost of their personal life. However, many in the profession aren't that self-sacrificing. They have learned how to teach in a "survivor" mode.

"Survivor" mode means you have created tricks of the trade or an organization system that lets you be a good teacher without sacrificing your personal life. In my case, I do my best trying to stick to my new personal policy of not taking papers home to grade, at least every night. I get on the task of correcting papers as soon as class has been dismissed. I stagger assignments and tests so that I don't overwhelm myself with a lot of work to correct on any one day. I even change what time of day I will give a test so that it will give me more time to check papers while they are doing independent work.

This has resulted in many positive results. My house and car are no longer cluttered with piles of paper I have corrected and I know at the end of the day which student owes me what assignment. I also know that, since I don't take papers home with me, if a student is missing an assignment, it's not because I somehow misplaced it at home.

Most importantly, I feel like I have a break from school and I am not sacrificing the time with my family or personal interests. I recognize that to be a good teacher you need to be a happy teacher and often that means not working ten hours every day.

Does survivor mode happen at the expense of educating students?

I don't think so, but in reality, teaching in survivor mode will probably not get a teacher chosen "Teacher of the Year."

When we heard Ron Clark speak, or if you read his books, you can tell that he has never operated in survivor mode. He never told us how many extra hours he spends beyond the teaching day. I think we can safely assume it takes many, many hours outside of his contract day. But because he such a dedicated teacher, I doubt he even thinks about it.

During his first year at the school in Harlem, he visited the home of every student before the school year began. I think he said that meant visiting the homes of 36 students. How much time do you think that took?

One time he went to a local convenience store and asked the clerks to help quiz his students on the styles of great artists by showing them flash cards he had created depicting works of art. At his request, the local supermarket renamed the aisles so his students would learn the streets in Washington, D.C. In order that his students can go on many field trips, he was constantly doing fundraisers or soliciting donations from businesses. And the list goes on in his quest to give all students the best education possible, with the price tag of his time.

I think most of the teachers who attended Ron Clark's presentation were overwhelmed by his dedication and results.

A week later, I was speaking with a teacher whom I work with about his speech. She told me it bothered her when other teachers dismissed his efforts as unrealistic when it comes to the real world of teaching. I disagreed with her. It is obvious that he puts all of his energy into teaching, without a wife or children who also need his attention at home.

Also, he never gave us an exact amount of time he had been teaching, but most estimates figure he had only been doing this between seven and ten years, not enough time for burnout to happen. *(Personally, I don't think Ron Clark will ever burn out on teaching, or at least won't admit it.)*

The teacher I was talking with felt the other teachers were just finding a way to excuse themselves from trying to be a better teacher. She felt it wasn't about what he did, but more about his desire that all students be successful.

While I agreed with her that a teacher doesn't have to go to this extreme to be a wonderful teacher and that it is more about having the right attitude when teaching students, I also felt our colleagues were right. Is it really fair to expect all teachers to put in the time that Ron Clark does? Does the path to becoming a truly "effective" teacher and not leaving children behind come at the expense of a teacher's personal life?

No, I believe there are many roads to Mecca, I mean good test scores, and there are many fantastic teachers who do it by teaching in their survivor mode. But then again, maybe I just might be living on de Nile, I mean, in "denial."

Mystery #13: Why do some teachers have an "Us vs. Them" mentality when it comes to their students?

In the course of human events, and very frequently in schools, there is a time when people have to take tests. That is just the natural progression of things. Teachers teach. Then students take tests to see how well they understand what is taught. There are "radical" educators who think testing is bad for students because it doesn't accurately demonstrate what the students have learned. I disagree but am not going to take the time to argue the pros or cons of either side at this point in the book. All I know from my few short years of teaching is that a written assessment, or test, is truly the most efficient way to see if a child is learning.

However, I've noticed, even with some really good teachers and teachers my own children have had, there is a pervasive attitude out there that I find rather perplexing. It is the common belief that it's only the student's fault when he or she does poorly on a test. I have often heard teachers make statements such as "I'm so mad at my class! They just did horribly on the math test." Or "I just don't get it. We went over and over the science material and they still didn't get it. I just don't think they tried." These teachers somehow make it sound like the students are purposely failing in order to get back at a teacher. It's sort of an "us vs. them" mentality.

I'm not saying that it isn't possible for a group of students not to try and therefore fail a test, but I don't think they do it to get back at the teacher. I like conspiracy theories, but even I have a hard time buying as fact that the class, collectively as a whole group, got together and agreed to fail a test, as the comments above suggest.

I don't think a lot of teachers have this attitude, but I have been present when teachers have innocently made these remarks. I find this peculiar, because when I see bad results on a test the first thing I think of is, "Wow, I must have done a lousy job teaching that lesson!" Well, that's not always true. I have also been guilty of thinking to myself, "Why do they hate me so much? Why did they do so poorly on this test after all the work I did teaching them the lessons?"

I understand, intellectually, if my class, as a whole, doesn't do well on a quiz or test, I first need to examine the test and see if it was a bad test. Then, if that wasn't the case, then heavens forbid, I realize it wasn't the students' fault, but must have been a problem with my teaching. Or maybe I rushed through it and didn't give them enough time and practice to really learn.

I admit, this is one of the most frustrating aspects about teaching, teaching your heart out and then giving a test and finding out that many students did not "get it." I have given science tests where, prior to the test, I go over every question and the answer for that test, and still most of the class does poorly. It drives me nuts!

But it's easy to forget that we are looking at things through an adult mind vs. the minds of ten-year-olds, twelve-year-olds or even sixteen-year-olds. Concepts that seem very easy to me, with decades of life experience behind me, do not come easy for children, even if they did hear the information over and over again.

I want to believe that I'm not a bad teacher and they are not dumb. Again, maybe it has to do with that most important first lesson I learned from my Education 101 class: often times, it's all developmental. That means, maybe you have to repeat things lots of times before it sinks in. (You might notice this "repeating" trait is something I have unintentionally incorporated into my writing. It's not that I think adults also need the repetition, it's just a habit I have.)

There is a more common reason why students fail tests, and it has nothing to do with how well the teacher teaches or "doing it to make the teacher mad." The reality is there are many students out there who don't care what they get on a test. Or maybe they care, but not enough to do the work it takes to pass. A teacher can't help those students. Sadly, it isn't about "us vs. them," but "them vs. them." What those students don't realize, as adults do, is that they are only cheating themselves by not putting their best effort into school.

Mystery #14: Why do some teachers teach the same way they have for 25 years?

The biggest problem you get with a very small portion of experienced teachers is that they teach the same way they taught 20 or 25 years ago. I've heard of a teacher who still believes that "whole language" is the way to teach language arts; despite the fact we know students need extensive phonics instruction. It's not that she doesn't teach any phonics, because she does. It's just that she still mainly uses strategies from back in the days when "whole language" was the way to do it. She also does the same bulletin boards and the same field trips that she has for the past fifteen years. Another teacher has used the same homework packet for five years, even though it's hard to imagine all of her classes have progressed at the same rate.

As I have mentioned, my own children had a teacher who made them do long laborious reading comprehension packets that had nothing to do with teaching them actual reading comprehension skills. These packets were just pages and pages of questions asking for details about the classroom novel they were reading. My son just hated them and would fill them out very quickly. Obviously, he got a "D" in reading comprehension.

But is that grade a real indicator of how well he read? It was a real grade that reflected his effort on these packets, but that's not what I wanted to know. I wanted to know how well he comprehends when he reads lots of different texts, not just a particular novel he may not have enjoyed. But this is the way she has taught all of these years, and this is probably what she will continue to do.

In education, it's amazing how someone can stick to old methods of teaching. It seems we are constantly being inundated with new ideas or ways to do things, thus our never-ending need for staff development. Sometimes I think students aren't achieving because we never give an idea a long enough chance to see if it will work. Just as it is reflected in society, in education too we want quick fixes to our problems.

While the constant reinventing of the wheel isn't good, neither is doing the same thing year after year. There is a fine line in knowing whether or not you should reinvent the wheel or just change it because it's flat.

How does a teacher know if he or she should change the way they teach? If a teacher sees real results that her students are learning, why change things? As they say, "If it ain't broke, why fix it." But if students are struggling, then it's time to try something new. The students' time in the classroom is too short and precious to waste it on lessons that might have worked ten years ago, but no longer do the trick today.

Mystery #15: Why aren't teachers supposed to yell at a class and, heavens forbid, say the "s" word? (Not that four-letter "S" word but, "Shut-up!")

He who truly knows has no occasion to shout.

— Leonardo Da Vinci

Parents might not know this, but a sign of a good teacher is one who has her class so in control that she never needs to yell at them or raise her voice. Of course, I think it's also a sign of a good parent, one who doesn't yell. Well, I guess that makes me neither a good parent nor a good teacher.

Actually, I have learned that yelling isn't the best way to get a child's attention. I know now that the best way to quiet a class is just standing there quietly with my hand up in the air. It is amazing how well it works. I learned this from my Harry Wong book.

Nevertheless, I have a naturally loud voice and it always sounds like I am yelling. (That's my story and I'm sticking to it.)

But heaven forbid you tell your class to "Shut-up!" Even if that's what they really need to do. I remember the first time I ever said that particular "s" word. It was during my first year of teaching fifth grade. Those kids just weren't being quiet. So I calmly said, "Please, shut-up!" and boy did I hear these gasps around the room.

"Mrs. Craig, you said the "s" word."

"Yes, I said shut-up. You all need to be quiet." (This is a horrible confession, isn't it?)

It worked, but I was just waiting for the call from some parent. I even wondered if it was grounds for getting fired. I know Ron Clark has never even thought of telling a group of students to "Shut-up, please" (I always ask politely.) For me, it just seemed like the thing to do. (So forgive me readers, for I know I had committed a teacher's sin.)

I am also guilty of saying another not socially acceptable word: "crap." Albert, a student you will be learning about in my "Student" chapter, had the messiest and worst desk I have ever seen. His papers and books were strewn everywhere. One day, I told him he needed to pick up his "crap" off the floor.

Oh, my gosh, did my other students freak out? That time I did get a call from Albert's mom wondering if I actually had said that to him. How could I lie? I had all of those witnesses. I confessed I did. She told me she would appreciate if I didn't use that kind of language again, because that's not how she likes her son being spoken to. The funny thing is, she would yell up a storm at Albert when he was present at conferences with her. But I understand why that was okay, because she is his parent.

Anyway, I apologized to her and have been careful not to use that word again, even though he has long been gone from my class.

I really don't understand what's wrong with saying these words. That's not true. I do understand this resorting to yelling and a poor word choice makes it sound like the teacher doesn't have control of the class and it shows a lack of respect to your students. And heavens forbid, even though many students show no respect to teachers, teachers must always be respectful towards students.

Mystery #16: Why do they put the "bad" teachers at poor schools and the "good" teachers at affluent, successful schools?

How else can it be explained why schools in more affluent areas do so much better in state assessment testing than the schools in low socio-economic areas?

Doesn't the government wish that this were true, that test scores are all about the teachers? But then again, I think they do believe that the "bad" teachers are at low socio-economic schools.

Just so you know, school districts do not staff their poorer schools with the worst teachers and the best teachers at the affluent schools. Nor is it true that most teachers at poor schools are new, inexperienced teachers. If my book could accomplish just one thing, it would be to help dispel the myth that "good teachers" work at "successful schools" and that "bad teachers" work at high-poverty, minority schools. This is why the issue of "merit pay" for teachers is becoming more popular. The problem is, this just isn't the case.

As you know, I have been a teacher at a Title I, or low socio-economic school, for over seven years. I work my heart out, as do the other teachers at my school, including some who have over 25 years of experience. Yet we are struggling to meet our goals. I resent the insinuation that a teacher from a more successful school in an affluent area could miraculously get the students at my school to suddenly perform better.

Contrary to popular opinion, successful schools are not all about good teaching. You also have to have students who want to learn, parents who help the students learn, and a culture that promotes education. We can throw all the money you want at high-poverty, minority schools but until there is some ownership on the part of the parents and students for better scores (if that's the criteria we are using for "success") then I think success will be elusive.

I would love to see some newsmagazine like *60 Minutes* or *Dateline* actually conduct an experiment where teachers from an underperforming school are switched with teachers from a school with some of the highest test scores. Would these teachers be able to get the students from the underachieving school up to the level of proficiency the government wants? Can they do it in one year?

And what about those students who would now be taught by the teachers from the "failing" school? Would their test scores go down, or remain the same? My guess is that test scores at either school will not be dramatically impacted by this switch in teachers.

I will partially get my "wish" of switching teachers fulfilled this new school year when a teacher from a more successful school and different demographics has decided to transfer to my school. It's not exactly a switch though, since one of our teachers will not be going to his school. Nevertheless, I will take what I can get.

The new teacher coming to our school is an experienced teacher and wants the challenge of working at a Title I school. It will be interesting to see how he adjusts to the different type of school. Will he be more successful than the teacher who left? Who knows, maybe I'll find out that it really is all about the teacher.

Mystery #17: Would schools be better without a tenure system?

Unlike being in the private sector/business world, teachers have a perk that sets them apart from most other workers, except maybe those who also work in large organized labor unions. Teachers have something called "tenure." Tenure means that after two or three years (depending on the state) of working for a school district in a probationary period, a teacher earns a very special sort of "job security." Teachers have to do some pretty horrible things before they can be fired or let go. That's why the teaching profession has this reputation of harboring "bad" teachers.

In an effort to right this wrong, and because "every student deserves a good teacher," California is putting on the ballot a proposition that will ask voters to change tenure from two years of satisfactory performance to five years. In my opinion, people are very naïve if they think increasing the length of time it takes a teacher to earn tenure is going to have any real impact on student performance.

I haven't heard of any teacher not getting tenure after their two-year probationary period anyway. The reality is schools need "highly qualified" teachers (by the government definition). It's usually difficult just to fill the open positions resulting from retirements or people leaving the field. With the demand for experienced teachers so high, I don't see that changing even if tenure isn't given until after teaching five years.

Most "bad" teachers are also pretty good about hiding their weaknesses. How are teachers evaluated? In our district, it happens when your principal comes in and watches you teach a prepared lesson. You have to be a really bad teacher to mess up that. Even if your lesson is less than stellar, most principals might give you a second chance or just chalk it up to stress. There might be an administrator who might not like a particular teacher and now can use this higher standard for tenure to get rid of him or her, but I would hope there would be safeguards built into the system to prevent this.

Most importantly, my theory is that most teacher burnout probably comes after ten years of teaching. That's when a teacher gets burned-out, is tired of caring anymore, and putting up with the ridiculous demands on teachers. By then they already have the tenure, so what difference will it really make whether tenure is at two years or ten years?

I think this idea of "tenure after five years" is much ado about nothing.

On the other hand, it might be bad for education. Teachers already are under constant scrutiny and the insinuation that we are at fault for the public school system, while putting no responsibility on students and parents. So if tenure is moved up to five years, we might find this "great" idea will backfire on us, when its not the "bad" teachers that leave, but the "good" teachers who have nothing to gain by hanging on and are fed with up with the whole system.

What about getting rid of tenure altogether? Now that's a different subject. It might have an impact on the quality of teaching, as long as administrators have the guts to let go of long-established teachers who are just going through the motions of teaching. But on the other hand, how can an administrator really know this is happening? What criteria do we use to determine that a teacher isn't doing the job? Do we base it on (gasp) "test scores?" I don't think so. As I have said before, often even bad teachers can look good with a class of really bright students.

I'm skeptical of the system changing even if tenure were abolished, because the reality is schools have the power, even with tenure, to get rid of bad teachers. Most school districts don't bother because of the burden of proof they have to come up with and it's just easier to keep a bad teacher than to find a good teacher.

Believe it or not, it would make me happy to be proven wrong, to see that administrations are willing to eliminate teachers who are not doing their job. Ineffective teachers make it harder for the other teachers who do try and want to give the education students not only expect, but deserve.

Mystery #18: Why does it seem that the government assumes it's "always the teachers' fault" when it comes to students achieving academic success?

As you know, this is my battle cry. Contrary to what the government probably thinks and contrary to low test scores, I will tell you that most teachers work very hard and give it their best effort.

If that is the case, one might be thinking, why then are so many schools not making the goals set up for them in the No Child Left Behind Act? Schools have the materials approved by adoption committees, they have the facilities conducive to learning and, the Lord knows, schools get billions of dollars from state and federal governments. So teachers must be at fault for not teaching kids what they need to know to be proficient in math and language arts. What other reason could it be?

For starters, could it be that the students themselves are to blame for their underachieving ways? Heavens forbid that could be the reason. This may come to a shock to many politicians, but some students come to school because they have to and not because they want to learn. They don't do class work and homework. I doubt those words are even in their vocabulary. And no matter what the teacher says or does to try to get them to care about test scores, they still aren't interested. I recently attended a regional math networking conference. We were asked to explain how we thought we could improve our math scores. A group of high school teachers all agreed they didn't know what they could do. They said their biggest problem was students' lack of ownership for the scores. The consensus was that most students don't care what score they get and many don't try.

So are teachers supposed to be miracle workers and make these students successful despite lack of effort on their part? If this is the case, I must have missed my credential class on "Miracles 101" for information on how to do this.

What about the parents? Don't they bear some of the responsibility to ensure that each student is up to par on his or her studies? Even though taxpayers are paying our salaries, the sad fact is that with so many students in a class, teachers can't do it alone. Sometimes parents have to put just as much effort into helping their child as his or her teacher does, especially if the child is not motivated when it comes to learning. That's just the cold reality of public education.

Mystery #19: Why would anyone want to become a teacher in this political climate?

As the pressure increases on teachers more and more each year for better test scores and students who can excel on standardized tests, it's a tough wanting to stay in teaching. This is particularly true now that many school districts are mandating to teachers, not just what to teach, but what to say when they teach, and the exact times they must teach certain subjects, and scrutinizing lesson plans to make certain that only the "core" curriculum is being taught.

Teaching used to be considered a creative field, where teachers would "design" lesson plans for presenting an effective lesson. It looks to me like those days will soon be gone. Now it's about administrators micromanaging classrooms in order that they have complete control of how a student is taught. This is probably an unfair generalization of the state of public schools. I'm certain that many school districts all around the country still promote creativity and innovation in the classroom. However, I see the trend, especially in "underperforming schools" of strict adherence to a precise program, one (of course) based on "scientific research" that will (of course) "get those test scores up."

Recently I read a Gallup Youth Survey that asked 1,000 kids between ages 13 and 17 what their career goal is. Surprisingly, teaching came in at number one, followed by being a doctor, then lawyer. Actually it isn't any surprise that teaching came in so high for teenagers. Teaching is the job they can most closely identify with because they know, or at least they think they know, what a teacher's job is. Part of the allure of teaching, and deservedly so, is the fact most teachers, like the students, get summers off. In that regards, it is a very good gig.

Even the very unscientific internet poll that asked, "My dream job would be in…" had teaching tied with medicine for first place. Go figure.

I am glad that people still want to go into teaching. The world can never have enough people who are intent on educating our future generation. It is a rewarding job, but as you can tell, there's also a lot of insanity mixed in. But then again, what job is perfect, right?

Personally, I wouldn't recommend anyone entering the teaching profession unless they really understood what they were getting into.

2

Reading & Writing

Reading is to the mind,
what exercise is to the body.

— *Joseph Addison*

Is there a correlation between academic success and how much a student reads? After all, it is really the foundation for learning all of the other subjects. Kids have to know how to read. In my experience as a teacher, usually the brightest students are also the ones who love to read.

Students + Reading = Jeopardy champions

For the record, I want to make it clear that I do watch the TV show *Jeopardy*. Ken Jennings, the all-time winning champion on this television game show, said one of reasons he is so smart is because he loves to read. Therefore, I understand the relationship between a student who reads and the student who is smart and academically successful. They are usually the same.

Why is it so important to read to children when they are young?

Have you ever wondered why some students are naturally born readers while others won't even touch a book? I have a theory coincidentally based on my own family situation. My daughter Jenna, who is in middle school, loves to read. I have never had to tell her to do her nightly reading. Jenna is also a fabulous writer. Of course, that's not surprising since she's an avid reader. I've heard the two skills seem to go hand and hand.

My son, Matthew, is two years younger than Jenna and he hates to read. Well, he will read non-fiction books like *The Guinness Book of World Records*. Still, picking up a book to read is not something he does willingly.

How could two children in the same household with the same parents be so different when it comes to reading? Some might argue that it's because Jenna is a girl and Matthew is a boy. Maybe it's because Jenna is the first-born of the family and they seem to be more self-motivated. But I have another theory.

From the time Jenna was little, I read constantly to her. Bedtime stories happened every night. Books were part of her daily routine. However, when my son Matthew was young, I was working part-time as a supermarket cashier and started taking my teaching credential classes at night. I just don't remember reading the stories to him like I did to Jenna.

Is it true what they say about the importance of reading to your children when they are young? My theory is maybe there is a window of opportunity that gives students an edge if they are read to from the time they are born until they go to school.

Okay, so maybe this isn't really just my theory or a mystery. I know experts always harp on parents to read stories with their children when they are young. It does set some kind of stage for them to be more motivated to read. I guess I should have believed "them."

I am a believer now, and often wonder if their hypothesis isn't also correct about how students from low income families, who don't indulge their children in a print-rich environment, are put at a disadvantage in school. If they aren't exposed to books at an early age, then when they come to school, the teacher gets the job of trying to force something that might have happened naturally when they were younger.

But then again, who knows. Even if I had read to Matthew, maybe he still would not have had that natural inclination to pick up a book and read. To those of you who have small children, don't leave it up to chance. Read with your children when they are young so if they end up not reading when they are older, you won't be faced with the parental guilt I have with my son.

Maybe I shouldn't feel so guilty. Does a lack of love for reading necessarily mean a child won't be a good reader? I used to think that since my son hates reading, and doesn't do much of it outside what I mentioned and his Sgt. Frog comic books, that Matthew is a poor reader. But then I received a bit of information that rather startled me. In our school district, all fifth graders have to take a reading placement test to determine what level of language arts class they should be placed in. If they are significantly below grade level, they are grouped in a class that will help them catch up with their peers.

After seeing my son's "D" grade in Reading Comprehension on his Progress Report from the teacher "I love," I decided to ask her for my son's score. Out of 55 questions, my son only missed four, thus placing him at the ninth grade level and above, in reading! And yet his teacher says he's a "D student"? And I thought because he doesn't "love" reading, he was also a poor reader. Shows you how much I know.

Mystery #20: Do teachers really believe a child has read all the books they list on a reading log?

Reading furnishes the mind only with materials of knowledge; it is thinking that makes what we read ours.

— *John Lock*

Most parents understand the importance of reading and a child's academic success. Okay, maybe I didn't provide real numbers, but we all know that research will support the claim.

Now, since a teacher can't physically be at their homes to see if students are reading, what can he or she do to make certain they are doing independent reading at home?

Well, she can't secretly videotape each student at their home reading; that would be too costly and an invasion of privacy. She could demand weekly book reports. (I'm sure there has never been a student out there who has written a book report on a book they haven't read.)

Teachers often track the amount of independent reading a student is doing by having them write the book title and the number of pages he or she has read on a piece of paper commonly referred to as a "reading log."

I have dealt with reading logs since my children have been in kindergarten. The teachers at my kids' elementary school have been good perpetuators of the "reading log." The school even used the logs as a basis for contests in hopes of motivating students to read even more. Often the reader who reads the most in a month is eligible for a drawing or a prize! Most teachers, just like my son's fourth and fifth grade teachers, make turning in this reading log part of their grade.

So what's my problem with reading logs? If the truth be told, this gripe is really coming more from the parent side than my teacher side.

I just can't believe that teachers really believe that students are honest on these logs. Why would I doubt the credibility of these logs?

One teacher who is NOT setting a good example

Okay, well maybe I'm going to be giving you too much information, but I've got to do it for the sake of proving my point. The reason I hate reading logs has nothing to do with my experience as a teacher, but my experience as a mom. I'm sorry to admit it, but I have let my own children write down books they haven't read.

It is true. I, a teacher, used to have my own children cheat, or at least fudge a little on them just because I knew, for some weird reason, his teacher would rather have a reading log that might be totally false than no reading log at all.

Why do I think that just because I have cheated on reading logs most students also cheat on reading logs? Oh, please. If a schoolteacher has her own son cheat on his log, why wouldn't she think that other parents/students do the same? The "good" parents, of course, never would, but some of us desperate parents have, especially if it avoids a lower grade for his or her son or daughter.

However, I am proud to report that actually I'm a reformed cheater. We don't lie any more on reading logs because I've decided to quit playing the "straight A" game. Nope. If my son isn't going to read, I'm not going to have him write down books that he hasn't read. He has to come clean and suffer the consequences of this reading neglect, which usually means his reading grade is lowered.

My point about reading logs is what's the point of them if some students can lie about what they read? The parents don't even have to be a partner in this crime. I spoke with a teacher who suspected that students were forging their parents' signatures or having other students sign off for them. What teacher has the time to worry about forged signatures on a reading log?

Do I have a better idea? Well, not exactly. I just think society wouldn't suffer if reading logs were eliminated from public schools altogether. In fact, it might even be a positive thing. Think of all the trees that would be saved and the more room there would be in landfills. Besides, just because a child writes down that he has read many books, doesn't necessarily mean he comprehends what he reads either.

Mystery #21: Do teachers put too much emphasis on just reading books and ignore other ways that children can learn to embrace reading?

If a teacher has the policy that reading at home is for a grade, as much as doing math problems, it does make sense that a student who hasn't done it should get "dinged" on their grades. I can't argue that this is an unfair punishment.

However, whether a child is from a low socio-economic family and wasn't exposed to books or a child from a more affluent, middle-class neighborhood who has his own library, it would be great if elementary school teachers saw it as their job to help students embrace books; to create a joy for reading, and not just punish them when they don't read. We all know, if you like doing something, then the odds are you are more motivated to do it. But sometimes that goal gets lost in the madness of "having" to read thirty minutes every night and writing down everything you read.

So how can we instill the joy of reading in this generation of non-readers? First, I think we need to acknowledge that any reading is good for a child, even if it isn't a book. I know my own children constantly spend time reading things on the internet. My son, because he loves video games, reads their massive strategy guides. Maybe it's not the same as reading a book, but we should acknowledge that this is reading for their enjoyment, and that's how you begin to instill a love for reading.

It doesn't have to be only about reading. Exposing children to new words to increase their vocabulary will help their comprehension just as much as if they read thirty minutes every night.

By my own admission, I was a strange child. One of the things I looked forward to every month was going to the mailbox and finding the latest edition of *Reader's Digest*.

It's not because I loved reading so much that I couldn't wait to read all of the articles. No, it was because they had a feature called "How to Increase Your Word Power," a test designed to increase your vocabulary. They listed a word and you had to choose from four words to come up with its meaning. Even though many of the words were way over my head, and probably still are, I liked seeing if I could guess the right answer. I also used to love reading the dictionary. Never did I realize until I became a teacher what a valuable service I was doing for myself by enhancing my reading and writing ability.

At our school, our students take a test on the computer that is supposed to determine their reading level. But this test doesn't ask questions of comprehension about a passage of text they have to read. No, it has either a sentence or a paragraph of text, then a blank line where a word is supposed to go. The student is given a choice of four words and has to decide which word works best in the sentence.

Now as an adult reader, it seems like a very simple test. Some of the choices they give are very obviously wrong. But I am amazed at how many words my fifth graders do not know. No wonder they do poorly on the reading tests based on vocabulary.

I have also discovered this phenomenon when we do our weekly spelling tests. I'm always surprised when I find students don't know words like "humor," "slope," and "flute," words I just assumed they would know. I was especially shocked when one girl asked me what a "rifle" was. Maybe in this day of semi-automatic weapons and no "Bonanza" television show, how would a student in the 21st century know what a "rifle" is?

A flaw of making kids read just for the sake of reading is that many students don't take the time to look up new words that they don't recognize in a text. As a teacher, we give them skills to try to figure it out, but I don't know how many average or below average readers do this.

At my school, where we have a predominant percentage of English Language Learners (ELL), they may know and use basic English well enough to communicate, but they really have a long way to go when it comes to vocabulary. In fact, I remember when one of my fluent English Language Learners asked me what a "shoulder" was? How many other fifth graders don't know what a shoulder is? This student said he had never heard it before.

Yet we give the same achievement tests to all students, who are assumed to be coming in at about the same level of vocabulary and prior knowledge. It just isn't the case. Many of my ELL students have parents who speak to them in Spanish and do not themselves have a good command of English vocabulary words. How are these

ELL learners expected to catch up with English speaking peers with just the instruction they are getting in class?

The more a student reads, the more words that student will be exposed to and the better the opportunity to increase their vocabulary. Skills that help students figure out the meaning by looking at the content are good for children, especially when they don't have access to a dictionary. However, teachers should encourage students to have a dictionary at their side when they read so they don't have to guess at the meaning of a word. And who knows. Maybe someday they too will look forward to trying the "Word Power" feature in *Reader's Digest*.

Is our society doomed to become a nation of couch potatoes who never read?

The man who doesn't read good books has no advantage over the man who can't read them.

— Mark Twain

Yes, many "experts" have pulled the alarm when it comes to reading in our country. They aren't just worried about children not wanting to read, but adults as well. There is a fear that we are on the road to becoming a nation of illiterate non-readers. Is there truth in these fears or are they just a ploy to make us feel guilty about one more thing in life?

According to a report released by the National Endowment for the Arts in July 2004, the number of non-reading adults increased by more than 17 million between 1992 and 2002!

Yikes! They report that only 47 percent of American adults read "literature" like plays, poems, and fiction, a drop of 7 points from the previous decade, which isn't too bad considering the big decrease in readers. Also, those reading any book, just not "literature," fell 4 points to 57 percent from 61 percent.

I love this quote from NEA chairman Dana Gioia, who said in

an Associated Press interview that "We have a lot of functionally literate people who are no longer engaged readers. This isn't a case of 'Johnny can't read,' but 'Johnny won't read'."

In defense of non-readers everywhere, look what books are out there. If it isn't a true confession from a celebrity, sports figure, or person associated with a criminal act, what choice do we have?

The decline in reading was greatest among people ages 18 to 24. Only 43 percent had read any literature in 2002, down from 53 percent in 1992.

All is not hopeless when it comes to reading. I also found a current Harris Poll that said "reading," yes reading, was the number one favorite leisure activity! (Of course we'd rather even read than do anything that requires movement.) Reading beat out watching television, 24 percent vs. 17 percent. (I'm sorry, but I no longer believe the validity of this survey.)

What was at the bottom of the list? Cooking has that honor, which I guess explains our society's love for fast food. (Okay, I really hate cooking too so maybe this survey is accurate.)

Mystery #22: Why do teachers use reading as punishment?

"Anthony, this is the last time I'll tell you to quit talking," said a schoolteacher somewhere across America. "You need to take a book outside and read during recess."

I don't know how common the above scenario is, but I know I have seen teachers who "punish" students by making them read at recess or while the class gets to do some other kind of activity. If you happen to love to read, is that really punishment? But as I have discussed, how many kids love reading?

I just find this a peculiar thing that teachers do. What kind of message are we really giving to kids? We want them to love reading, but yet if they are being punished, part of the punishment is reading? Actually, I know this isn't the intention. Making kids read while they are on "punishment" is a way to turn something bad into something good. Instead of just sitting there, now the child can at least they can use the time for reading.

Writing curriculum mysteries

**When something can be read without effort,
Great effort has gone into its writing.**

— Enrique Jardiel Poncela

Enough about reading, it's time to move on to another one of my favorite topics, "Writing in Elementary School." I apologize in advance that I also don't have a "Writing in Junior High School" or a "Writing in High School" chapter, but those are not my areas of expertise. Actually, one could argue quite well, as I confess later on, that I am also not an expert in "Writing in Elementary School."

To support the fact, I had to rewrite this chapter, and in part my point of view about writing instruction in elementary schools, after I attended a series of teacher training classes at the beginning of my second year of teaching fifth grade. What do you know? I actually learned something I can use to help me become a better teacher.

But first, I will share with you my own personal writing epiphany, or "How I found the courage to write this book."

Mystery #23: Is it true that "Those who can, do; those who can't, teach." (And those who can't teach, teach gym?)

"Those who can, do. Those who can't, teach." (And of course, to quote Jack Black in the movie, *School of Rock,* "Those who can't teach, teach gym.")

No, eight words have been so haunting to me since I've become a fifth grade teacher. I don't know if most writers have to get an epiphany in order to start writing, but I know I did.

I will never forget standing up in front of a class, teaching a writing lesson with the support teacher who comes in to help one hour a day, four days a week.

She, like most teachers in education, is very big on having students prepare a graphic organizer to help organize their thoughts into either a paragraph or multi-paragraph composition. One of the students asked if she had to use the four-square box graphic organizer passed out to all of the students.

I told her, "Well, if you think you can write without one, go ahead and try."

Well, that was a mistake. My support teacher quickly snapped back, "What are you telling her? Of course, she has to use one. Everyone has to use one. She just can't write down her thoughts."

I asked, "Why not?"

She replied, "Because that's not the way real writers write. They don't just write down what they are going to say."

"They don't?" I inquired.

"No, they don't!"

I couldn't let it drop. "Are you telling me that all famous writers use a graphic organizer to write?"

"Well they might not use a graphic organizer, but I know they all organize their thoughts into some format before they write."

My response: "Some of my best friends are famous writers and none of them use a graphic organizer. They just start writing on the computer to get their thoughts down!"

Actually, I wanted to tell her that, but I didn't because it wasn't true. And I didn't know that she wasn't right. All I know is, I love to write and I seldom, prior to a writing project, sit down and organize my thoughts. Nor have I ever used a graphic organizer. (Okay, I hope you're not thinking maybe I should be doing that.)

I really resented her telling me something has to be done a certain way when in reality she really didn't know either.

But there's more to the story than that. The reality was, I was having a terrible problem teaching writing to my class. It's not that I couldn't, it's that I didn't want to. I was embarrassed when I heard a fellow fifth grade teacher tell me how her students write every day. I seldom made my class write.

And I knew what the problem was. I wondered about the saying, "Those who can, do, those who can't, teach?" When the support teacher in my class said she knew how all writers wrote, I had my moment of truth. I said to myself, "What am I doing here? I can't teach writing, I need to be writing. I am a writer!"

The very next time I was off-track, I wrote the first draft of this book in its entirety. (If you noticed, I said first draft. It has taken me many drafts to get it to this point.)

So there, I hope I have proved that old adage wrong: yes, those who can teach, can also do. At least I thought this was the case until I heard an author on a talk show say that, "Those who can, do, those who can't, write." Hmm, I just can't win, can I?

Mystery #24: Do teachers really believe students will become better writers if we force them to write phonetically spelled sentences in kindergarten and first grade?

I have a hard time with elementary school administrators thinking that kindergartners through third graders need intensive writing instruction at this age and that it actually gives them the foundation for being a good writer later on in life. I don't know if I'm bothered by the emphasis on writing in the early elementary school years because I am a writer or if I would have been bothered by it even if I weren't a writer.

I think the real reason I have a problem with writing in these early elementary grades is because back in the dark ages when I was growing up, I wasn't expected to write phonetically spelled sentences in kindergarten and I still learned how to write.

I don't even know how much credit I can give to my high school

English teachers. I do give Mr. Ervin, my high school English teacher, credit for teaching me grammar and word usage skills. For me personally, it wasn't until college that my writing skills gelled. All of a sudden, I got it. But NOOO! Now in today's public schools they have to "get it" in first grade?

Another effect from this ridiculous push for elementary school kids to write is that as a fifth grade teacher, not only do I get a classroom of kids who get frustrated when they write, they hate the idea of writing anything. Educators want so much for kids to love reading, well the same should be said of writing.

I don't care what the research says, I will never, ever believe that by starting children writing in kindergarten and first grade we will have a nation full of better writers. I think the opposite is true. I think because there is so much pressure for students to write in school, people grow up hating writing and therefore will do anything to avoid doing it.

I just don't understand this big rush to make kids write. I think good writing happens as a person matures and forms more coherent thoughts. Why pressure them when they are so young to do something they will eventually learn how to do as they get older? Not only that, the results will be better if it's taught at a maturity level where they really understand the concept.

So am I saying we shouldn't teach writing in elementary schools? Absolutely not! I think by fourth grade, once they have a command of their reading and *spelling skills*, and with the proper instructional program, even 8- and 9-year-olds need be able to learn how to write sentences and paragraphs.

Mystery #25: Why do they think writing is so important in the early grades that educators even encourage the use of "inventive spelling"?

It is a damned poor mind indeed that can't think of at least two ways of spelling any word.

— Andrew Jackson

Have you noticed that Americans can't spell today? I won't say all Americans, but probably those who were told if they didn't know how to spell a word, it's okay to just spell it out phonetically. This might be an "okay" strategy if you don't know how to spell one or two words. But in kindergarten, kids don't know how to spell, period. They know how to sound things out. I'm sorry, but good writing isn't just about putting a pencil to paper and expressing your thoughts. Good writing is about content, word choice, organization, and conventions like spelling words correctly.

Still we have this push for kindergartners and first graders who aren't developmentally ready to write yet, and also don't know how to spell many words. So what do we do? Teachers encourage students to just spell it out like it sounds. It's called "inventive" spelling and it lives in public schools all across America. I think it sets a bad precedent for writing instruction. It is really hard for a fifth grader to break the habit of just spelling words out phonetically. Despite spelling lessons and spelling tests, most of my students automatically revert to spelling out words phonetically. I am amazed at how many words, some even very simple, they still spell by sounding them out.

Hello! Even though our country has been experiencing a huge influx of illegal aliens from Mexico and Central America, we do not speak Spanish (yet), where often words are spelled exactly the way they sound. With some exceptions, many of our English words aren't spelled like they sound. You have to know how to spell a word correctly. But what are educators more worried about? "They don't want the child to get discouraged with writing because they don't know how to spell the words."

This is silly! Hasn't anyone thought that maybe we should wait until they know how to spell words before we worry about making them write? Don't we realize how hard it's going to be to break kids of the habit and teach them that they just can't spell words the way they sound?

I may not remember much about elementary school, but I do remember it was emphasized that all words needed to be spelled correctly. If we weren't certain how to spell a word, then you looked it up in a dictionary, using phonics to help you figure out how the word is spelled. For the most part, I am a very good speller. Thank God my small country school hadn't heard of inventive spelling.

More importantly, thank God for spell-check on computers, not just for me, but for all Americans who were taught to "spell things out like they sound."

Mystery #26: Why do they think writing in a journal will help students learn how to write?

Why didn't my fifth graders come in writing good paragraphs? Maybe because some of their teachers prior to fifth grade confused writing in journals with writing instruction?

What is journal writing? It was really big when I entered the teaching profession. Journal writing is where you give a topic to the class, such as, "If you could bring one thing with you on a deserted island, what would it be and why?" Then the student spends thirty minutes just writing down their thoughts.

The big thing: journal writing is not to be corrected for errors, but is only judged by content. We don't want to discourage our young writers and have them think writing has conventions you have to follow.

So what's wrong with writing down this free-flow of thought

without regard to form or grammar? Shouldn't a child be expected to stop and analyze the world around them? Yes, that would be good, if that's what children really do with journals. Most students I know just write anything down because they know they aren't getting graded on the organization or conventions of writing. I call this a waste of valuable instructional time.

Also, most students hate writing in journals. Why? Because they are smarter than adults and realize journal writing is a waste of time. It does nothing to improve a student's writing ability and, in fact, sets a bad example of what is expected in good writing. Since their prose is never checked for spelling or grammar errors, then they won't learn what mistakes they have made in their writing. In my opinion, writing in journals is a waste of time in an already very crowded academic day.

Why do teachers in elementary school (I hope they don't use it in the higher grades!) use journal writing? First, because it's an easy way to say your class is doing writing. Secondly, most teachers probably don't like to write themselves or know how to teach writing, therefore using journals becomes that much more attractive.

Writing in schools should be done with the purpose of teaching students how to construct sentences and organize thoughts. If students want to write in a journal they should do it at night in the comfort of their own home where it truly is a private collection of their thoughts and will not be read by their classroom teacher.

Mystery #27: If writing is so important to a student's success, why didn't they show us a really good way to teach writing in our credential classes?

While it was true I had a hang-up about teaching writing because that's what I really wanted to be doing, if the truth be told, I also was one of those teachers who did not know how to teach writing.

My problem is that I love to write, but it's a mystery to me how I do it. All I know about writing is the words come out of my brain and onto the computer without any type of graphic organizer. I then do *lots and lots* of revising until it has the right "sound." In fact, I don't understand why we think it's fair to judge students on writing exams like those in the Standardized Aptitude Test (SAT), when even professional writers might have a hard time composing a multi-paragraph essay in a minimal amount of time. Good writing is actually the result of rewriting, not getting it right the first time. At least this is how it works for me.

How do I know what needs to be rewritten? Again, I don't know. I reread it, and then it just sort of happens. Just as some people have a talent for hearing musical notes, or sounds, a writer needs to develop a talent for hearing words and being aware of organization. Good writing happens when it "sounds" good.

So how do I teach that to ten-year-olds?

Luckily for me, I was at in-service training class when one of our staff development coordinators mentioned she was going to be holding a three-day training seminar on a program designed to show teachers how to teach writing to elementary and middle school students.

It is a program called "Step Up to Writing" and it was developed by a middle school teacher in Colorado who came up with a simple way to break writing into specific parts. It is a very easy, methodical way to organize your thoughts and then finally turn these thoughts into sentences and paragraphs.

I think the story behind it goes something like this. One year after the Colorado seventh grade writing assessments were graded, only about 75 students in the whole state had passed the test with flying colors. I believe 23 of those students were in one teacher's class. They went to her to find out her secret. She shared her system and, thus, a super writing program was born.

If you want more information on Step Up to Writing, you may visit their website at http://www.stepuptowriting.com.

I started using this method my second year of teaching fifth grade and what a difference it has made in how my students write. In fact, instead of being embarrassed about their writing, I now openly share writing samples from my class with other teachers.

For me, it also took the mystery out of writing. I finally know how to teach to students who don't have a natural inclination for writing. It also showed me that, yes, fifth and fourth graders can learn how to write a decent paper.

So, maybe then I have also changed my opinion about having second and third graders write because maybe it's not all about being developmentally ready? Not really, I still think the time would be better spent on math or reading instruction.

I admit though, since I haven't taught either grade level, maybe I'm not aware of what they can accomplish in their writing or how it fits into the big scheme of things. But I will tell you one thing, until they know how to spell a lot of the words they use in their vocabulary, I think teaching writing too young can be very detrimental.

Mystery #28: Is teaching students how to write one of the worst jobs in education?

Often we hear reports in the media that college remedial writing classes are usually jammed. College educators are quoted as noting how poor the writing skills are from some of the brightest students. Even the SAT has added an intensive writing test to emphasize the importance of good writing skills. (Or is it really designed to help college admissions offices know how many remedial writing instructors they will need for the fall school year?)

If public schools have emphasized writing skills since kindergarten, how could it be possible there are so many students with such poor writing skills?

Even if you have a great program like the one I mentioned above, the one thing that can really help students with their writing is going over it individually and telling them what they need to work on. But do you know how much time that takes? Do you know how much time it takes just reading, in my case, 33 essays and then also correcting them for errors and suggestions for improvements? It takes a very long time.

I don't know how high school writing teachers do it with 100–150 students a day. It has to be one of the hardest jobs to do well in education.

When I asked a high school teacher, she said, ironically, it wasn't that bad because by the time they get to high school, they should know what they are doing. Then maybe being a fifth grade or junior high school writing teacher is the worst job, because, let me tell you, these students are clueless on how to write a good essay. But if they didn't have a good instructor teaching them what it takes to write well, why should I expect better results?

It's no secret what will help students learn how to write well. It takes time with a teacher who gives constructive suggestions on improving their writing and giving them lots of time for rewriting papers. Even a professional writer needs a good editor to help him or her fine tune his or her writing. The mystery with teaching writing in public schools is how is a teacher supposed to do it with so many students in a class and in so little time? I guess then it isn't a mystery why many students need remedial writing classes when entering college.

Mystery #29: Why do reading, writing, and math curriculum happen at the expense of other subjects?

The best educated human being is the one
who understands most about the life
in which he is placed.

— *Helen Keller*

I am not the perfect teacher. I am the first one to admit it. My classroom is too noisy. I don't put up pretty bulletin boards. I hate doing small group differentiated teaching. I don't make my kids do reading logs and write in journals. Plus I don't follow the order of the textbooks.

The one thing I pride myself on is that I pretty much teach to our core curriculum and the California State Standards. Even though there isn't much time in the day, I do try to teach all subjects. I am one of the few teachers that feel that although language arts and math are very important, they are not the only subjects children need to know.

One of my biggest gripes with teachers is that many feel it isn't necessary to teach the whole curriculum. I'm speaking specifically about those elementary school teachers in fourth and fifth grade who spend all of their time on reading, language arts and math and don't bother teaching the ugly stepsister subjects of science, social studies, and physical education. The common excuse is, "They will pick up that subject later on at a different grade level because we just don't have time to do it all." I have even had a fourth grade teacher who didn't teach fractions, because "they will learn it in fifth grade." This kind of thinking is insane.

I don't know how common a practice this is overall in public schools. But if it's a problem at even one school, it's a problem that needs to be addressed.

Why does it happen? In the push to get higher reading test scores, teachers devote more and more time to language arts. In my case, my school district is mandating that language arts instruction be at least two-and-a-half hours a day! That doesn't leave much time to teach math, science, social studies, P.E., and break for lunch.

The other teachers at my grade level came up with this plan that next year we should only teach social studies and science twice a week, for 45 minutes a day. I probably should be grateful that at least they are making room for science and social studies. But the problem I have with their idea is, I will only be able to teach social studies and science for only one-and-a-half hours a week? I teach both subjects a minimum of thirty minutes EVERY DAY! Why should I have to change that? Plus I also feel it's not fair to the students, you can't do justice to either subject by only devoting 90 minutes a week to them.

With so many subjects to teach in only a given amount of time, I know first hand, it seems we can't do everything. At a staff meeting we were taught about "selective abandonment." This means you have to decide what subjects you're going to spend the most time on and which ones are sacrificed. Many agree that social studies and science seem to be the most expendable. But are they really the subjects that can be left behind?

Many schools dictate that students must be given at least thirty minutes a day devoted to Sustained Silent Reading (SSR), or time where they are given a chance to read quietly by themselves. I understand that this is often the only time that a child will pick up a book and read it. So how can I knock this?

I knock it if it means it's taking time away from another subject I could be teaching. I ask myself, "Which will benefit my students more: Reading silently for 30–40 minutes, which they could do at home, or teaching a social studies or science lesson where they are going to have to read information out of a textbook and will gain prior knowledge for future topics? I really look at these subjects as an extension of language arts anyway: learning how to read expository or informational text. I feel I'm giving them a skill they will need when they are in middle school or junior high school.

Other teachers don't see it this way. They feel it's more important for students to read a book. I have even heard some teachers say their students "aren't able to read their social studies textbooks anyway."

Perhaps they are right. How sad. How does this happen that by the fifth grade they can't read their social studies textbook? When will they be ready?

Also being sacrificed is physical education. Because I personally work out six days a week, I give time for P.E. almost every day. I think I'm the only fifth grade teacher at my school who does so.

Many think P.E. is very expendable but I think kids need a movement break to help them learn better. Our state also mandates that we give students 200 minutes of P.E. every ten days.

Why do they specify an amount of time? Because fifth, seventh, and ninth graders take a state P.E. test. The results for last year showed only 25 percent of all students meet the criteria of being a "fit" child. (Are any of us really surprised at this? I think not.)

So how many California schools actually give their students the mandated amount of P.E. time? According to one consultant for the state Department of Education, only about 25-30% do. The rest, 70 to 75 percent do not. Some districts are trimming physical education classes to pack more instruction time into the day.

This is a mistake. Regular exercise is not only good for the body, but for the mind. According to a report published by the state of California and discussed in an editorial piece published in the Riverside County's *Press-Enterprise*, "schools with more physically active students tend to rank higher on California's Academic Performance Index."

It is wrong to opt out of teaching certain subjects just because they are deemed unworthy of the precious time that students get for instruction. Yet many teachers are doing this not to be insubordinate, but with the blessing of their school, the school district, and the politicians who wrote the No Child Left Behind Act. The government even recognizes that an intensive language arts program might have to happen at the expense of other subjects! This is really sad.

The cost vs. the benefit of silent reading

I truly don't know if sustained silent reading in my time-deficient school day is the best use of academic time. Often during SSR, I watch students who do a pretty good job of faking it when it comes to quietly reading a book.

I think I learned in a business class that businesses have to weigh the cost of something vs. the benefit. It is called the cost/benefit analysis.

It shouldn't be any different in schools. The "cost" of an instruction or lesson is the amount of time involved teaching something. The "benefit" of the lesson is how much learning is happening through that lesson being presented. Teachers need to get the most "bang for the buck" when it comes to lessons.

Do teachers ask themselves whether the benefit of a project, lesson, or strategy is going to be equal to or better than the amount of time it takes to teach it? Is the thirty to forty minutes a student spends on independently reading more valuable than the direct instruction of social studies or science, which will give them prior knowledge they will use in future subjects? In fourth grade, students are supposed to learn California history. I believe if they don't learn it there, they might not pick it up again until high school, if even then.

In defense of teachers everywhere, I truly understand the time concept. There really doesn't seem to be enough time to teach, and teach things well, in all of the subjects. Maybe we do need to use "selective abandonment." Besides, the argument goes, math and English are truly the most important subjects.

But does language arts really deserve two-and-a-half hours of uninterrupted instruction at the beginning of the day?

In my school district, they want us to set aside the first two-and-a-half hours of each school day for uninterrupted languages arts instruction. What's wrong with that? When you consider that language arts lessons involve reading, writing, grammar, and spelling, that doesn't sound like something unreasonable. No, it doesn't. I have a problem with having to do it in one uninterrupted block of time at the beginning of the day. Haven't they thought that maybe students might do better with math instruction first thing in the morning when their mind is fresh and able to handle complex math problems?

Why does it have to be "uninterrupted?" Too much of anything can be overwhelming. What would be so wrong with teaching something else and then going back to one of the elements of language arts? I'm sure they will tell me that "research" shows this is the best way to teach language arts. That's what schools base all of their decisions on, scientific research.

I just question whether it is really true. I just see it as another attempt to micromanage classrooms because school districts are overcome by this fear of accountability demanded by the state and national governments. They are constantly trying to "prove" that they are doing their best job making sure kids read well and it sounds pretty convincing when you can say "all of schools devote two and a half hours of uninterrupted language arts instruction."

What about the "gap" problem created by this elimination of teaching certain subjects?

One of the great things about being a kindergarten teacher was that I had students who all came in at about the same level. With such a push for preschool, there were actually some very bright kids who already knew a lot of the kindergarten curriculum. In reality though, while that was nice and made our job easier, it really was up to us to teach them the alphabet, sounds, printing, and numbers. We didn't have to worry about a teacher not teaching a subject because, in most cases, there is no prior teacher to a kindergarten teacher.

However, even before I became a fifth grade teacher, I heard that a big problem with moving up grade levels was that you now have a lot of kids at different levels. Not all of your students are going to be functioning at a fifth grade level. In education, we refer to areas of the curriculum that a student didn't quite grasp at a grade level but are moved on anyway as creating a gap. A great example would be in third grade all students should be fluent in knowing their multiplication tables. If they leave third grade without this fluency, it is going to be more difficult for them in fourth grade where it is assumed they know them and need the information to do functions like double-digit multiplication. If they still didn't learn them by the time they reach fifth grade, they are really going to struggle because now they are expected to multiply and divide fractions and we don't have time to go back and do third grade math.

I use the example from math because this does seem to be the area where not understanding a concept really comes back to hurt the student's ability. However, gaps in education can occur in all subjects.

Who is to blame for these gaps? Is it the student's fault for not trying hard enough or just because he or she didn't get it the first time? Is it the parents' fault for not providing additional help when the student needed it? Or is it the student's previous teachers' fault? Maybe they didn't focus on an area or, worse yet, didn't have time to teach it.

In my current class, I have students who are reading at a second and third grade level. I am still expected to teach them fifth grade standards, not to re-teach third and fourth grade standards.

Sometimes I'm not given a choice. It's not unusual for me to have to re-teach a fourth grade concept because most of the students forgot it. I can accept that. What drives me absolutely insane is when I have to teach a fourth grade concept because their teacher said she "didn't have time" or thought, "Oh well, they will get in fifth grade."

Much of education, at least in the elementary grades, is built on a spiral of knowledge. You learn phonics in first grade, and then pick it up again in second grade adding some more details. You even get phonics in third grade. Because education is so developmentally based, if they didn't get it in first grade, maybe they will in second grade. But to not teach something at all is putting the next level teacher at such a disadvantage. It is so unfair.

What makes it even worse is when you have a class where some students were taught a particular concept by their teacher, but students from another teacher's class weren't taught the same thing. So now I have to waste the time of students who already know it, by starting all over again for those who didn't have it before. Yep, this is how it goes.

The purpose of this spiral curve is to build prior knowledge for a student as the child goes up the ladder. Yes, I understand firsthand the concept of "not enough time." But if a teacher makes an arbitrary decision to omit something because they feel it's not important, it makes the next teacher's job that much more difficult. And again, we don't have enough time to be playing catch-up in school any more than we already do.

Once we had a fourth and fifth grade class at our school where the students were grouped together by their low reading ability. The emphasis in their curriculum was getting them up to par to have them reading at the grade level they are supposed to be at. The emphasis was truly on language arts. But did it make sense to do this at the sacrifice of science or social studies?

I accept the fact that getting students up to their reading grade level is a worthy goal. Still, I can't help but wondering whether we are doing it at the expense of the sixth grade science or social studies teacher who will get them next? I don't know, maybe emphasizing their reading skills will actually help the sixth grade teacher more than their learning about how our country was created and formed and building a vocabulary of words from these curriculums. Fortunately, we have discontinued this program.

With such a biased attitude towards language arts, I can't imagine what it must be like being a high school teacher in a non-language arts area. I can only imagine that it's not fun trying to catch up ten previous years' worth of lessons that the teachers below them didn't have time to teach, or didn't feel were necessary.

Even if an elementary school teacher doesn't think about how his or her decision will affect another teacher along the line, there might be a bigger price we pay as a nation, one that has nothing to do with building prior knowledge.

If we sacrifice social studies instruction in elementary school, what message are we giving students? We need to instill in children early on in life the importance of valuing and appreciating this great country that we live in. It is important that all students learn how our nation was formed and the sacrifices so many made so we could have so much today. To instill a strong sense of patriotism in our rising generation will produce far more benefits than silently reading a book ever will.

3

Next stop:

The Twilight, I mean the Homework Zone

My world of teaching turned upside down when my principal, my wonderful principal, Robert Gordon, called me into his office one spring day and told me to look at this large white board where he was figuring out staffing for the new school year. Noticeably absent from the kindergarten teaching positions was my picture. He had moved my photograph down to the bottom of the board under the words "Fifth Grade."

I truly thought he was joking and started to laugh.

"That's funny. Me, a fifth grade teacher?"

"You don't understand. I'm serious. I want you to teach fifth grade next year." Mr. Gordon went on to explain that he thought I would be a great fifth grade teacher.

I replied that of course he would say that! It's hard to fill fifth grade positions and that spring we had three fifth grade openings. I wasn't going to be fooled by his flattery.

Mr. Gordon insisted that this was not the case. He truly felt that not only would I do a good job, but that I might actually like fifth graders.

I told him he was nuts! There was no way I would move out of kindergarten, especially for a fifth grade position? I wouldn't even substitute in fifth grade because, well frankly, how could I like them when I was afraid of fifth graders!

Divine intervention or just coincidence?

The following Sunday I went to church. For the record, I consider myself a spiritual person, not a really religious person, or even a regular churchgoer. However, something that day told me to go church. I didn't know until I got there that the sermon of the day was "Leaving Your Comfort Zone." The pastor's message was simple: sometimes it's God's will for us to leave our comfort zone because he has better things planned for us.

That sermon really hit home. I felt the message had to be only for me. The next day I told my principal, "I'll do it! I'll leave my comfort zone and take that fifth grade position."

Goodbye "Comfort Zone," Hello "Twilight Zone"

I am amazed how appropriately the introduction to a television show described my experience as a fifth grade teacher.

"I unlocked this door with the key of imagination. Beyond it is another dimension: a dimension of sound, a dimension of sight, a dimension of mind. I moved into a land of both shadow and substance, of things and ideas. I had just crossed over into... the Twilight Zone. (I mean teaching fifth grade.)

Or even this one works.

"There is a fifth dimension (grade) *beyond that which is known to man. It is a dimension as vast as space and as timeless as infinity. It is the middle ground between light and shadow, between science and superstition, <u>and it lies between the pit of man's fears and the summit of his knowledge.</u>* (Boy, doesn't that describe how I felt!) *This is the dimension of imagination. It is an area which we call "The Twilight Zone,"* (or teaching the fifth grade)!

Actually, teaching fifth grade was a good move for me. In fact, I love fifth graders. The pastor was right. God did have better things in store for me.

The truth be told, I was ready to move on. I was becoming weary of the kindergarten curriculum. If I had to show a student one more time how to make the number "3," I was going to scream.

In addition, during my last year of teaching kindergarten, due to financial problems our school district was going through, they had increased the size of the class from 20 to 30 students. Did they increase our academic time? No. It is very hard giving kindergartners the attention they deserve when there are so many of them. As a fifth grade teacher, I would have 33 students, but at least they could read and write.

A final reason for being eager to move to a higher grade level was, secretly I always wondered if I could handle students older than six years old.

I definitely wasn't in Kansas, I mean, kindergarten any more

While I love, and prefer, being a fifth grade teacher, I suddenly saw public education in a different light. I was in world where I saw that teachers held firmly to traditional educational institutions like homework, tests, and projects like U.S. State Reports. Yet on the other hand, we were having in-service training about learning how to use new textbooks and curriculum, the latest methods that produce effective teaching, such as small group differentiated learning, and new theories on how kids learn. Educators everywhere are fixated on finding the holy grail of teaching: discovering the key what will make test scores go up. (For the record, now that I have to teach students who take the state assessment test, I want to know that secret too.)

I don't know if it is because of my varied employment history, or just the fact I'm a contrarian, but I have always seemed to question the way things are routinely done. My favorite question seems to be "Why?" Why do we do it this way? Even as a kindergarten teacher, I seemed to be the "odd woman out" when it came to doing things.

For instance, when I started teaching kindergarten, it was a standard practice to present a "Letter of the Week" lesson plan. During that week, students learned how to print that particular letter, learn the sound of the letter and do fun projects connected with the letter.

My son and daughter made a "Mom's Memory Memento" for me during the letter "M" week.

But as a kindergarten teacher, it made no sense to me teaching only one letter a week. First, it will take 26 weeks to go through the whole alphabet! That's like a whole school year. How are you going to teach them to read and write if you don't get to the letter "u" until the 21st week? Also from my experience, I saw that often if you pointed out the letter "c" to a student in week 13 when you are studying the letter "m," they don't remember it even though you had spent a whole week on it.

I never could teach that way. Thanks to my good friend and mentor Maureen King, who introduced me to the Zoophonics program, I saw how students could learn all of their sounds within the first 12 weeks, putting them easily on the road to reading. Fortunately, I don't think "Letter of the Week" still happens in kindergarten classes anymore. (At least, let's hope not.)

As a new fifth grade teacher who didn't know anything about educating 10-year-olds, that first year I started teaching fifth grade the way fifth grade is usually taught. But it didn't take me long to see flaws in the way some things have always been done. This, in fact, was one of my motivations to write this book: to encourage parents to look at our 20th century educational practices in the light of the 21st century. The first practice that seemed to me to need revising was this century-old concept of "independent practice," commonly referred to as homework.

Mystery #30: Does the concept of homework still work in the 21st century?

Some will either think this is a very bold or very stupid suggestion. How could homework not be a very viable practice for our 21st century students? Everyone knows the more students practice on work from their day's lesson, the better or more proficient they should become at it, and doesn't homework ultimately prepare them for their future in the work world?

How could I even begin to think that homework should be eliminated? I guess because of my own personal perspective, and honestly, it is a battle I am tired of fighting. I get tired of having students show up to class without their homework. I am tired of seeing homework done by an older sibling. I am tired of spending so much energy on worrying about homework.

Actually, I'd better be careful here. I think it's against the law for a teacher to publicly come out against the sacrament of homework. However, for the record, I hate homework!

If you have children, or ever had children, I don't need to tell you that our society, schools, teachers, and even parents have a love affair with homework. Teaching strategies may come and go, but one thing remains constant, teachers have always given kids homework.

We know almost all kids hate homework. Parents on the other hand are more confused when it comes to homework. They hate it if it is a subject their child is having problems with and they can't figure it out either. Or they don't like it on nights when there are non-school things to do. But for the most part, I think parents really love homework. They associate it with good teaching.

Case in point: Often schools and teachers are judged by the quantity of homework they give to students. Frequently, I have heard from my friends and acquaintances comments like this, "My child's middle school is really tough. You should see all the homework they get each night." Or, "I'm concerned about my child's teacher; she hardly gives any homework."

We also know that in other parts of the world where academic standards are very high, namely Japan, students are given lots of homework and their tests seem to prove there is a relationship between homework and successful learning. But in Japan, not only do they give homework, struggling students attend a juku school at night where they sort of "cram" more instructional time in until the student can master a skill. Now which do you think helps those students more, the homework or the juku school?

In theory, homework is a very good idea. Learn something at school, then take it home and not only see if you can you do it by yourself, but practice doing it. It is common knowledge that the more you practice the better you will get.

The problem with homework comes in when one of those steps is lacking. The most common one is the student thinks he/she understands it in the classroom, but when they take it home, it seems like a foreign language. *(Of course this is okay if homework is a foreign language.)* So what does the student do now? Obviously, they ask mom and dad for help. This is the scenario that happens in many households.

Parent: "Have you done your homework yet?"

Student: "No, I don't understand it."

Parent: "Let me see it." (Student shows homework to parent who doesn't understand it.)

Parent: (Not wanting the child to know he or she doesn't get it either, the parent replies) "Didn't your teacher go over this in class?"

Student: "No."

Results: #1) Student does it wrong. #2) Student doesn't do it and gets penalized by teacher.

A "smart" student goes to school and tells the teacher he couldn't do the homework because he didn't understand it and neither did his parents. Of course, he better be certain that it's something the parent really didn't understand. Sometimes a teacher will be sympathetic to his plight, then let him slide on last night's assignment. Usually, we teachers know when we are trying to be scammed and the real excuse was laziness.

How many parents know a lazy child out there? Please raise your hand. (Uh huh, just what I thought. I see lots of hands out there. You may put them down.)

The government's solution:
"Helping Your Child with Homework"

So important is homework, the U.S. Department of Education has prepared a 25-page publication, called "Helping Your Child with Homework." It covers everything you always wanted to know about homework from just "Why Do Teachers Assign Homework?"

to how to "Encourage Good Study Habits." It is a must for any parent of school-age children and is available on the No Child Left Behind's web site at http://www.ed.gov/pubs/edpubs.html.

I will share with you some highlights of this very fine publication. Let's start with the most important question, ***"Does Homework Help Children Learn?"***

"In the early grades, homework can help children to develop good study habits and positive attitudes. From third through sixth grades, small amounts of homework, gradually increased each year, may support improved school achievement. In seventh grade and beyond, students who complete more homework score better on standardized tests and earn better grades, on the average, than do students who do less homework. The difference in test scores and grades between students who do more homework and those who do less increases as students move up through the grades."

Makes sense to me.

"Why Do Teachers Assign Homework?"

"Teachers assign homework for many reasons. Homework can help their students

- Review and practice what they've covered in class
- Get ready for the next day's class
- Learn to use resources, such as libraries, reference materials and computer websites to find information about a subject
- Explore subjects more fully than classroom time permits;
- Extend learning by applying skills they already have to new situations;
- Integrate their learning by applying many different skills to a single task, such as book reports or science projects;
- Teach them to work independently; and
- Encourage self-discipline and responsibility (assignments pro-

vide some children with their first chance to manage time and to meet deadlines.)

- Can help create greater understanding between families and teachers and provide opportunities for increased communications."

For something that can do so much good for children, I bet a child is going to have to spend a lot of time working on homework. Absolutely not! The publication goes on to say, *"National organizations of parents and teachers suggest that children in kindergarten through second grade can benefit from 10 to 20 minutes of homework each school day. In third through sixth grades, children can benefit from 30 to 60 minutes a school day. In seventh through ninth grades, students can benefit from spending more time on homework and the amount may vary from night to night."*

One caveat: It does say that when you add nightly reading onto these totals it might just push the time a bit beyond the amounts suggested here. (There's always a catch, isn't there?)

In a perfect world, homework is a great thing.

Yes, homework, in theory, is a very good thing and one would have to be well, a moron, not to fully support it.

Hello, I would like to introduce myself. I guess you can call me "moron." As I explained, it's not that I hate the concept of homework, I just have some major issues with it as I have seen it in practice as a teacher. I also question the real benefit of homework vs. the "cost" of doing homework. We know children in underperforming schools get homework, just like students in the performing schools, so why aren't their tests scores higher like the students at the achieving schools? (I know it must be those "bad" teachers at the underachieving schools. They probably are giving them "bad" homework?)

Even though most parents might think homework is a good thing, in reality, even they have issues with it. In fact, in the very first pages under "Homework: A Concern for the Whole Family," one of the principle motivations for preparing this guide was to address parent concerns surrounding homework. It states, *"At parent-teacher meetings and conferences with parents, teacher often hear questions such as:*

- How can I get Michael to do his homework? Every night it's a struggle to get him to turn off the TV and do his homework.
- Why is Jonathan getting so much homework?
- When is Suki supposed to do homework? She takes piano lessons, sings in her church choir, plays basketball and helps with family chores. There's hardly any time left to study.
- How can I help Robert with his math homework when I don't understand it?"

Whether you are a teacher or a parent, we recognize that homework is great in theory, but it is often difficult to fit it into real life situations.

Mystery #31: Who made up the rule that after working all day, a parent now has to spend their nights helping a child with homework?

Or in defense of the "uninvolved" parent

This might surprise you, but I think being a parent, especially a parent "involved in your child's education," is a tough job. So I sympathize with those parents who are guilty of slacking off when it comes to helping their children with homework. I am a teacher, so I should be eagerly awaiting the chance to help my own children with homework, especially since I know the value of it. Yet ironically, after working all day, homework is the last thing I want to worry about especially when there is dinner to prepare and a dozen other things to deal with.

Even if my children are capable of doing it on their own, since it is "independent practice," I still don't like dealing with the "Is your homework done?" routine. It's just one thing in my life I could do without. This sounds so horrible coming from a teacher, doesn't it?

I am curious how many other parents out there feel the same way, or just take it in stride that homework issues are simply another part of parenting.

Maybe I hate homework because I see so much of it as a teacher. Sometimes, I just want a break from school and teaching.

Needless to say, I know it sounds like a big cop-out to say that, because parents are busy or tired from working, students should get a pass on homework. But that's not what I'm suggesting.

Okay, I can't fool you. I do want a life without homework. I want our nights to be like they are when the kids are on vacation; relaxing and stress-free with nothing better to do than watching our favorite reality show.

Do I want it even if it comes at the expense of my child's education? If I were totally honest, yes. All right, I guess not. Besides, I'm sure the twelve years they are in school will go by very fast. Then I can have my homework-free nights forever.

Mystery #32: Which is more valuable to the student: participating in outside activities after school or spending time doing homework?

Play is often talked about as if it were a relief from serious learning. But for children, play is serious learning. Play is really the work of childhood.

— Fred Rogers

School is very important, but is it everything? What kind of society would we have if children didn't take piano or dance lessons after school? With so many children dealing with weight issues, what would happen if parents had to make a choice between Little League or soccer, and homework? Even though much is written about the over-scheduled child, in reality it is good for children to have outside areas of interests beyond the school day.

As for me, and speaking only as a parent now, it used to drive me nuts when my son was in baseball. We had practices and/or games three nights a week. I'd come home tired, but oh wait, Matthew didn't do his homework. Matthew eventually quit baseball altogether because he got tired of doing it. And I was happy to be done with the madness of fitting everything in at the end of my very long workday.

Thankfully, most parents are not as selfish as I am. They bite the bullet and put up with hectic activity schedules because they feel, in the long run, activities and homework are both important aspects of a child's life. Sometimes there has to be a fast pace and hectic lifestyle for the long-term benefit of the child.

With this being said, I also hope those parents are scheduling in the important things in life. You know, things like time for playing, conversations with parents, and time to just do nothing, including homework. Who needs a childhood that is as stressful and hectic as our adult lives can get? If we haven't taught our children to stop and smell the roses, can we really say we've done a good job parenting? I don't think so.

Mystery #33: Why is it the kids who do the homework are the kids who don't need it and the kids who need homework are the ones who don't do it?

This is the biggest frustration for me personally, as a teacher, about homework. The students who always do the homework are usually the kids who don't need to do the homework. The students who need to do the homework are the ones you have to fight, beg, and bribe to get the homework in.

These homework slackers are also the ones who don't work hard in the classroom and need the most help. Chances are, if they try doing the work at home, they probably don't understand it when they get home. So then mom and dad get mad at the teacher because they feel like they are the ones teaching their child. What they don't realize is that if their child paid attention in class maybe they might understand it.

Most homework slackers don't admit to mom and dad that they have homework. I have had this scenario happen to me, as a parent, more times than I care to admit. It goes like this.

Mom: Have you finished your homework?

Son: I did it at school.

Mom: You finished all of it at school?

Son: Yep, it's in my desk at school.

Mom is relieved there is no homework battle tonight.

When the child comes to school the next day, without homework of course, what's a teacher to do? If you're in the elementary grades, you can make them stay in at recess or lunchtime. Then again, the teacher is also being punished because those are her/his breaks too. However, teachers have to be selfless because we cannot leave children behind, even if they want to be left behind. But then again some teachers, like my son's, would rather give zeros than have them even complete it at recess.

Not all students who do not turn in homework are homework slackers. There is another kind of student who doesn't do homework, but has a better reason for not doing it. This is the student who takes it home and realizes he or she didn't understand the lesson. Maybe mom and dad can't help out either. What does a teacher do with this child? Also punish them? Shouldn't teachers have one set of standards? No homework means no homework. Or do you give some students a pass on missing homework because "It's okay if you didn't do the homework because you didn't understand it and nobody at home could help you either." Chances are the slacker doesn't know it either, so do you give them different forms of the same punishment?

Oh, it's just too confusing to me and another reason why I hate even dealing with homework.

Mystery #34: Why do many teachers never even look at homework except to see if a student has turned it in?

As a parent, I always assumed that when my child did homework, they would either go over it the next day in class or the teacher would check it to make certain they understood the concepts. When I became a fifth grade teacher, I discovered that might not have been the correct assumption.

I have had the good fortune of substituting in other fourth and fifth grade classrooms at my school and other schools. Most teachers, I have found, are big believers in homework.

I was surprised to find out what happens with all of the homework these kids work so hard on at night. One teacher told me, *"Just check it in, then throw it away. I never have time to go over it."* Then another teacher said, *"Just mark it off that they did it, then return it back to them. We don't have time to go over it in class."*

I was so surprised. How could they make students do homework, then just dismiss it as nothing? How did they find out if someone was having a problem? Wasn't that a goal of homework?

I'm not saying all teachers treat homework this way, but I bet many do. I casually asked other teachers what they do with their homework. It was very rare to find a teacher who actually checks the homework they assigned. The one teacher who did was a fifth grade teacher and that's how she spends her evenings, going over all of the homework. Obviously, her children are grown so she does have that luxury.

Ironically, and in fairness to all of the teachers who don't check the homework, I truly understand where they are coming from and don't blame them. At night I am already grading class work that might have to go into the grade book. How could I possibly also check the homework? Even though I may get a lot of time off, they don't pay me enough to work a 12-hour day. And what am I supposed to do with my own family, and helping my own children with their homework?

To me, I have a problem giving homework just for the sake of homework. I have a conscience that would make me feel guilty about expecting students to do this work after school, knowing that I will never look at it or maybe not have enough time to even review the work in class. I understand that most teachers don't give a grade to homework, because it is only supposed to be practice. Is it fair to penalize a student if he or she gets home and realizes at home that they don't understand what they were doing? Or is wrong home-work better than no homework? I think to most teachers, it is.

A homework grade then isn't really a grade for doing a good job on independent practice, it is a grade for being responsible. If this is the case, why should a homework grade even be included in the fi-nal grade of the student? Aren't grades supposed to be about where the student stands in knowing the material, not how responsible he or she is? I bring this issue up again in Chapter 7 when I discuss the problems with grades and the grading system.

Another problem with homework

So let's say I'm a teacher who believes it's important to check all of the homework that comes in. How do I do this?

As a fifth grade teacher, homework needs to be a daily thing. It is to check for reinforcement of that day's assignments. Let's say our lesson for the day was putting fractions into lowest form. I give out the homework and the students turn it in the next morning.

I now have two options. The most logical thing to do is to go over the homework together as a class and check it. If we check it during the day, that is going to take up valuable time for our new lesson. After giving the new lesson, I want to give practice prob-lems. This is when I now have a chance to help students who are not getting it. With 33 students in a classroom, I can spend a lot of time on this guided practice.

In my real world, I just don't have time to review the homework, teach and practice a new lesson, and still cover five other subjects in a single day.

My other option is to wait and take it home that night and check it. Let's say I wait to correct the homework at night. If I do that, how do I know what to teach that day? Do I go ahead and do a new lesson only to find out that night when I'm checking their homework that they didn't get yesterday's lesson?

Of course, if you don't want to take it home and you don't want to spend the time in class, you can always do the third option: just check it in and throw it away. Maybe a teacher doesn't need to feel guilty about doing this. The teacher will find out when she gives the test how well the students did and understood the homework.

To be honest, then why even bother with homework? It is the one "mystery" that just seems to haunt me.

Mystery #35: Why do some teachers assign totally worthless assignments or stupid projects as homework?

Teachers shouldn't give homework just for the sake of giving homework. It has to be meaningful. One could say that the quality of homework assignments is often in the eye of the beholder. As a parent, I really have a hard time with "projects." Not all projects, just stupid ones. You know the kind I'm talking about: Make a sample of what you think a person living on Mars would look like or dress-up like the people who came over on the Mayflower.

I also think teachers are hypocritical when it comes to projects and totally overestimate what elementary school children can do on their own. They say they want it "kid-done," but when it comes in looking like a piece of crap, they probably give the student a lower grade.

The teachers at my children's elementary school all champion the project bandwagon. There wasn't a year where they didn't have to do a multitude of projects. Fourth grade was a good year for projects. They both had to do a California relief map, which I actually thought was cool, and a state parks project, or mission, which I thought wasn't cool. One year, my son worked six weeks on an "invention" that was due a couple of weeks before we took one of our month long breaks. (He was enrolled at a year-round school.) Did he get a grade for it before we left on vacation so he knew that his hard work had paid off? No, in fact, I don't remember ever seeing a grade or evaluation for that particular project.

My theory is that some teachers like projects because it is an easy way for them to assign homework, i.e., students have to work on their project. From my parent perspective, I also notice my children seem to get a lot more projects after the state testing because I think the teachers are just tired of teaching.

Some projects are actually mandated by the state or even school district. In fifth grade, students are required to do science fair projects. I hate making my students do them but I do because the scientific investigation is part of the fifth grade science standard. Do I encourage students to do them by themselves? No way. Even though, ideally, teachers want the student to do it all alone, in reality, we want nice looking projects that will represent the class and school well. I tell my students from the beginning, mom and dad need to help you with this.

Ironically, what do I get? Totally kid-done projects. Isn't that the way it's supposed to be? Not in the real world. I understand the value of science fair projects doesn't depend on whether the student wins a prize or not, however schools want to be the residence of students who do good, award-winning projects that they can be proud of. This, honestly, usually happens only with the assistance of an involved parent or older sibling.

I will probably never have a student who will win a science fair project prize, even though they probably should since they best represent how a typical fifth grader does a science fair project without any help from a parent. I did have about three students who had projects that you could tell the parent assisted in. By no means did those parents do the whole project. When I asked the other students whose projects were really bad why their parents didn't help, their reply was, "They said it was my project and that I had to do it." Who can argue that?

Can I feel better knowing that my fifth graders probably learned more by doing their projects alone? Personally, I don't think so. I think students learn more if there is parental involvement. They learn even more by watching mom and dad do it. Besides, what really is important in learning is how well you retain the information. When they have their own kids, then they will get their chance to prove they know how to do a science fair project. Isn't it wonderful how it all works out!

One more problem I have with "projects," at least in my own classroom, is projects are like homework; they aren't worth the battle of getting kids to do them if there is no parent support behind them. Even though I demanded that every student turn in a science fair project or they would get an "F" in science, I still only had 23 out of 33 students who turned one in. On the day another teacher's science fair projects were due, she only had three students ready to turn a project in.

A support teacher and I spent six weeks of classroom instruction reviewing how to do a research paper, a requirement for each science fair project. Guess how many students turned in a research paper? Maybe two. About seven students half-heartedly attempted one, but I think I only had one that came in with the required bibliography. It is very frustrating for a teacher. I had to ask myself, with these students needing so much help in other areas, why did I even waste my time on science fair projects?

Another project that I don't understand: in California a fourth grade social studies standard is California history. Many students are expected to build or recreate a mission. How educational is that? Will they someday be called upon to build a mission in real life? I know, it's probably not the end result that's valuable, but just the process of figuring out how to do it.

A common fifth grade project I don't make my students do is a "state report." A state report is where the student must pick one of the fifty states and do a research paper on it. They need to find out about their economy, their geography, and any other pertinent information about that state. Although I see the value in a research paper, I don't make my class do a "state report." In fact, I am the only fifth grade teacher at my school who doesn't have her students do one. Am I too easy on my students? No. They are too busy learning the states and capitals, which is a part of the fifth grade social studies standards. It says nothing about having students do a "state report." Not only did my son have to learn all 50 states and capitals, plus postal abbreviations, he had to do two projects related to a state, all in the course of three weeks. I also know teachers who only make their students do a state report and never teach the state and capitals. Yes, a research paper is a fifth grade writing standard but they get to do one when they do their science project. If I had time, I would love for them to pick one state and have them research it. Who knows, maybe one day someone might even decide to move to this state because of their fifth grade report.

Some projects really do have a place in our public schools, but frankly, in this day and age of accountability and working at an underperforming school, I don't have the luxury of spending time on something that won't directly benefit my students on their assessment test. Welcome to the world of teaching at an underperforming school in the 21st century.

Mystery #36: Does your child's teacher give meaningful homework?

Not grading homework, or giving lame assignments just so the teacher can say he or she gives homework, defeats the purpose of homework. Even in our friendly manual, "Helping Your Child with Homework," it states:

*"Homework helps your child do better in school when the assignments are **meaningful,** are completed successfully and are returned to him/her with **constructive comments from the teacher.** An assignment should have a specific purpose, come with clear instructions, be fairly well-matched to a child's abilities and help to develop a child's knowledge and skills."*

This is exactly what homework should be. Check your own children's homework. Can you honestly say the homework your child is bringing home has a specific purpose and then is returned with constructive comments from the teacher? Or is it just busy work so the teacher can say she gave out homework? And what about correcting it? Does it really get corrected or does a checkmark just go into the grade book?

How many parents really think about these things when it comes to our children's homework? We just assume the teacher knows what he or she is doing.

So before you "brag" about all the homework your child has gets, make certain it is really independent practice that will help him or her in class and not just busy work that the teacher can just check-off and throw away.

Mystery #37: Are teachers who do not assign homework bad teachers?

Absolutely not! Another worthy goal I have for writing this book, besides convincing the public that the failures of schools is not the fault of the teachers, is to dispel that myth that "good teachers give out lots of homework." This just isn't the case.

My daughter, who is in middle school, rarely has homework. Her friend, who goes to a different middle school not far away in the same town, gets lots of homework. It probably isn't a coincidence that her friend's school has the best middle school test scores in the city. Is there a correlation between giving lots of homework and better test scores or academic success? One would probably infer that, after all, the more students practice math or reading skills, the better they should become at them.

But I'm not so quick to make that connection based on homework alone. Her friend's school also sends Progress Reports home every week via email. More importantly, this school has an academic climate that permeates the teachers and the students. They expect a lot from their students and from the parents. This school is successful not just because of the amount of homework they give but because of their expectations. Not only do they have these expectations, the students and parents have bought into their goals. This is how the "home works" into creating a successful school, and not just about the amount of the "homework."

From discussion with my friends who are parents, I think there is a trend that teachers aren't giving as much homework. Many parents comment their child doesn't seem to have a lot of it. I think teachers are becoming more realistic about all the nagging and energy spent in creating and checking homework, and wondering whether it is really worth the effort. Also, as I pointed out in my own class, I would really rather see my students be productive in the classroom where I can assist them, and not leave it up to the parents at home who might be too busy to help or who might not understand the assignment.

So don't worry or condemn a teacher for not giving as much homework as the next teacher. As long as your child is learning in the classroom, and doesn't need the extra work, things will work out fine. But what if you do want your child to have extra work? By all means let the teacher know. Chances are, she will be happy to get some practice sheets together.

Mystery #38: Am I saying we need to completely forget about homework?

Well, in my own "perfect" world we would, but since I teach in the real world I have found even I, a teacher who despises homework, still make my own students do it. With so much to do, and the fact that I try to teach science and social studies every day, there just isn't enough time for students to complete all their work during the school day. Just like their teacher, students often have to take work home too. Of course, they also need to study for tests. (Not that I think they actually do.)

I do not usually assign an extra homework packet that they have to complete in addition to their unfinished class work. I am grateful if I at least get class work returned to me. With this policy, I also find that students seem to be more on task and try to get as much work done as they can during the day. They know that wonderful feeling of going home and not doing homework and they like it.

Of course, not every student in my class is motivated to work hard during the day. There are still the ones who will mess with anything inside the desk, or who want to talk to a neighbor, or will just sort of sit there staring into space. If the work isn't finished at home either, then I tell them, "If you're not going to work on my time, then you work on your time" and they have to stay in at recess and/or lunchtime until it is finished.

By eliminating frivolous paperwork at night, there is another fringe benefit to my homework policy. It has been discussed that the more a child reads, the better he or she becomes at it. Since my students usually don't have much homework, spending the 30 minutes a night reading doesn't seem like such a big deal.

Defenders of homework say homework is good because, ideally, it gets the parents involved. This is true. But as I have discussed, sometimes even the most involved parents just don't have the time or energy to oversee their child's or children's homework every school night.

I suggest to my parents that if they really want to know what is going on in their child's classroom, they need to ask to see the completed work that has been checked. Nothing tells a parent more than when they see on a corrected paper that a child only got 7 out of 30 math problems right. It is at that point in time the parent needs to intervene and sit down with the child and help him or her figure out why he or she doesn't understand the subject and not wait for homework to come back that might not have even been corrected.

Homework and the "Work Ethic" theory

The best preparation for work is not thinking about work, talking about work, or studying for work: it is work.

— William Weld

As you can imagine, I haven't met many teachers, and maybe even parents, who buy into my theory that the "only good homework is no homework." They all feel homework is essential in developing character and a good work ethic when children become adults. After all, they tell me, "When we're adults, we all have to do work that we don't want to do."

True. But how do they really connect homework with a good work ethic? I'm certain there are many adults out there who have been fired from a job because of doing a bad job at their work. I bet most of those adults not only received homework, but completed it. I also bet that there are many students out there who just hated school and seldom did homework, but bust their buns on a job because they know they have to in order to earn a paycheck. I just don't buy into this theory that students need homework because it will make them a better person or a better employee. One's work ethic depends on the character of the person, what kind of job a person enjoys doing, and how badly a person needs the money. It's a stretch to say a child who does his homework will automatically have a good work ethic.

Would my students be more successful if I gave the more homework?

I probably haven't made many believers in homework convert to my side. In fact, you might even want to ask me, "Debra, you complain that your students aren't succeeding on their test scores. Did you ever think that maybe if you piled on the homework, then maybe test scores would improve?"

Yes, I have thought about that. However there are fifth grade teachers at my school who do give out more homework than I do and our test scores are all comparable. I'm just not that convinced that homework is the key to academic success.

Still, I am thinking, what if I'm wrong? Maybe I should become the "Homework Queen" and be known for the vast amounts of homework I give. Who knows, I just might find that homework is really worth the hassle. Nah, I don't think so.

What isn't a mystery?
How students would fix the schools

I couldn't include this as one of the mysteries of public education because I don't think it's any mystery how students would fix schools. In the school district where I teach, the majority of schools struggle to have our low socio-economic students improve their test scores. They decided to go straight to the students and get their suggestions on improving schools and test scores.

What was their reply? They suggested changes such as no homework, shorter school days, and of course better school food.

See, even students agree with my idea that eliminating homework is a good idea. (Actually, now I think I'm worried about my idea.) Seriously, this is a different generation of students. We can try all we want to insist they follow the rules and traditions that we grew up with, however, they haven't been raised that way. Okay, sure some have, but a lot more of them haven't.

Mystery #39: Is there a better idea out there than making students do homework?

It looks like some high school students are making their "no homework" fantasy into a reality. Once I was substitute teaching for my friend who supervises a high school "On-campus Intervention" class. This is where disruptive students and rule violators go when they get into trouble. I happened to glance at a memo another teacher had sent her. The teacher was complaining that *out of 27 students, only one* had turned in the homework assignment. I could feel the frustration in her letter. She didn't know what to do.

I'm not saying adults need to abdicate our power to students, but at some point we have to choose our battles wisely. What should our priorities be? Is this battle with homework really the best use of a teacher's energies?

I think the "Serenity Prayer" needs to be hung in every classroom across America. In case you aren't familiar with this classic piece of inspiration by Reinhold Niebuh, here it is.

**God grant me the serenity
to accept the things I cannot change;
courage to change the things I can;
and wisdom to know the difference.**

My favorite idea that would replace homework

My daughter, the real writer in the family, won an essay contest sponsored by the Veterans of Foreign Wars. At the banquet where she picked up her award, I sat next to some parents who had recently enrolled their children in a new charter school. At this school, all classes were an hour-and-a-half long and the school day didn't end until 4 p.m. Why? So students would have enough time to do homework at school with the teacher! The parents loved it. Now when their child came home from school, they could relax with the rest of the family.

What a concept, huh? If only the rest of public education could be so bold. Maybe my ideas aren't so farfetched after all?

4

Students & Parents

Children are the messages we will send
to a time we will never see.

— John W. Whitehead

Mystery #40: Does a teacher have to love kids to go into teaching?

We have an after-school video club that tapes a morning announcement that airs on Friday mornings. On their last segment of the school year, they went around and interviewed some teachers at the school. Their first question was, "What's the best part about teaching?" Of course, every single one said something about "the students being the best part of the job." (Hmm, I thought the best part of teaching was the paycheck or all the vacation time we get. Only kidding.)

How can you not like kids, especially if you are a teacher? It's probably not a good idea to go into teaching if you can't stand being with children all day. Unfortunately, some people don't find this out until they become teachers.

Luckily, I haven't met too many teachers like that. I did read an opinion piece whose writer felt that the best teachers are those who don't like kids. His theory had something to do with the fact that teachers who like kids are more nurturing. He felt that what students really need are teachers who are tougher and not so nurturing. This definitely is a unique perspective.

Personally, it is true that with all of the madness teachers must deal with, working with the students is probably the best part of the job. Some are nice, some are very smart, and some are obnoxious.

As a teacher, we "see" children from a vantage point not available to most people. I put "see" in quotation marks because there are many things we don't actually see about our students but can figure out by the way they do their work, the way they come dressed to school, and the way mom and dad talk to them. You also see who isn't in their lives, often it's dad, but many times it's mom and dad. I have had many students being raised by grandparents, and many by foster families.

This book is about "Mysteries of Public Education," but another book could be "Why do some children have such a tough life?" It's really hard for me to feel sorry about my teacher's lot in life when I know how some children live. I have had students who have one or both parents in jail, have restraining orders against a parent, who have witnessed or even been a victim of domestic violence or sexual abuse, who come to school with inappropriate clothing for the weather, and live in homes that often have the electricity and phone cut off for lack of payment. One year I had a kindergartner who was living in a car with her unemployed mom and seven-year-old brother. It's also not unusual to have students who live in motels "temporarily."

Once I had a student who had been to five different foster homes in one year. In fact in the short two months she had been in my classroom, she had switched again. Was this girl a monster? Not at all. She had issues, but I thought she was a very sweet girl.

That's why I think it's fascinating that our government wants to lump students together and say, "Teach them all the same thing, with the same amount of time, and then we want them ALL to achieve the same measure of success by spring when the state assessment tests are given, despite this background and baggage students bring to school with them. I agree we shouldn't leave them behind, but sometimes small successes are the best we can do.

Mystery #41: Why are there so many disruptive students in schools?

"Disobedient children":
Nature vs. no nurturing?

Teaching would be much more tolerable if all we had to do was worry about rude comments students make about the size of the teacher's derrière. While it has been said that working with students is the best part of the job, to be perfectly honest, sometimes a student can be the worst part of the job. Ask any teacher and I bet they will tell you they have had their share of behavior problems. There are a lot of difficult students out there. I think it's depressing that many of my memories aren't from all the wonderful students who have been in my classroom, but from the ones I wished weren't in my classroom.

Why are there so many children with behavior problems in our public schools today? I'm not an expert in this area but my guess has to do with the parenting, or lack of parenting, going on. By my own admission, parenting is a tough job and I don't even think I am very good at it. I know I'm guilty of spoiling my children by buying them the latest gadget and wanting to give them everything they want, except discipline. But there is a controversy on how to do that. We know schools aren't allowed to hit children, but many psychologists or family counselors will tell you neither should parents, even if it's just a quick swat on the behind and the child deserves it. What's a parent to do? Oftentimes as teachers we figure out they probably don't do anything. If a child wants to rule the roost in the classroom, chances are it is because they get to do it at home.

Sometimes it's not just a lack of parenting skills, but a lack of a stable home life. Then again, I've had some pretty rotten kids, who have great siblings who are model students, with loving, caring, involved parents at home. I can never figure this one out except to think that, despite the genetics, each child is a unique human being.

I would imagine that ever since there have been public schools, there have been students who cause chaos and don't want to learn.

I know, with every new school year, the question that is often most asked among teachers about the end of the third day of a new school year is, "So how is your class?" (Students are normally very, very good that first day of school.)

Occasionally, a teacher will respond, "Oh, they are very bright. It should be an easy year." Or, "They are pretty low. I have a lot of work to do."

But that's not what we want to know. We want to know what their behavior is like. From personal experience I can tell you that you can expect a much better year with a below average class with great behavior than a high achieving class with bad behavior. In my two years as a fifth grade teacher, I have experienced both.

It is amazing how just one disruptive child can cause the rest of the class to lose valuable instructional time. The big problem is, there never seems to be just one disruptive student. In my first year of teaching fifth grade, I would say I had three students who were just awful, another three almost as bad, and another three who had good days and bad days. The rest of the class was usually just wonderful. But it's those "bad" kids that make it hard on the rest.

Don't think that misbehaving children are only found in the upper grades. Two of the most out-of-control students I have ever taught were kindergartners. There was even a kindergartner in Florida who was so out of control that the assistant principal brought in the police who used handcuffs to restrain her. Luckily, I didn't need to use such drastic measures with my own kindergartners-from-hell. Believe me though, it's not that I wouldn't have loved to or that they didn't need it, it's just that even I think handcuffs might be overkill.

Come to think of it, maybe handcuffs would have been a good idea for my first out-of-control kindergartner named Michael. He was in my class during my second year of teaching and from the beginning he was very defiant and wouldn't sit still. One day he got up and took a pencil sharpener from his backpack and stuck his finger inside of it. Immediately, I took his backpack and sharpener away from him.

Michael then had this huge tantrum. He kept shouting, "Give it back to me. It is mine." I told him "No, you're going to hurt yourself." He kept demanding I give it back.

When I didn't, he went into the kindergarten kitchen area and started throwing everything, the dishes, the blocks, the toys, even play furniture. The other students became scared. He was definitely out of control. I called an administrator who removed him from the class. This was all because I took away the pencil sharpener he wasn't allowed to have because he might have hurt himself.

Yet what did mom say. She called me a racist and said I "didn't know how to teach black kids." Three years later when her son was still having problems with academics and behavior, she confided to his second grade teacher that Michael would never do well at this school because "Mrs. Craig poisoned all the other teachers to be against him."

Cody: The Kindergartner from Hell

His name was Cody and he was a cute little boy. He had big brown eyes, beautiful eyelashes, and chin-length curly hair. He also was very smart and spoke as if he were 16 years old, not the 6 years that he was. Some might argue that Cody even behaved more like a teen-ager than a kindergartner. Sometimes he would be so evil, I wondered if he was the devil incarnate.

Cody would spit on children, purposely trip them, cut their hair, mark on them, and say and do very mean things to other children. He could also cuss up a storm. When asked why he did these things, he often replied, "The devil told me to do it."

It wasn't surprising that Cody wasn't the ideal student; he didn't have the ideal home life either. His mother was on drugs and had abandoned him as a baby. Grandma had been raising him since birth, and she herself wasn't in good health. Grandma was also a caretaker to a former boyfriend who had been in a motorcycle accident and became disabled. She had very little money, but always made certain Cody had the things he needed, except maybe clean clothes. She had her plate full and it was hard for her to handle Cody. And Cody was a handful.

I had tried all sorts of teacher tricks to get Cody to turn around. We tried the positive motivators like giving stickers if he had a good day, extra snacks, and extra free time. Grandma of course would bribe him with a trip to Chuck E. Cheese Pizza if he had even one good day. But he seldom had one good day.

We tried the negative stuff, like taking away recess, making him sit by himself, and of course time-outs. Things would work for a little while, and just when we thought he was changing, he would do something mean like pull a chair from under a student about to sit down. I wondered how I was going to teach 29 kindergartners and deal with Cody for a whole school year.

As a teacher it doesn't take you long to believe in God, or good karma, especially when one of your "behavior problems" moves away. After living in our city for 16 years, Cody's grandmother moved out-of-state to Arizona with him at Christmas break. Even though I am honest in saying I was glad he was going to be another teacher's problem, there was a part of me that was sad to see him move. As a teacher, you always wonder in the back of your mind, could I have been the teacher who could have made a difference in this child's life? Because he had moved away and I had so many failures with him while he was in my class, I knew I wasn't that teacher.

I gave Cody a going away gift of a backpack with some school supplies in it. I even put paper and some stamped envelopes with the school's address on them, and told grandma we wanted to hear from them. Neither she nor Cody ever did write. I can only hope for the best.

Mystery #42: Why did they have to banish corporal punishment from public schools?

The big difference between kids behaving badly 100 years ago and now is that, back in the good old days, if a student misbehaved he got a time-out with a hickory switch or some other instrument good for giving a quick swat.

I have spoken with teachers who have taught a long time and they think that student behavior seems to be getting worse. Is there a correlation between the banning of corporal punishment and this increase in bad behavior? Could it be that maybe it's because today it's the schools and teachers who are the ones in fear, in fear of lawsuits if they discipline Johnny when the parents don't think it's necessary?

For the record, I really don't think it's a good idea to punish children, especially when they are not your own, by hitting them. However, it must have been nice to have something to threaten kids with that they would be afraid of and thus be motivated to change their behavior.

It's pretty common knowledge that in public schools these days the schools are pretty powerless when it comes to discipline. The worst part: kids know it. Sure, there are the students who don't want to get after-school detention, or suspended, or the ultimate penalty, expulsion. But there are lots of kids out there who it just doesn't bother, and they tell us that every time they get punished. I also find it ironic that often schools resort to suspension and ultimately, expulsion to punish a student. Isn't this what the student want, not to attend school? As adults, we may worry about things like permanent records and think being removed to a continuation school is punishment. But do we really think it bothers or worries habitual troublemakers? I don't think so. Yet this is the "punishment" they get.

There was a third grade teacher at my school who had a student with major behavior problems. He was disruptive, belligerent, and didn't do his work. He basically did whatever he wanted, when he wanted. This included standing up and doing arm farts, screaming, breaking pencils, and just creating a scene.

Just a few days after we had replaced our fifteen-year-old carpeting, a substitute teacher had the students paint outside and threw away the used painting materials in the wastebasket. When they were getting ready to go home, this child got upset at something and dumped the trash can on the floor with all of the painting trash inside. Needless to say, the new carpeting got paint on it.

Of course, he has missed recess, field trips, sat in the office, and had several suspensions. None of this behavior was grounds for expulsion. Luckily, they moved this child into another teacher's class. Then he became her problem. Sadly, this is the way most schools handle behavior problems. Ship them off to another teacher; maybe he can do something about it. Fortunately for our school, this cycle was broken when his family moved out of the area.

A punishment that doesn't involve a hickory switch

High schools have the right idea for a short-term solution by putting discipline problems in a very strict and structured class, usually called "On-Campus Suspension." But you can't make the student stay in there forever. What then?

California needs to get tough like Texas. According to my sister, who is a fifth grade teacher in Texas, a child gets three strikes, and then he is out. I'm not talking out like moved into some other poor teacher's classroom to disrupt her class. I think she said "out" to a school for students with behavior issues.

Actually, I think that's even too easy. First, maybe the child really doesn't belong in a classroom environment. Maybe he's acting out because a classroom is just too structured for him. But by home schooling him, the parent could design a curriculum that would keep him focused and interested in school.

Secondly, by home schooling this child, it takes him out of the classroom and now the other students in class can learn without distractions.

Thirdly, home schooling the child would let the parent see what it's like teaching a belligerent child. It's called payback. This would be particularly good if parents are in denial over their child's behavior. If they think it's the teacher's fault, then why don't they see first-hand what it's like to be their child's teacher? Is this what they call "poetic justice?" No, I think you can just call that "teacher justice."

I know home schooling is not a realist solution for many working parents. What then? Let's give them a voucher and tell them they can enroll in a private school or a school for misbehaving children. So what if this is also an inconvenience to the parents? Let's get our priorities right. It is better to inconvenience parents of a disruptive student than the education of 32 other students in the class who are there to learn.

Mystery #43: Do public schools soften our children by not wanting to hurt their self-esteem?

We worry about what a child will be tomorrow, yet we forget that he is someone today.

— Stacia Taucher

Let's see. There's a school (or school district) that won't permit teachers to use red ink when correcting papers because it might make the students feel bad. I was once told in a staff development class if I were to make corrections on a student's paper, I should ask the student for permission first. (This is a true story.) Some schools give everyone an award at end-of-quarter ceremonies because they don't want anyone to feel like a loser. We don't think students can handle more than 180 days of school a year or be in class until 4:00 p.m.

Do I think schools coddle students? Yes, I do to an extent, but I also think it's not as bad as it used to be. I also think it depends on the geographical area of the school and the socio-economic make-up of the school. My theory (and it's only a theory) is you probably find more policies concerned with self-esteem at higher socio-economic schools.

What do I base my "theory" on? It's just a hunch I have. It's also based on a story I heard. There was this teacher at a Title I school and she actually called a student a "loser" to his face. I know it sounds horrible but she had a good reason to do it. This is the story.

A fourth grade girl came into her classroom and said, "The principal wants to see Beatrice." Thinking there might have been a playground violation earlier, the teacher dismissed Beatrice. A couple of minutes later, the fourth grade girl frantically returned to the classroom telling the teacher, "That boy lied to me. The principal doesn't want to see Beatrice, he did. Now he wants Beatrice to come behind the building and talk and she doesn't want to go."

The teacher obviously ran out to see what was going on. When she confronted the boy, who happened to be out of his fifth grade classroom, he denied his deceptive plot to talk to Beatrice. The boy, with an attitude, kept shouting at the teacher, I did not do that. The witness said she wouldn't have made that up. The teacher knew she was telling the truth because she knew it would be pretty difficult to make up a story like that.

The teacher then proceeded to tell the fifth grader he was a "loser for lying like that and he needed to stay away from Beatrice." The boy was suspended from school for one day for his actions. He ended up getting suspended many times for his chronic lying problem. Still, some teachers felt her "loser" comment was inappropriate for a teacher, however I'm glad I said it, I mean, the teacher is glad she said it.

Good or bad, no, not all teachers or schools coddle students or worry about their self-esteem. In defense of worrying about a student's self-esteem, there are some kids you can tell get nothing but verbal negativity at home. And then they come to school and get it there too? I think this is the reason many schools do worry about hurting children's feelings. After all, they are just children and many do have a tough life. Many times teachers really don't know which student could really use some tender, loving care so they feel it's only right to give it to all.

Nevertheless, I still think schools need to be tough with students who are habitual rule violators and behavioral problems. Why sugarcoat it? A student who lies about the principal wanting to see a girl just so he can talk to his fifth grade "girlfriend" is a loser.

Mystery #44: Why do people outside of education think that teachers just want to "drug" their disruptive students and don't believe that ADHD students suffer if they are not treated?

We in the teaching profession have had it ingrained in us that we are not medical doctors, therefore, we cannot make a medical diagnosis. But I will tell you, it doesn't take a medical doctor or a rocket scientist to know which students have Attention Deficit-Hypertension Disorder, also referred to as ADHD, and how totally disruptive those students can be in class.

Teachers and administrators get some really bad press because parents and some child experts think all we want to do is drug our "bad" students. They think we think this is the solution to all of a student's misbehaving. Many experts don't even think ADHD is a real disease.

I may not be a medical doctor, but I do know that when a child can't sit still, can't keep quiet, and can't get his or her work done, something is wrong. We may not want to label children, but I will tell you this type of behavior is not the norm. In fact, Michael, the student I told you about earlier, was diagnosed with ADHD but mom "didn't want to drug him."

Do I personally want to go around and medicate all of my students who are behavior problems to make them zombies? (Hmmm, I'm thinking. Only kidding.)

Of course not. Do I want to see children who can sit still, do their work, and actually focus and learn? Absolutely! I don't care if that child has to wear a pincushion on his head, if it works, then do it. Something has to be done to help the child. Unfortunately, the one thing that seems to help children with ADHD the most happens to be prescription drugs designed to offset the disruptive and negative behaviors.

In defense of parents who don't medicate their children, I do understand. Who wants to feed their child a steady supply of a prescription medicine? Yes, these drugs may make the student focus and sit still; however they also create side effects that may bother the child. The common ones I have heard about include a loss of appetite and a feeling of drowsiness.

Yet I am still amazed when I have parents tell me, and parents tell other teachers, that they do not want to see their child medicated, even if it's just for a short trial period. Aren't they even curious about what a difference it might make at school? Don't they think it would be interesting to see if the child not only learned more, but enjoyed school more because he wasn't always getting in trouble?

I accept a parent's decision not to medicate a child for ADHD, but I think it comes at the cost of a child's education. Even if parents accept that fact, is it fair to keep the other kids in the class from learning because their child is out of control? I think not.

In my career as a teacher, I really hadn't had that many students with ADHD, except Michael, the kindergartner who liked to throw furniture. Then in my first year of teaching fifth grade, not only did I get to be stressed out by a new curriculum and a new kind of student, I also got an "initiation by fire" of what it's like to teach an older student diagnosed with ADHD.

Let me introduce you to Albert, a student who could be the poster child for ADHD. I have changed his name to protect his identity. However if a student from my school reads this book, they will know who "Albert" really is. Most kids know "Albert." You could even say that Albert is almost "famous" in the part of town where my school is located.

The "legend" of Albert

Let me share with you the story of my "all-time favorite" student, Albert. Albert had been diagnosed as having ADHD by his doctor. As I said earlier, he could be the poster child for ADHD. He didn't sit down, he wanted to talk all the time, he wanted to make comments about everything, he wanted to joke around, and he wanted to keep others from doing their work as well. Did he complete any assignments? Hardly ever. Did he take his medication? Hardly ever.

He had his moments when I did like him. Sometimes I felt sorry for him because not only did he have ADHD, he had a pretty strange mom. This student was even identified as qualifying for the Gifted and Talented (GATE) program.

So what kind of grades did this gifted and talented ADHD student get? Straight Fs. Actually, because I felt sorry for him, sometimes I gave him Ds. Did I mention that the year he was in my classroom was his second year in fifth grade? That's right, he had been retained at a different school and, according to that teacher, his mom wanted him retained at our school since they lived across the street from our school. I couldn't blame his low grades on poor attendance. Much to my chagrin, he had perfect attendance.

Why didn't he take his medication? The excuses ranged from it made him tired, or he lost his appetite, or he just plain forgot.

The naïve person that I was, I thought it was good for Albert that he was in my class. I had spoken with his previous year's fifth grade teacher and there weren't many kind words he could say about him. Maybe I would be the one to rescue Albert from another failed year at school. (Then for my next miracle, I will be ready to solve our problems in Iraq.)

I tried everything to make Albert successful because, remember, we can leave no child behind! I modified his work, I let him get up and move around if I wasn't talking, I let him pass on certain assignments. My ultimate solution: He was a huge rap fan. I told him if he would stay in his seat and work, I would let him bring his Walkman to class and listen to it all day.

I thought I was a genius. With that Walkman on, he just sat there. Literally, he just sat there listening to the music and didn't even bother with the class work. Still, it allowed me to teach the rest of the class. For a little while anyway.

After we came back from our month-long March break, for some reason he became out of control. He stole yearbook money that belonged to another teacher; I think he stole pants from another student's home, and he was very defiant.

The first four days back from our break, I had a conference with at least one of his parents each day after school. Even though we had found the stolen yearbook money on Albert, his dad believed his story that he was just holding it for the person who really stole it. He believed this despite the fact I had three independent witnesses who saw Albert take it.

Mom showed up at one of these meetings, where the assistant principal was in attendance. She wanted to put her two cents worth in and ranted about how I was such a "terrible teacher" because I even let Albert bring his music to school. What kind of teacher would ever allow that? Funny, she had thought it was a good idea at the time. All of a sudden, I felt like I was on trial.

Nothing got resolved from these meetings. I think Albert got worse because he saw how his parents were taking his side. Still, I moved Albert to the farthest place away from the other students in the classroom so I could keep him from distracting them.

When mom found out, she was furious! During the next school day, luckily while I was at lunch, she comes storming onto our campus. Remember, she lives directly across the street from the school. She went to my classroom and started pounding on the door. The noon duty officer called me in the teacher's lounge and told me I had a parent looking for me.

When I saw it was Albert's mom I was livid. When she saw me, she raced towards me. My principal was on the playground watching students at lunchtime when I ran up to him, before she got to me. I told him I had had enough of Albert and his family, I wanted him out of my class immediately. Of course, she comes up to him and tells him how horrible I was to move Albert by the door. She was trying to talk to me as well.

I told her, "I have nothing to say to you; I just want Albert out of my classroom!"

She said, "Good. Because you're a horrible teacher and I want him out too!" For once we could agree on something.

After my seven months of hell with Albert, he was moved appropriately to the GATE classroom. He lasted seven days in that class until that teacher said he wasn't going to put up with him either. Luckily, the school year was almost finished. Albert completed the rest of his fifth grade year at home.

So did Albert change his ways once he went to middle school? I don't believe so. Two of my students who were at the same middle school told me that their teacher was going to speak to the principal because he was tired of having another teacher send Albert to his class all of the time. But remember, we cannot leave any child behind.

The flip side to an ADHD case

I had another student in my class, this time a girl, who was focused and very smart. She always turned in her work and was a "straight A" student. At parent-teacher conferences, as I was giving her parents a glowing report, they remarked that she'd been that way ever since they put her on medicine for her ADHD. I was shocked. I never would have guessed this girl had ADHD. I mean, never would have guessed. But mom and dad relived what it was like for her in kindergarten through second grade. She wouldn't sit, she was very disruptive, and she wouldn't get her work done. It took a while to find the right prescription and the right dosage, but as they say, the rest is history!

Now do I think Student A could make the turnaround like Student B? Perhaps, but I really don't know. They were two very different children with very different kinds of parents.

If I had a child who had an ear infection, I would give him antibiotics. If I had a child who was diabetic, I would give him insulin.

If my child had ADHD, I want to think I would have no problem putting him or her on whatever medication is out there to help solve the problem. Even if I didn't like the idea of a prescription drug, I would try to find something that would work. But who knows, maybe it's not as easy as it seems.

Mystery #45: Why don't they teach in our credential classes how to make all students care about school and value education?

People who enter the teaching profession have probably one thing in common. They care about and value the importance of education. Teachers need lots of higher education to enter their profession so it helps if they like school and learning.

Therefore, one of the most frustrating aspects about being a teacher is teaching to students who really just don't care about school. They just sit there, many lost in their thoughts, doing something else. You see it in their faces, the blank stares, the yawns, the sighs, and they put absolutely the minimum effort they can into their work. Their grades are mainly D's and F's or maybe an occasional "C" if they put a minimal amount of effort into a subject.

This isn't anything new. I understand that kids have hated school ever since there were schools to hate. Luckily, not all students share this apathy. We do get those bright-eyed and eager students who do love learning and find school fun.

It's just too bad there isn't a way to motivate all students to get some joy out of school. I think that's what they expect us teachers to do. Actually, that's not quite right either. They don't care whether students have a joy for school, they just want those test scores up. Somehow, I think the two are related. Once again, I need to recall the Serenity Prayer: God grant me the serenity to accept the things I cannot change; courage to change the things I can; and wisdom to know the difference.

Parents

Perhaps parents would enjoy their children more if they stopped to realize that the film of childhood can never be run through for a second showing.

— Evelyn Nown

Mystery #46: Why do schools have to be afraid of parents?

Does it have anything to do with the fact that some parents sue schools when they don't get what they want?

LOS ANGELES (Reuters)—*Cartwheels and handstands have gotten an 11-year-old girl temporarily bounced out of her Los Angeles-area school.*

Deirdre Faegre was suspended for a week after repeatedly disobeying school officials who told her not to perform gymnastic stunts during lunchtime.

"Our first concern is the safety of all children," San Jose-Edison Academy Principal Denise Patton told the San Gabriel Valley Tribune. Patton said Deirdre could accidentally strike another student, or injure herself, and other children could get hurt trying to imitate Deirdre, who has been doing gymnastics for five years.

Deirdre's father, Leland Faegre, said it was absurd to suspend his daughter for doing gymnastics when students were allowed to play basketball and other sports.

"Contact sports, apparently, are fine. But this one is so dangerous it requires the cartwheel cops," Faegre said.

What is absurd about this story is that his daughter doesn't know how to follow rules or orders from adults and her dad is defending her. How did he miss the point completely that this wasn't about "cartwheel cops" or whether or not contact sports are more dangerous but still allowed? This is about insubordination and the safety of other children.

I would like to introduce both of them to "Kalia," a student in my class who learned first hand what can happen when you do cartwheels. You see, one afternoon when Kalia should have been at home, she came back to school to play on the playground.

As I was getting ready to go home, her sister came up and said, "Kalia was doing cartwheels and hurt her ankle." She was in a great deal of pain so I ran to the office to call her dad to pick her up. Kalia had broken her ankle.

The parent in the above news story, I'm sorry, seems like a jerk. I have even heard reports that he was thinking of taking some kind of legal action. Thank God his daughter goes to a private school.

However, public schools have their own share of controversial parents.

It is a sad commentary that instead of students being "afraid" of schools, school administrators and districts in the 21st century have become afraid of parents. Parents who are unhappy seem to think that a lawsuit is the best way to make a point.

I never have had a parent sue our school because of something I did, but I did have one who threatened to sue the school because her child caught head lice. Another parent didn't threaten a lawsuit, but she wanted some kind of justice against me. She was upset when I referred to her daughter as a thief. Other kids saw her take things, and we found the items in her daughter's backpack. Mom said she wasn't a thief; she just likes to take things from other kids. She eventually became satisfied by having her daughter pulled from my classroom.

Parents have sued over transportation, food, and dress code issues. Now they are even suing over what kinds of games can be played at P.E., and on top of the hit list is dodge ball.

As a fifth grade teacher who regularly commits the crime of letting her students play dodge ball once a week, I must agree that it is a rough sport. But to sue the school district, possibly collect money, and ban other students from playing it seems like a drastic measure to take. In this era where kids aren't getting enough exercise, I find it ironic we would prohibit them from playing dodge ball, a game they love. A teacher does have to be there to enforce rules and sit out the kids who are playing too aggressively.

Lawsuits on P.E. activities are admittedly rare. Guess which area prompts the most lawsuits against schools?

Disciplining students. That's right. According to the *"School Superintendent's Insider,"* a newsletter for principals, they even had a feature article called *"10 Ways to Get Parents on Your Side and Avoid Lawsuits When Disciplining Students."* (Feb 2004). The article illustrated how the fear of litigation is interfering with everyday disciplinary decisions in our public schools and making it increasingly difficult and costly to maintain order in the classroom. "Even if a court ultimately rules in your favor," the newsletter notes, "lawsuits protesting school discipline can drain your budget and your staff morale." That's wonderful news isn't it?

It's not just the threat of lawsuits that makes some administrators nervous, just the idea of speaking with a parent causes some principals or assistant principals to break into a sweat. I knew a teacher who had a problem with a student behaving badly. It came to the point he needed help from the administration so he went to the assistant principal to ask him to speak to the parent. What did the assistant principal tell him? "I'm not going to call that parent. I don't want to get yelled out by her. You can take care of this." So the teacher was left with handling the problem.

Granted, this is an isolated case, however, I'm sure it happens in schools all across the nation. If administrators are afraid of dealing with parents, why would we expect the students to be afraid of the administrators?

Mystery #47: Why do some parents habitually let their kids stay home from school because they don't feel like going to school?

Here is a true story that happened at my school. We had seven days before our month-long break and I had lots of teaching I was trying to get in before we left. As I was leaving school that afternoon, a girl about high school age rode her bike up to me while saying, "Look, Alex! Here's your teacher."

Alex is a student in my class who had been absent the last three days. He rode up to me and I asked him, "Why haven't you been in school?"

His sister replied, "Mom said we could all stay home for a few days."

I asked her, "Was your mom sick or was there another reason why you couldn't come to school?"

"No. We just didn't feel like it."

They just didn't feel like going to school. But remember, I can "leave no child behind."

The most important thing a parent can do is to make their child or children come to school every day unless, of course, they are ill. I say this not just because it means more money for the school; I say this because I can't teach a kid who isn't there.

Sometimes a parent doesn't have a choice. But my suggestion to all parents is, please try not to schedule non-illness related appointments during the school day and don't let a child skip school because they stayed up late and are too tired. I'd rather see a sleepy body in that chair than no body in the chair.

I work at a year-round school. Basically, we go to school for 12 weeks, then get four weeks off. It's actually a great schedule. Yet, I get amazed at how many parents will still take their child out of school for vacations or, the real killer, so they can go to Disneyland or some other amusement park! They use the excuse, "We just want to go when it's not busy." At a year-round school, at some point in their off-track time, Disneyland isn't going to be busy! Yet, there they go, off to have a good time at the expense of their child's education.

Sometimes parents don't bring their children to school because the parent was too tired or overslept. I've worked a graveyard shift before and I know you are tired when you get off. But, hello, you are an adult. As an adult it is expected that you stay awake until you drop your child off at school.

Do you think Alex above is an isolated incident? Hardly. Also that year I had a student named Allison, who started after the school year began. I met her mom and we chatted a bit. Allison came to school that day, then I didn't see her for another two weeks. I thought maybe Allison didn't like me as a teacher, but it turned out what Allison didn't like was going to school.

In fairness, for those first two weeks she was gone, she did bring a doctor's note saying she was sick, so I just chalked it up as she had bad timing getting sick.

Even after Allison was well, she only came to school maybe two or three days a week. When I got her cumulative file from her old school, I couldn't wait to see what her attendance was. The previous year, Allison *missed 68 days* of school and attended school for only 102 days. When I asked her why, she said, "My mom doesn't want to take me." Despite my pleading and reminding mom why Allison needed to be in school, she still missed over 48 days of school. I am glad to report that her attendance did get better during our third trimester. Why? One factor was, a new girl moved into the area and became good friends with Allison. She encouraged her to come to school every day.

Another reason her attendance improved was that, when we started our third trimester, the students were told about their end-of-the-year field trip to Knott's Berry Farm. I had informed Allison because of her poor attendance, I couldn't see letting her go unless she had perfect attendance. That meant two months of no absences. So did Allison go on the field trip? You bet she did and mom came along with her. Go figure.

But Allison and Alex weren't the only students with poor attendance that year. I also had students who missed 15, 20, 22, 25, 26, and 44 days of school. It was enough to make me paranoid and wonder if I was the reason these kids were staying home all the time. Luckily, when I looked at their permanent records, they all had a history of missing lots of days of school.

Some states do have laws that will punish parents for things like excessive tardiness or absences, but how many school districts really have the guts to prosecute a parent? Yet remember, we can "leave no child behind," even those students who have parents that choose not to take them to school!

There is another important reason absences are bad for schools. It is because, in California, schools get paid only when the student is sitting in that seat at school. Even if the child has a legitimate reason for being out, for instance because of illness, the school still doesn't collect the money. Mystery 59, in Chapter 5, shows just how much students' absences in one classroom can cost the school district in revenue it won't be getting.

In Los Angeles, rumor was that there was going to be a race riot at schools between Hispanics and African Americans on Cinco de Mayo. Thousands of students didn't show up that day because they were afraid of the violence. It was estimated that Los Angeles Unified lost approximately $700,000 in revenues on that day alone from absent students.

I'm not suggesting that students should risk their lives just so schools can get money, however, I just wanted to show how much excessive absences can negatively impact the finances of a school district.

As a parent, I must confess, I have let my children miss school for reasons that probably weren't good ones. I'm not proud of it, however, it isn't something I have done often. All I ask is that we all try to get our children to school every day.

Mystery #48: Why don't parents read the information that is sent home from school and then respond quickly to requests from the school?

Want an easy way to be an involved parent? Check your child's backpack on a daily basis and see if there is any information from the school you might need to know. Okay, I take back the part about it being an easy way. I've had to check my son's backpack and it can be scary. I've also presented evidence that I am guilty of not reading everything that comes from the teacher.

We have a "Flex Wednesday" once a month where students are released at 11:30 a.m. instead of 2:20 p.m. Flex Wednesday is the third Wednesday of every month and has been happening for over two years. Prior to each Flex Wednesday, the office sends out reminders that their child needs to be picked up from school early that day.

Yet, it never fails, each Flex Wednesday there are probably 10-15 kids whose parents or babysitter are late in picking them up. It is simply amazing.

An involved parent will also look for memos that need a parent's response. I've actually given up on collecting surveys from parents. No matter what I bribe the students with, parents at my schools seldom return surveys.

Mystery #49: Why don't some parents show up at school events or worse yet, why do they leave early before the program has finished?

As a teacher I'm not very fond of having to put on school programs. In this day and age of accountability, it takes away a lot of academic time from students. Fortunately for us, we aren't currently required to put on a play or program; we just have Back to School Night and Open House.

With that being said, I know a lot of schools across America probably still do things like Christmas programs (excuse me, I mean "Winter Programs") or plays. Nothing is more disheartening to a teacher than to bust her buns on a program or a play and not have parents show up.

Taking a child back to school for a school function not only shows your child you believe their school is important, but it shows them you think all aspects of their life are important.

Many parents reading this might be thinking, "What parent wouldn't take their child to a Spring Program or Literacy Night or to a son's or daughter's athletic event?" You would be surprised how many don't attend things their child might be participating in. I know it surprised me when I became a teacher.

Just as bad are the parents who show up to see his or her child perform, then leave right after their child performs. This is so rude, and that is so wrong, and yet it has happened at almost every school event I have attended.

During the time when we did put on programs, my daughter and I attended one at my school that was being performed by a different track than the one I was on. The theme was "musicals" and some teachers put a lot of effort into it.

The night of the performance our multipurpose room was packed. But then the strangest thing started to happen. Because there was no "whole group" final act, when one grade finished, the parents of those children got up and left. When the next group finished, the very same thing happened. By the time the fifth graders had performed, the auditorium was almost empty except for the parents of the children performing and a few others who stayed until the end.

The really depressing thing was, it was a great program.

Because my school has many immigrant parents, maybe part of the problem is a "cultural thing." Yet my daughter attends an average, middle-income school and parents still were walking out of her band program after their child had played. What's their excuse, except that they were being rude?

There are times if you aren't feeling well or if the family has other commitments that you have no choice other than to leave early. These are legitimate reasons for leaving early. Nevertheless, just ask yourself how you would feel if you had worked very hard on a program, and people not only didn't care enough to stay, but walked out just as you were going to perform. I think it is called the Golden Rule, or "do unto others as you would have them do unto you." Parents should not only teach it to their children, but practice it as well. A good place to begin is by staying for the entire performance of a program or play.

Don't forget to attend informational nights as well

Parents shouldn't just attend the entertaining school programs. I mentioned above, in our school district we have a "Back to School Night" to talk to parents about what to expect during the coming school year. I so badly want my parents there that I spend about $200 and make "goody bags" for my students whose parents show up for Back to School Night. The other teachers can't believe I do this, but I look at it as a good investment. I want my parents there so I can tell them what to expect and what I need from them for the upcoming school year.

I know many parents have long commutes, or might go to night school, or work when these events are held. These are all valid reasons for not showing up. Parents probably have lots of legitimate reasons why they don't attend school events, but I always wonder how often the excuse is, they are tired and they just don't want to come. That's not a good enough reason. Remember, your kids aren't going to be in school forever. Parenting is all about sacrifice and sometimes that means the ultimate sacrifice: giving up an evening of television.

Mystery #50: Why don't some parents feel the need to get involved with school organizations or support fundraising efforts?

We have about one thousand students enrolled at my school.

Yet, guess how many people are actively involved in the Parent-Teacher Association (PTA)?

A hundred? Fifty? Twenty?

Try about five people. That's right. When it comes to doing a lot of the legwork of planning fundraisers and helping out with things like planning a yearbook or holding book fairs, there's probably about three to five people who do everything. They get so burned-out that they usually quit after one year of volunteering.

We do have more parents who have bought memberships for our PTA. I think that number is around 50 but, when you consider how big our school is, that isn't even very many. Every new school year, it's the same thing. The staff and administration wonder if our school will be able to find enough people to volunteer for PTA. It might take a couple of months, but we usually pull it off.

I know lots of people work and cannot take the time to be a PTA officer. That's okay. But maybe there is some other way you can help by donating prizes, or helping at one event, or doing some kind of work at home.

I'm not suggesting everyone needs to be an officer in a school parent-teacher organization, but at least join it. Also, you don't have to organize the fundraiser, but at least buy something.

One year we had a fall fundraiser. Any classroom that had 100% participation, meaning each student only had to sell one item, would get a pizza party and five playground balls. Kids love playground balls.

However, I guess they don't love them enough because despite my motivational speeches and pleading, only 14 out of 32 students sold anything. And it wasn't like everything was real expensive. My son's school, which I should add is a magnet school, used the same company for a fundraiser and I brought twenty packets of cool feathered gel pens. My class loved them. I recommended that they just buy *one*, not the twenty packets I had purchased.

Yes, my school is considered a low socio-economic school, but they were only $5.00 each. If each family bought just one $5.00 item, imagine how much money that would result in vs. not giving anything. Maybe I'm out of touch with their reality. Maybe $5.00 is too much to spare for some families and I wouldn't expect them to sacrifice grocery money for a fundraiser. Nevertheless, there are many more families who probably could afford it, but choose not to help out in any small way.

I know it's not the kids' fault; it's the parents who just don't understand the big picture. Fundraisers let schools have some neat extra stuff, like assemblies, field trips, and certain instructional materials that are not covered in our school budget. If everyone pitches in a little, a lot can be accomplished.

Mystery #51: Why do some parents forget the importance of a proper bedtime, a good breakfast, lunch money, and school supplies?

There are some other simple things parents can do to help their child do better in school.

For instance, it would be nice if you could get your child to bed at a decent time. Studies have shown that we are a sleep-deprived nation and I can tell you firsthand that it isn't only adults who aren't getting enough sleep. The culprit is usually television, but the real villain is parents who aren't monitoring how late it is and allow children to go to sleep way beyond a decent bedtime.

In addition to making sure they get enough sleep, try your best to get them to eat breakfast before they leave for school. I know my daughter hates to eat breakfast, but I offer it to her every day. Even if you can't make breakfast for your child, set them up in a breakfast program at school or have food in your house that they can prepare themselves. I can't tell you how many times we hear from students how hungry they are in the morning.

Once more thing, speaking of food, please remember to give your child lunch money. A small school district near where I live is in debt $8,000 over two years because of unpaid school lunches. Obviously, this amount isn't from low-income students, because they receive free or discounted meals. This deficit is from students whose families supposedly can afford the $1.50–$1.75 cost per lunch. The district even sent 800 letters to parents about these debts, but had little response in collecting past due monies. This is really depressing.

If your child needs school supplies and you can afford them, please make it a priority for them to have pencils, pens, and paper not only for school, but at home.

I have a student in my class who has never brought his own paper or pencils to school. I know his family because I have had two of his siblings as a kindergarten teacher and they seem like responsible parents. Maybe they believe it truly is the school's responsibility to provide a free education, and that includes supplies. Maybe they just forget. Maybe the student doesn't tell them what he needs because things are tight financially at home. Whatever the case, I supply him with the materials he needs to help him get his schoolwork done.

Besides pencils and paper, a dictionary would be a really nice thing for students to have at home. Add a thesaurus to your library and your child has no excuse not to write an interesting essay. (Providing they have a teacher who knows how to teach writing.)

If you get a letter from the school saying your child needs glasses, please do your best to get them as soon as you can.

This past year, I had a child who needed glasses to see the board. Even though I let her sit in the front row, sometimes she still had to get closer to see what I wrote. The school nurse sent home a note at the beginning of the school year letting her parents know it was important they get their daughter glasses.

Still, week after week, she showed up without glasses. When I asked why, one time she replied, "My mom doesn't have the time." Another time was, "I lost my pair last year so she said I can't have another pair." I asked her if money was an issue and she replied no.

After a phone call to her house, her mom assured me she would get them. The week before we tracked off, almost three months later, this girl finally had her glasses.

Mystery #52: Why don't we make it clear to parents that if a child needs help academically they are the ones who have to do something about it, not just the teacher?

An Open Letter to All Parents,

(especially those who have written letters to Time Magazine complaining how teachers expect parents to do their job):

Dear Parents:

Let me tell you the reality of being a teacher. I have a class of 33 students. My second year of teaching fifth grade, at least three-fourths of the class struggled with basic fifth grade skills, in both math and language arts. I didn't have any students who you might call "high achieving." I had at least eight students who were extremely low in ability, and truthfully probably didn't even belong in fifth grade.

I would love to spend even five minutes helping each student individually and sometimes in math I have done that. However, to do that with 33 students means that it takes up 165 minutes or two hours and forty-five minutes, almost one half of my school day, on one subject. You can see I don't have the luxury of doing this very often.

It would be great if I could tutor your child after school. However, during my planning period, I really do need to use it to get ready for the next day. There are many teachers at my school who do their planning period after school hours so they can tutor. I apologize I am not one of those teachers; I too have a family at home waiting for my help with their work.

Therefore, if your child needs additional help, you can see it is very difficult for me as one teacher to help everyone that needs the help. Yes, I am getting paid by your taxes to teach your child. I do the best I can in the time allotted.

This is why you hear the constant teacher mantra of "parents have to get involved with their children's education." The reality is, we do rely on parents to help do our job. I'm not asking you to come in and teach the other 32 kids; I'm only asking that you help your *own* child, even if it means you have to morph into a math tutor at night.

If you see a way I can thoroughly service the needs of every student in a reasonable amount of time, please send the information to the address in the introduction.

Thank you,
Mrs. Craig

Wow, I waited a long time to write this speech. This isn't just a speech I give to parents, it is one I repeat to myself. My son was failing fifth grade math. At first, it infuriated me to think he could be failing math when it used to be one of his favorite subjects. I decided his teacher was probably going too fast and not explaining things well enough.

Then I stopped playing the blame game and remembered my speech. It didn't matter how he got to the point of failing, my immediate concern was what I was going to do to get him caught up. The answer: I spent hours while we were off-track re-teaching the things he should have learned. I did it willingly and without begrudging the teacher (okay, maybe there was just a little bit of bitterness.) I was lucky I had the time to do it, yet even if we weren't off-track, I would have had to find the time to do it. It's all part of priorities and being a parent.

I am not asking any parent to do what I am not willing to do myself, because of a work schedule or other commitments, you aren't able to help your child, let the teacher know. Maybe he or she knows someone who can help, or even might volunteer a day or two a week after school. Often churches provide after-school tutoring not just for members of the church but to students in the whole community. Remember, the squeaky wheel gets the grease and it's your responsibility to let the teacher know you are trying your best to make your child successful.

Look at your child's progress reports or report cards. Is he or she missing assignments? Is your child's behavior preventing him or her from learning? Does your child simply not understand the subject? If the teacher doesn't hear from you, he or she probably will assume it doesn't bother you what kind of grades your child is getting. This is what we mean by "getting involved," not just joining the PTA. Remember: Don't wait for the teacher to do something about your child's education, become not only an involved parent, but a down-to-business parent.

I had a student one year, a fifth grader, who couldn't do simple subtraction problems. I'm talking subtraction problems using simple two digit numbers. When I watched him try, he started from the left side of the number instead of the right side. He also didn't know any of his times tables, yet he was in the fifth grade. Remember, we can "leave no child behind." Obviously, here is a case where he was being left behind in math. His reading skills were fine, but his math skills were non-existent.

Actually, it is a tragedy that a fifth grader could get this far without the necessary and basic math skills. Who failed him? Was it the public school system or was it his mom?

Once he entered my class, it didn't matter. What mattered was how I was supposed to get three years of math caught up in a matter of four months? So what did I do? While the class was doing fifth grade math, I had some second and third grade sheets I was tutoring him on.

His mom had told me they were trying to help him at home, but unfortunately, I didn't see the evidence of it. Mom thought he had a learning disability in math, but come to find out that wasn't the case. What this student had was an aversion to math. He hated math and didn't want to do it. Only after I really got tough with him, and quit feeling sorry for him, did I start to see improvement. It is amazing how taking away recess and lunch recess can make a student learn to like math.

Was I able to get him up to a fifth grade level? No. When we came back from our break, he had moved. I couldn't help but wonder what was going to happen with his math skills now? It would be great if teachers didn't need the help of parents in educating students. Unfortunately in many cases, it just doesn't work that way.

Mystery #53: Do teachers really hate parents?

Again, while I was working on my umpteenth revision of the book, *Time* magazine had a cover article called, "What Teachers Hate About Parents." It was a very good article giving parents an insight into the world of teaching. It gave anecdotal stories about experiences teachers have had with parents.

For the record, teachers can't hate parents; we need their help too much. However, this doesn't mean that some parents don't drive us nuts. The bottom line is, it has been shown that the more involved the parent is with the child's education, the more successful the student is. So it is really in the teacher's best interest to work with parents. Teaching also becomes a much easier job if the teacher has the support and cooperation of parents. Teachers only dislike parents who aren't involved in their child's education or, in the case of my son's teacher, parents who complain too much about their child's education.

Mystery #54: Do teachers care whether parents like them?

Do you know that the first week of May is "National Appreciation Week for Teachers"? Have you even sent your child's teacher something on this day? Have I, or any teacher I know, ever received a token appreciation from a parent during this week? Does it bother us? No, I don't think it does. Besides, many teachers are also mothers and we already understand that sometimes a show of appreciation doesn't come with the territory.

Secretly, whether we will admit it or not, I think all teachers want parents to like them. I will even go further and say each of us hopes parents think we are a good teacher, even if they never tell us. And even though we don't know what to do with all the bath salts, candles, and "#1 Teacher" paraphernalia we get at Christmas or the end the school year, we still like getting it. Well, some teachers don't. I knew a teacher who requested a donation be made to her favorite charity instead of getting any more gifts. That is a nice gesture, but to be honest, so is a gift certificate to Staples or Office Depot.

Actually, most of us are not that shallow. I think the best gift a teacher can get is one at the end of the school year when a parent or student gives you a simple thanks for trying hard to be a good teacher.

5

Money and Public Education

Mystery #55: Why do they pay teachers so little money?

> To fulfill a dream, to be allowed to sweat over
> lonely labor, to be given a chance to create,
> is the meat and potatoes of life.
> The money is the gravy.
>
> — *Bette Davis, The Lonely Life*

So why do teachers get so little gravy?

I'm sure everybody thinks they should get paid more than they do. Exception: When I was a supermarket cashier, I felt overpaid when working on a major holiday. On holidays like Christmas, Thanksgiving and the Fourth of July, retail clerks made triple time, or about $45.00 an hour. Of course, it is a drag to work on a holiday when you have family around, so I could justify it and felt like it was a reasonable amount of compensation for our sacrifice.

In California, as teachers go, we are among the highest paid teachers in the nation and I am very grateful. In fact, there was a teacher who left my school to teach in Florida and she made at least $10,000 less than what she was making in California. (Of course after reading that columnist's article from Florida, I can understand why that is.) Some teacher pay scales around the country are very low considering the fact this is a job that requires a college education.

For example, *Parade* magazine every year does a special report on "What People Earn." It tries to give a sampling of a variety of jobs from people all across our nation. They make it clear that this is "just a salary roundup and is not a scientific study." Nevertheless, before I was a teacher, I used to love seeing what other people make.

But since I've become a teacher, now I only get depressed. Do you know that Sponge Bob Square Pants made $1.5 billion dollars? Not that I expect teachers to make what a cartoon character does, but still that is pretty amazing.

Back to the real world, salaries ranged from John Travolta, $25 million, to Lance Armstrong, the professional cyclist, who makes $19 million. Wait, I did say the "real world" didn't I?

Here's a real world figure. The teacher they mention from Alabama made $29,500, $300 lower than the airport screener from Bakersfield, California. Gee, I wonder how much college an airport screener needs? Also, my 22-year-old niece works at an investment company and, after only one year, she is pulling in $40,000 a year and she doesn't have a college degree either.

There also seems to be a huge discrepancy in teacher pay depending on what area of the country you work in. I remember reading in *USA Today* a letter from a man who was bemoaning this fact. He said his teacher friend, who works in Pennsylvania, along with his wife who is also a teacher, were earning a combined $120,000 a year. They also got compensated extra for doing extra duties like being the teacher chaperone at evening sporting events and leading extracurricular activities or clubs. This is the part I loved, his wife also got a full time aide!!!! (Wow that would be so neat.)

The man writing the letter was from North Carolina and his wife was also a teacher. They were only making a combined total of $70,000 a year. His wife also got an aide, for a half day, but the aide was often pulled away to be a substitute teacher. (I'm still jealous.)

Now I couldn't decide whether or not I should mention this letter because if you look at these combined incomes, it kind of shoots the argument down that teachers are underpaid. But we must remember, these are combined income totals and, in the case of the North Carolina teachers, that means each only averages about $35,000 a year. That again is not a lot of compensation and not much more than a baggage screener. (In defense of baggage screeners everywhere, I'm glad they make what they can make, because that is a job I would not like doing.)

What seems to be the mystery is why teachers don't command bigger salaries, considering not only the amount of education we need but the importance of our job. I understand that we are not in the private sector. We are beholden to taxpayers for our pay. Yet there are other government employees, like politicians, who seem to think they deserve more money and they give it to themselves.

There is the cop-out excuse justifying teachers' lower wages: It is, "Teachers only work nine to ten months or about 180 days a year." Just like those Florida letter writers were saying, it's just part-time work. And how many days do politicians really work?

I'm sorry. Even working only 180 days a year at $29,500 is not a good deal for a professional occupation like teaching, which requires so much higher education and often working long days. The woman in this picture was only 25 years old, so she obviously is at the bottom of her pay scale.

The people who say we have no business complaining about our salaries, because of the time off we get, don't take into consideration all of the extra time we do put in when we are working.

There are lots of jobs that require working outside of the regular workday, but often there might a reward, if not monetarily, then in the form of promotion, or you make a large enough salary to justify the overtime.

In the case of teaching, it just comes with the territory and we aren't compensated in any way. My local newspaper reported that some teachers are spending lunchtime and hours after school tutoring students to help increase their test scores. They aren't compensated for that; they do it because they want to help students.

The biggest adjustment in going from teaching kindergarten to fifth grade is all the paperwork. While in some regards I think teaching fifth grade is easier than kindergarten, now it seems like I always have things to grade. The worst is grading the students' writing. I always save that for weekends.

Since we can't get more money, I have a great idea. In lieu of a pay raise, they could just give us aides like the teachers in Pennsylvania or an assistant who could do the grading of papers, copying lessons, and putting up bulletin boards. I like that idea a lot.

Many schools, like my own, that do not have money to pay for aides, have come up with their answer to getting help for teachers. My sister who teaches in Texas says her parents come in and help her with some of her extra duties. (It must be nice.) At my school, we are signed up with the local college and university's work-study program and get college students to help teachers at our school.

The good thing about it is, you can get access to lots of college students. The bad thing is, you can get access to lots of college students who aren't very dependable. Sometimes a teacher is so desperate for help, a bad assistant is better than no assistant.

There is a way teachers could get rich if they followed the advice of a letter writer to a newspaper. It was one article I didn't clip, but I remember his premise. He said that teachers should get paid an hourly rate per each student they teach. I can't remember the exact rate he came up with but the annual salary for a teacher would have been $200,000 a year. Now that's a salary I could live with.

Mystery #56: Why do teachers not only get low pay but then still have to spend money on school supplies?

One day while I was making a trip to my local office supply store to get some writing folders for my class, I ran into another teacher from a different school district. She commented that there are not many occupations where you have to bring your own supplies to work. "Can you imagine if an office worker had to supply his or her pens, staplers, and copy paper?"

She had a point, even though I knew it wasn't quite that bad for me. We do get a $300 annual budget for schools supplies like pencils, erasers, paper, and markers. As I have mentioned, I am constantly amazed how many of my students never bring a pencil or a sheet of paper to class despite my pleading that they really need to bring their own supplies and to have some at home as well.

Yes, I do work at a Title I school but, please, we do have a Wal-Mart in our town where they could buy a 99 cent pack of pencils or a $1.29 ream of notebook paper. And sometimes prices are lower than that if you stock up during the "back to school" sales.

Spending a lot of money on supplies is by far not a universal thing all teachers do. I would imagine you see it more with elementary school teachers than high school teachers. Some spending might also be for supplies that are not obviously needed, and is probably considered "discretionary" spending for things they don't really need.

Walk into any teacher's supply store and you will find the coolest stuff. Okay, maybe my class doesn't really need the Bingo Fractions game, but I just know it will help them learn their fractions better. Not only are there things that will make our lessons better, but they have pencils and stickers to reward students for good behavior. A teacher needs self-control and restraint when shopping at a teacher supply store or else there goes your whole paycheck. Well maybe it's not that bad.

Of course, I do know teachers who absolutely refuse to spend any money for supplies or motivational prizes. I am not one of them. In kindergarten, I spent a fortune on reading books, extra snacks for students who habitually forgot their snack, stickers, learning aids, craft supplies, and photocopying. My costs have decreased as a fifth grade teacher, somewhat, but I still buy books, teaching guides, and spend tons of money on motivational rewards (now it's usually pizza party money) to get them to learn more and behave better. My other two big expenses are playground balls and tissues. I can't believe how many tissue boxes fifth graders go through. I have asked for donations and probably ten parents in my class have responded.

So if you really want to do something nice for a teacher, just ask if there is anything simple that you can donate to the classroom. It might not be something as basic as a box of tissue, but whatever you can help out with will be greatly appreciated.

Mystery #57: Do politicians really believe that test scores will go up if teachers' salaries are based on merit?

Our society often rewards the "gifted and talented" in many industries. The major league hitter with the powerful bat is the one who gets the mega-million-dollar contract. The actor who motivates the public to buy movie tickets is paid millions of dollars per movie. The chief executive officer who commands a multinational company to climbing profits is compensated for his business acumen and leadership skills.

The teaching industry also has many "gifted and talented" teachers in our schools. I already described one, Ron Clark, but there are many more who will never win the Disney teacher-of-the-year award although they are just as deserving. These are the teachers who have the right combination of niceness vs. toughness and present lessons that don't just cover the subject, but inspire students to learn. They make teaching look effortless while never complaining about all of the extra hours they put in on their nights and weekends. There are many teachers like this at my own school, and I am in awe of them.

The big difference between talented teachers and talented people in other industries is that they are not compensated for their gifts. This isn't fair. So why aren't they compensated more? It is because in these other industries they have a way to quantify in dollars what the worth of a talent is. In teaching, it is based on a quality that can't be measured in dollars.

But it can be measured in test scores? No, it cannot. This is a myth people who aren't in education want to believe. For one thing, children are not some parts on an assembly line, coming into your classroom with the same dimensions, talents, and attributes. Students are different depending which area you live in within a city, let alone which state you live in. Also many of the talented teachers teach in kindergarten and first grade where students don't take state assessment tests. How would they be evaluated?

So then, maybe teachers should be paid by how much growth they make from year to year? But that isn't going to work either. Each year, we get a class to teach that is totally unique and different from the previous year's class. "They" are going to compare maybe a higher achieving class with the next year's lower achieving class? That really makes sense doesn't it?

This is the basic problem with the premise of merit pay for teachers. There just isn't a fair way to determine who gets more money. So while it might surprise you to know I agree with many politicians, including California's Governor Arnold Schwarzenegger, that "good" teachers deserve more money than "bad" ones, I don't see any way of quantifying what a good teacher should earn vs. a bad teacher.

Furthermore, I think it's insulting to teachers that people think money is the key to motivating teachers to work harder so their students will succeed.

As I have mentioned several times now, I personally, and most of my colleagues at my "underperforming" Title I school, already bust our buns trying to get students to succeed. Even though many of us may not be "talented" teachers, that doesn't mean we don't give it our best effort. Most of us already spend long days and nights, as well as our weekends, creating lessons aimed to get those students to that much sought after "proficiency level." Unfortunately, it must not be enough, because according to our government we haven't met our target goals.

The general consensus seems to be that all we really need is that money "carrot" dangling in front of us, and then maybe we will work even harder so that we will finally achieve the success that has been so elusive at my school.

This may come as a shock to many politicians, but as a public school teacher for seven years, I haven't met any teacher who went into teaching "for the money." Yes, it would be great to get paid more, but I would gladly give up any monetary reward if, instead, for one year I could have a class of 33 students who were all motivated to succeed in school. Or how about students that I didn't have to prod, threaten, or bribe to finish simple class assignments. Actually, what I would really like is a class of 25 students, even if some don't have the desire to learn.

If that's too much to ask, then how about parents who make certain the child has school supplies at home, a good breakfast on the table, and send their child to bed at a decent time? Or how about parents who themselves value what a good education can mean for their child?

Yes, contrary to what our federal government feels, parents and students do in fact bear some of the responsibility in students' academic achievement. Believe it or not, there is only so much a teacher can accomplish, with or without the incentive of merit pay.

But since we can't control what parents or students do, the government could still help out, and I don't mean by enacting such inane legislation as the No Child Left Behind Act or now this idea of merit pay.

Instead of putting so much energy into testing, maybe the government could give us a simpler set of academic standards that are realistically doable in the current academic year. The current policies make me feel every day is a race against the clock trying to cram so much information into lower achieving, oftentimes language-challenged students. This in the end results in students becoming a sort-of "jack of all subjects, but master of none." (Actually, with so much to teach, I know they don't even become a "jack of all subjects"; that's why they are failing.)

Better yet, what about this earth-shattering and novel idea: instead of increasing salaries for merit, why don't they give all teachers more money and make kids go to school for more than 180 days a year. Not that I personally want to do this, but maybe students need to be in school longer than 180 days. My guess is a longer school year might even encourage those burned-out teachers to retire earlier.

The teachers in the Denver Public Schools system willingly decided to move towards a pay system that takes into account student growth, market incentives, evaluations and teacher knowledge and skills. Noticeably absent is a merit pay system solely based on how well your students do on the standardized test scores.

I just think to be fair that if teachers' salaries are going to be based on merit, so should politicians'. Why don't we judge them on how quickly they balance a budget and keep spending under control? While we're at it, let's throw in a bonus if their constituents can increase their incomes every year, thus resulting in a larger tax base for the state. And they would get docked pay for every family who needs to rely on government services.

I suggest if anyone wants to do the math in regards to teaching, they look at my formula: Money plus Merit equals More Dedicated Teachers Who Will Leave the Profession.

Mystery #58: Should teachers who work at low socio-economic or troubled schools get more pay, also referred to as "combat pay"?

Absolutely! Well, as long as they consider working at any Title I school qualifies you for that pay. Seriously, even if my school wouldn't qualify for any kind of "combat pay," I still think that teachers who work in areas where students don't come with built-in family support and an environment of promoting education, they do deserve more money because it is a much harder job. Of course, teachers from more affluent schools might argue that it isn't easy putting up with pushy, over-involved parents either. That may be true but the bottom line is often kids from poorer areas also have more gaps in their education by the time they get to your class and that makes it much harder to teach what you're supposed to be teaching.

Believe it or not, this is an issue that even U.S. Education Secretary Margaret Spellings agrees with. Here in part is an excerpt from a press release I found on the Department of Education web site.

> *"We must treat our teachers like the professionals they are," U.S. Education Secretary Margaret Spellings told more than 300 educators and others attending the April 2005 Milken Family Foundation National Education Conference in Washington, D.C. "That means we must reward teachers who make real progress closing the achievement gap in the most challenging classrooms."*
>
> *Further, public school systems often do not reward those teachers willing to take on the hardest assignments: "Teachers with the skill and desire to close the achievement gap find themselves drawn away from the schools that need the most help. Many school systems even offer de facto incentives for teachers to leave these schools." Such a system often has "devastating results" for students who fail to learn and energetic teachers who find their dedication to help the most needy underused.*
>
> *To address the problem, President Bush has proposed a new $500 million Teacher Incentive Fund, Spellings said. The fund will provide states with money to reward teachers who take the toughest jobs and achieve real results. Spellings noted that, according to a recent study by the bipartisan Teaching Commission, 76 percent of Americans and 77 percent of public school teachers supported incentive pay.*

On the surface, "combat pay" does make sense. But my enthusiasm for the idea of combat pay was dampened when I heard a fellow teacher recommend a different solution. She didn't want more money because she didn't feel that would really help those kids. Her suggestion was the money needed to go towards something like smaller class sizes that would benefit kids directly. I had to agree with her wholeheartedly. As I pointed out before, even if I was paid more or had the incentive of getting paid more, I don't know how that would help me become a better teacher. However, even though I would like fewer students in a class, I'm not convinced that smaller class sizes always bring the higher results we expect. Maybe a monetary incentive to entice those "talented" teachers to a low-income school is the best use for the money.

Mystery #59: How much money do we need to give schools so that they can quit blaming their problems on "not enough money"?

Dollars have never been known to produce character, and character will never be produced by money.

— *W.K. Kellogg, I'll Invest My Money In People*

Before I begin this mystery, I need to make some apologies. I apologize to my fellow teachers and union leaders who feel like I am letting them down with these remarks I am about to write. I apologize to my school district for not pushing their "money" agenda. I apologize to my principal and fellow teachers for any embarrassment I might cause due to my stand on this topic. I also apologize to the non-California readers for making some of my "mysteries," like this one, so California-specific. I apologize to my mom and dad, wait, they aren't in education. Never mind. Enough apologies.

With all of that being said, I am still going to tread delicately because, to be honest, I don't want any disparaging remarks to hurt my potential book sales.

Here it goes. At the time of this writing, there was a controversy over how much money education was going to get in the new California state budget. The proposed budget for public education for the 2005–2006 fiscal year is ... 61 billion dollars! That's right, not $61 million, but billion. Granted this isn't just for grades kindergarten through high school, it also includes colleges and universities. So the big pot of gold has to be divided among many hands. This is especially true considering that approximately 80% of the education's budget goes towards labor costs.

Several years ago the voters of California approved a proposition that if revenues increase, so would the budget for education, regardless of the need. But as many of you might have heard, California has not had the rosiest financial picture the last few years. Because of errant spending by irresponsible politicians, we have had to borrow money to balance the budget.

Even though revenues may have increased this past year, there still doesn't seem to be enough money to go around. Last year the governor told "education" that he needed to take away some of their funds, with the promise it wouldn't happen this year. As things would have it, revenues are still trailing expenditures and he couldn't make good on this promise. Even though it is true that education is not getting their "legal" amount, the governor is giving education a boost in the budget. But of course our teachers' union is furious. They are now on the warpath, or more appropriately, the media path, denouncing the governor and his budget.

I'm the first one to say that spending for education should be a priority. However, I really think getting the state's financial picture back in health is a pretty good use for the money as well.

This is one of the biggest mysteries I have when it comes to public schools. How much money do schools need before they can quit blaming their problems on "not enough money"? Is there some magical amount that will fix our problems with public schools, or does more money always mean that our educational system will get that much better?

If "more money" does translate into better schools, does Washington D.C. have some of the best schools? According to the most current statistics from the National Center for Education Statistics (NCES), Washington D.C. is one area that has the highest "expenditures per pupil." I personally don't know if this is the case. I guess I would have to ask people who live there.

Compared to other states, the most recent statistics by the NCES shows that California's "dollars spent per pupil" is not only below many states, but it is below the national average. Our average dollar spent per student usually hovers around $7,500 per student while the national average is about $8,000.

Hopefully, this will change with the new budget proposal. According to the California governor's web site, they state that "Despite the fiscal challenges facing California, the kindergarten through 12th grade (K-12) education budget augments core instructional programs through an increase of $1.8 billion in total revenues to public schools. As a result, total per-pupil expenditures from all fund sources will exceed $10,000 for the first time. Total per-pupil expenditures from all sources are projected to be $9,864 in fiscal year 2004–05 and $10,084 in fiscal year 2005–06." That's amazing. Schools will be paid *$10,000 per student*. But again, while we can only hope this will happen, unfortunately nothing is set in stone.

So let's just take a look at how much money my classroom gets paid based on the old figures of $7,500 per student. That means for my classroom with 33 students, if everyone came to school every day, the school would get $247,000. Of course, this total is far from a reality. Last year, six of my students missed a total of 152 days. The other 27 students added 121 days of absences for a total of 263 absences. Let's say a school gets around $44 a day for every child who attends, then all of those missed days results in my classroom losing $11,500. That's leaves my classroom with a total of $235,500.

My salary is $55,000. A former trustee for a community college informed me that the benefit package teachers receive brings that figure up significantly, as much as $15,000.

Not only does each school have to pay for it's own support staff like office workers, custodians and cafeteria workers, they also have to contribute to the salaries and benefit packages of district personnel. In this former trustee's local school district which has daily attendance of just over 3,000 students, she told me these expenditures include 84.6% toward salaries and benefits for staff. This includes teachers, program coordinators and administrators, all classified service personnel including bus drivers, librarians, custodians, maintenance personnel, secretarial staff, paraprofessionals, warehouse clerk, directors and Board of Trustees.

Books and materials comprise 7.3% of the total expenditures with services making up the remaining 8.1%. Books and supplies include all curricular materials, and office, custodial and transportation supplies. Services and operating expenses include conference and travel for professional development activities, memberships in professional organizations, liability and student insurance, utilities, repair and maintenance contracts, consultant services, legal and audit fees, and costs for communication services (postage and telephone).

Granted, there are a lot of expenses with educating our children. No wonder schools need so much money. So if we deduct my salary with benefits, or $70,000 from $235,500 (the approximate amount received after absences), that leaves $165,500 from one classroom which will help pay for everything else. From a layman's perspective, that doesn't sound too bad, especially when you multiply that figure by all of the students in a school district. However, considering when you add up all of the expenses associated with running a school district, it probably isn't as much as it seems.

So is the person who complains about teachers not making enough money, also the same person who is suggesting that education is getting too much money? No, I am not saying that education is getting "too much money," because I don't know how much money it needs. But I am also a taxpayer who realizes that there are lots of government agencies clamoring for our tax money. If education really needs the money the most, then I guess we should give it to them. But before we do, I just want someone to assure me that it will be put to good use in a way that will help my students become successful.

Can't we all just get along?

—Rodney King

I don't want to offend the teachers' union whose job is to look out for the interests of myself and education. However, it does upset me to think that other taxpayers could get the impression that "education" is being greedy. The ads on television have teachers, especially those "teachers of the year," decry our governor about his budget plans. To protest the governor's proposed budget, some teachers have done rude things like disrupt his speeches and in one case, turned their backs away from him during a college graduation ceremony. These were members of the college faculty who did this. Isn't that a grown-up thing to do during students' special day of graduating from college? I'm all for free speech, but they should still use good judgment when showing their disapproval with the governor's plan.

My take on the budget situation is, I don't think the governor is trying to hurt children or education, but is actually looking out for the best interest of all Californians. Maybe right now that means education has to limit how much of they budget they get.

Besides, I don't think there is anything out there I could "buy" that would improve my students' test scores. I guess that's not really true. I would like a lot fewer students, or mandatory after-school programs for struggling students, and more time so kids can learn. These are all things that would cost money. But funny, I haven't heard the teachers union or legislature mention these things in their ads. Is that why they want the extra money? Then I might be for more money allocated towards education. I'm just tired of hearing this constant complaining that we need more money. Why don't they also tell us what it will be used for?

Our union could also ask for things that won't cost money. For instance, why don't they ask the legislature to make kindergarten mandatory, instead of voluntary? Or as I explain in Chapter 6, California needs to push the date up when students are eligible to enroll in kindergarten from December 2 to September 1st to get four-year-olds out of kindergarten. These are two solutions that can help schools without costing extra money.

In addition, private schools operate on a fraction of the budget that our public schools do and they seem to graduate smart and successful students. How do they do it? They pay their teachers very little money for one thing. How do they get away with that? Is it because their teachers don't have "credentials?" No, it's because their teachers don't have a teachers' union. I know a teacher who teaches at a private school in my town who only makes $25,000 a year. She's also been teaching for ten years. What would a public school teacher in California be making with that type of experience? Probably between $55,000–$60,000.

Private schools also have a lot fewer students to educate. However, the most important reason why private schools can do it for less is because they have plenty of the one commodity many public schools lack and something money won't buy: they have involved parents.

My husband tells me someone he works with sends his children to a small Catholic school. Besides paying the $350/month tuition for each child, the parent must do 30 hours of community service at the school every month or their tuition is doubled. The service can range from helping out with the gardening to tutoring students in the classroom.

But it goes beyond just having parents help out at the school. These are parents who are paying money for a child's education that they could be getting free. You know these parents are going to do what it takes to make certain their child gets that good education they are paying so dearly for.

Even though public school parents don't have to pay for their child's education, imagine if this same community service requirement was made for them? How great would our public schools be and how much money could they save if parents volunteered to do some of the jobs that the school district pays staff to do?

I wish this were a perfect world where everyone had enough money for their needs, including all government agencies. However, this isn't a perfect world and sometimes we just have do the best with what we do have.

Mystery #60: If some states give part of Indian gaming proceeds and fifty percent of their state's budget to education, why do schools still need to rely on school bond measures?

Finance is the art of passing currency
From hand to hand until it finally disappears.

— *Robert W. Sarnoff*

"Santa Claus" paid a visit to our district last year and he was very generous. All of the older schools got new carpeting, and playgrounds at elementary schools received modern updated equipment. We now have money for all sorts of projects like fixing water fountains and putting up outdoor shades for eating areas, things that the district couldn't do because there just wasn't enough money in the budget. He is also giving us three brand new elementary schools.

Of course, "Santa Claus" really didn't give us the money for all of our new things. Then did our school win the lottery? Or was the money from people who played the lottery because you know that's why we let the lottery into California: to give our schools "extra" money. No, this money wasn't from our share of these almost mythical lottery proceeds.

My school district owes their good fortune to the taxpayers of the city of Moreno Valley who approved a very generous bond measure to help out our schools. That's the only way we were able to do so many of the larger maintenance repairs among other things, by the goodness of the taxpayers' pocketbooks.

I understand why bonds need to be passed to build schools, because it is extremely expensive to build new schools. What I find fascinating is that, despite all of the money that schools receive annually, we still need help from bond measures to upgrade and maintain the schools already in place.

I don't understand why it is this way, just that this is the way it is. So remember, if you care about schools, vote "yes" on any bond measure that helps schools out.

Mystery #61: If Title I schools already receive more money from the federal government for having more low socio-economic students, why are those students still lagging behind in test scores?

If we assume that money is the key to successful schools, why then aren't the Title I schools the best schools in the country? They have been getting extra money from the federal government for years.

It's ironic how public schools work. The poorer your students are, the richer the school becomes. That is because the federal government gives additional money to schools based on how many students qualify for the free/reduced lunch program. The more students who qualify, the bigger the amount of money the school receives.

The school I work at has been a Title I school ever since I have worked there. In addition to the money we receive from the state of California, we receive approximately an additional $300,000 on top of that for being a Title I school. We get this extra money every year as long as our students qualify the free/reduced lunch program.

What do we do with all of that money? For the past two years, we used it to fund three full-time credentialed teachers and a part-time clerical assistant. Obviously these salaries, which include payroll taxes and other benefits, took a big chunk of the money. What was the purpose of hiring these teachers? To help the classroom teachers do writing, and some reading, lessons on a daily basis. Did it raise our test scores? No, not exactly. And was that a good use of the money? Some might argue that it wasn't if it didn't raise our test scores. As for me, it did help me grapple with my not-being-able-to-teach-writing problem.

Title money was also used to purchase more instructional materials and provide money for teachers to attend conferences, among other uses defined by the federal government.

In addition to Title money, my school was also a recipient of a three-year magnet school grant program a few years back. Over the course of three years, five schools in the district each received just under a million dollars each. Now that's a lot of money.

What was the money used for? Again, the money could be spent only in accordance with how we spelled it out in our grant proposal. The majority of the money went towards the administrative costs of hiring two full-time people to run the program. Our magnet school was based on publishing and television production, so we purchased lots of computers and other cool technical equipment like cameras and editing machines.

Magnet school grants are designed for various reasons but honestly, I think ours was designed to "attract white students into a minority neighborhood." Did it work? Hmm, no. But it wasn't the fault of the magnet grant. Our school was already at capacity.

Our grant ended a year ago. Often when the grant money ends, so does the interest in the program. Fortunately, we have a teacher who has been very good about using much of the broadcasting equipment and under his guidance students produce a weekly television show.

Despite all of this extra money Title I schools receive, in my district which elementary schools have the best test scores? Not surprisingly, the non-Title I schools. It just goes to show all of us, that being successful in education isn't just about getting more money. Even at the Title I schools that are successful, is it because they used their money wisely? Perhaps, but a better guess would be it is because they found a way to get their parents more involved. To quote the MasterCard™ commercial, "That is priceless."

Mystery #62: Before asking for more money, can teachers' unions honestly say schools are using wisely the money they are already getting?

Another person's secret is like another person's money: you are not as careful with it as you are with your own.

— *E.W. Howe*

Maybe we as citizens and/or parents should quit putting our heads in the sand when it comes to money and public schools. In California, all schools are required to complete a State Accountability Report Card (SARC) on how their money is spent. Maybe we parents should be just as concerned with how the money is spent in our school district as we are about test scores. Yes, it is very easy and great for parents to jump on the "we need more money for our schools" bandwagon. But a better thing is that parents know exactly where the money is going that a school district already gets and a plan for how to use any extra money that they want.

Why is it so easy to forget that this money that schools want isn't coming from some invisible source or some rich uncle who died and left the government billions of dollars? It is coming out of the citizens', yours and mine, pocketbooks. We also need to remember that our taxes not only support education, but many other worthy services. Before any parent goes asking for more from the government, they'd better be ready to ask themselves, how much are they willing to fork over from their own family budgets. Now, who thinks we need to give more money to the government?

Mystery #63: Why are some school districts top-loaded with administrators?

Actually, this might not really be a mystery. Teaching is a really tough job. My theory is most administrators were probably former teachers who were smart enough to know they didn't want to stay in the classroom forever. Getting an administrative credential or whatever education you need to get a job qualifying you for a district office job is the best way to get out of the classroom, but stay in education. The best part is, you're in education but you have no lesson plans to make, no papers to grade, no parent conferences to hold, and no test scores that hold you accountable.

Except for being a place to put burned-out teachers, I don't really understand why school districts need so many administrators, especially since most just function to make a teacher's job harder. (Only kidding.)

When school districts hire administrators, does it come at the expense of valuable programs like music instruction or after-school tutoring? One of the employees in my school district felt so and sent us all an email bemoaning the fact when extra money was found, instead of reinstating the elementary school band program, they hired four more administrators. I don't really know if this was the case, but I do know our district's financial health has greatly improved yet there are no talks of reinstating band at the grade school level

We take our fifth grade classes to Knott's Berry Farm for an end-of-the-year celebration. Knotts also invites schools from around Southern California to perform musical programs for the visitors at the park. The afternoon we were there, I saw three wonderful groups, all from private schools. Is anyone in public schools really surprised by this? I know I wasn't.

I've got it. What we need are administrators who can teach music, band, or art at schools all around a school district. Not only will they be out of the teachers' hair, they will actually be doing something beneficial for the students and will really deserve their high salaries.

Mystery #64: Why do administrators need higher salaries and get better perks than the teachers who work in the classroom?

There is a superintendent of a school district not far from where I live who will be earning $1.2 million over a course of four years. They even offered him a signing bonus. This administrator of 19 elementary schools will be making $70,000 more than the governor of California who oversees a whole state. Another superintendent in a school district along the southern coast of California reportedly gets $250,000 a year, not including his benefit package.

Why do these men get paid so much as superintendents of public schools? The school boards must think they are worth it. The irony about the pay of the first superintendent, supposedly summer school in the entire district had to be cancelled because they didn't have enough money. Go figure that one out.

I do not know the answer to this "mystery." I wish someone would explain it to me.

To be honest, I know these superintendents' pay are not "typical" salaries. But then again, I don't know what administrators like him or ones who sit in the district office earn compared to teachers but I have a hunch it's more than most teachers make. Some might even get perks like a car or business expense account. And wait, they need an office and furniture. Who's going to answer their phones and file and type the memos they send to principals telling us how we better get those test scores up? They have to have a secretary and maybe she needs an assistant.

As I have explained, all of this stuff costs money and lots of it. Is this the reason why schools need more money? With our president, politicians, principals, and parents, teachers already have enough people telling us what to do and how to teach. I don't think schools need any more administrators, no matter how expensive or cheap they come.

Mystery #65: Should schools pay high school students money as an incentive to stay in school?

A letter writer to a newspaper had an interesting idea about how we could curb the rising dropout rate for minority high school students. Of course, it does come with a price tag. His idea is that these students need to see firsthand the economic value of an education. So why not pay them a performance and attendance-based salary. Their report card is no longer just a report card, but a bank statement. Since it is just his theory, he didn't go into more details on how much he thinks schools should pay for good grades or attendance.

He concludes that many minority students do not have good role models when it comes to teaching them the relationship between education and income. As we all know, most people in society are given financial incentives to do well; we call this a "paycheck." So why not pay poor children, the people who can use it the most, for staying in school and doing a good job academically? Who knows, it might just be a solution that brings more results than hiring any more administrators.

6

Kindergarten:

Has California, and all states, learned everything they need to know about kindergarten?

Mystery #66: Why does California, or any state with a late admissions date, think four-year-olds belong in kindergarten?

> Say you're sorry when you hurt somebody.
> Wash your hands before you eat. Flush.
> When you go out in the world, watch out for
> traffic, hold hands, and stick together.
>
> *— Robert Fulghum*

Back in the eighties, Robert Fulghum wrote a best-selling book called *All I Really Need To Know I Learned in Kindergarten.* In one of the chapters, he described how what we learned in kindergarten is really the essence of being a good person. Things like "share everything, play fair, don't hit people and put things back where you found them" were at the top of his list. (Noticeably absent was "writing phonetically spelled sentences.")

A clever passage is quoted above, and in many regards, holds true today. Fulghum's book was published in 1986. I became a kindergarten teacher in 1998. My, my, how kindergarten changed in those 12 years.

I still taught the kids to share everything, play fair, clean up your mess, etc. He also mentioned in his passage about taking naps, however, I'm afraid there is no time for naps in the 21st century kindergarten. Kindergarten has become more about work, and not about playing.

I don't necessarily think that change is bad. I believe experts say that our brain is capable of the most dramatic learning in the first five years of life. I have even read that our memory peaks at age five. Therefore, by raising our expectations for kindergartners, it is truly amazing what these little five-year-olds can accomplish.

So then what's my problem with our modern day kindergarten classes? (At least the ones in California, because I don't think any other state is stupid enough to have such a December 2nd cut-off day for entry into kindergarten).

Well for one thing, kindergarten is no longer just a place to pick up socialization skills as Robert Fulghum's passage suggests.

The 21st century kindergartener is expected to count to 100, add, subtract, and of course read books and write phonetically spelled sentences. So why are we letting four-year-olds into kindergarten to hold back the progress of the more capable five-year-olds?

That's right. I am prejudiced against four-year-olds. Not all of them mind you, just the ones who enter school too early. I don't mean pre-school, because that is where all four-year-olds belong. But we need to keep them out of kindergarten.

Sure you may think your four-year-old is brighter than the rest, but I'm telling you from personal experience, every child born in late September, October, and November will benefit more by being held out and doing an extra year of preschool.

Mystery #67: Is pushing kindergartners more into academics actually beneficial for them?

But it's not just the four-year-olds who could benefit from "slowing down the academics push." In my Education 101 classes we learned that there is a childhood developmental timeline for what children can accomplish and what they cannot at a particular age level. From personal experience, I will tell you that calling them all five-year-olds doesn't mean they are all developmentally at the same level. There is a big difference between a child who is 4 years and 11 months and one who is 5 years and 6 months. For the most part, the older the child, even if it's just a matter of months, he or she will be able to do more. Just because you raise the bar and some kindergarteners can write a phonetically spelled sentence doesn't necessarily mean it's a good thing to teach everyone how to do it.

Of course there are exceptions to the rule. One year my best reader in kindergarten started school at the age of four and he had a late October birthday. I've also had a January born student who was the last to read. But again, these are anomalies. It is safe to say that the older the child is, the more prepared he or she will be to handle the rigors of kindergarten.

Why should we be putting academic pressures on little minds that don't need the pressure? Has it been proven that the earlier the child learns to read and write the smarter he or she will be? It didn't seem to hurt my generation of kindergartners who were given this first year of school to learn how to play together, sing songs, and clean up our messes instead of blending sounds to make words. Rumor has it that many of us were still able to go to colleges and graduate.

The ironic thing is we have increased the academic load on these children but, in most states, still only give them half a day to learn what students used to learn in a full day of first grade.

So then do we need all-day kindergarten classes? Well, only if students are guaranteed to have more time for fun and less time for academics. My fear is that once "they" expand the day, "they" will want them to learn even more.

Being older is better

This isn't just my opinion. The U.S. Department of Education's Office of Educational Research and Improvement did a study in 1998 on a class of kindergartners entering school. The study was called the Early Childhood Longitudinal Study, Kindergarten Class of 1998-99 (ECLS-K). The results of their research were printed in a report called "Entering Kindergarten: Findings from The Condition of Education 2000." A big difference between their research and my own personal experience has to do with the age of the students being studied. The admission age cut-off date for these particular students was a very reasonable September 1st. Also school started in the fall, unlike it does at a year-round school where three-fourths of the students start school in July. So this study is based on comparing mostly five-year-olds. In California where we have such a late entry date, we have a much higher proportion of four-year-olds. Not only that, some kindergartners could be four years old one-third of their kindergarten year if they happen to attend a year-round school that starts in July.

One might think the results of the ECLS-K study would not show as big of a difference as I have seen in the classroom, since 91% of the students in their study were at least five years old. Yet, even then, the advantage of being an older child was dramatic.

Here is the breakdown of the student's ages in this study.

- 63% were between the ages of 5 years and 5 years 8 months.
- 24% were between the ages of 5 years 8 months and 5 years 11 months.
- 9% were only 4 years old.
- 4% were already 6 years old.

The ECLS-K findings support my theory and other research that older students often have advantages with respect to the knowledge and self-regulation skills they bring to the classroom. Here are the results I am taking directly from this study.

Older kindergartners are closer to being able to read.
- Seventy-three percent of kindergartners who are about to turn 6 at the start of the school year are able to identify letters by name (i.e. reading proficiency level one), whereas only 56 percent of children who have not yet turned 5 are able to do this.
- Twice as many of the older than the younger children are at reading proficiency level three: they are able to associate letters with sounds at the beginnings and ends of words. Twenty-two percent of pupils about to turn 6 can do this, compared with 11 percent of those about to turn 5.
- The small numbers who are at an advanced reading level is four times larger among the older than the younger children. Four percent of pupils about to turn 6 can read easy words by sight, compared with 1 percent who can do this among pupils about to turn 5 or who became 5 within the past 4 months (May-August births.)

Older kindergartners are closer to being able to do arithmetic.
A similar positive relationship between knowledge and age was found with respect to proficiency in early mathematics skills. Here the average older pupil is at a higher proficiency level than the typical pupil in the youngest age group. Specifically:
- Two-thirds of those about to turn 6 are at mathematics proficiency level two. They are able to read numerals, count beyond 10, recognize patterns of figures, and compare the relative lengths of objects. By contrast, only 42 percent of those who have not yet turned 5 can do these things.
- Two to three times as many of the older than the younger children are at the third mathematics proficiency level: they are able to read two-digit numerals and recognize the ordinal position of an object.
- The proportion at an advanced mathematics level is 4 to 5 times larger among the older kindergartners.

The study also states that older kindergartners know more about nature, science, and human society. Not surprisingly, older children also have more advanced motor skills. This holds true for both fine motor skills, which means it will be easier for them to color, cut, and print, and gross motor skills, such as walking backwards or hopping on one foot.

Older children are more socially adept and less prone to problem behaviors. Most importantly, older children are more persistent, meaning they exhibit a more positive approach to classroom learning tasks.

What does this all mean?

For one thing, it proves that if our kindergarten classes become too academic, many students will become frustrated. It puts them in a position of always having to play "catch-up" with their older classmates. More importantly, if you live in a crazy state like California that has a totally insane late admissions date, research shows it would be in the best interest of your child if you don't start him or her until they have reached five years of age. It is better that he or she is the oldest in the class than the youngest.

Mystery #68: Is there a connection between California's low test scores and their admission date for kindergarten?

Again, a word about California. California historically has been lagging behind I think 90% of the other states when it comes to their students' test scores. Hmm, I wonder why? I wasn't able to find out if any other state has such a ridiculous late admission date for their kindergartners. I somehow doubt it. There were talks a long time ago about changing our enrollment date to September 1st, but, of course, what politician was willing to take the chance of making angry a constituent who was looking forward to that free daycare called public education.

What those politicians don't realize is just what I mentioned above. For the most part, the four-year-olds become five-year-olds who are stilling trailing the six-year-olds. And when they are in the first grade and finally turn six, they are still trailing the seven-year-olds in the class. It takes many years for the cycle to be broken, if it really ever is.

My own stepson, Jonathan, graduated at the age of 17. He has an October birthday. Even in his senior year of high school, he didn't seem to be as mature as he should have been and made lots of foolish mistakes. One might argue, "Debra, that's just called being a teenager." That may be true, but I can't help thinking if he had started school later, he might have had a different story to tell.

Mystery #69: Could California raise their test scores without spending any extra money?

Half of California's budget is allocated towards education. Yet it's ironic that the one thing that could help us the most in our quest for higher test scores wouldn't cost us a dime. All they have to do is raise that admission date to at least September 1. It's not the only thing they could do but it would be a good start: making sure all students were able to get a good start on their formal education. If they did that, who knows, I might just go back and become a kindergarten teacher again.

Mystery #70: Do children who go to preschool really do better in college?

I mentioned earlier that kindergarten teachers *love* students who have attended preschool. It makes their job so much easier. So I'm an advocate of sending children to preschool.

At the time I was writing this book, there were ads running on television touting the huge benefits a child gains by going to preschool. I think they mention statistics that a child that goes to preschool is more likely to go to college.

I do not doubt this is true, but I just think it's a stretch to give preschool all the credit. Are they really insinuating that the instruction is so valuable in preschool that it sets them up throughout their educational journey to end up in college?

Have they ever thought that it might not be the instruction a child receives in preschool, but the fact that parents who push education at the earliest age are the same parents who are going to push their children into college?

I just think credit should be given where credit is due. It is the parents who send their child to preschool, not the act of going to preschool that is responsible for the statistics that most preschoolers graduate from college. It is the parents who set the stage that education is a priority, whether the child is four or eighteen.

I find it ironic that people in California have the nerve to push for mandatory or even voluntary pre-school, when currently even kindergarten isn't mandatory. I'm all for preschools if it means they finally have a place to put all of those four-year-olds who don't belong in kindergarten.

7

Miscellaneous Mysteries

Mystery #71: Why don't most teachers give grades based solely on how well a student knows the subject, but also on how responsible he or she has been in class?

> Success and failure. We think of them as opposites, But they're really not. They're companions—the hero and the sidekick.
>
> —*Laurence Shames*

Grades are to teachers as money is to politicians. They have to give them out. What's the point of teaching if you don't have some way to conclude how well a child is learning? For me, grades also tell me how well I'm teaching.

Most teachers are very quick to remind parents and students that, "I don't give grades, the student earns the grades." That would be great if it were true, but it's not. Teachers "give" grades out every day based on things other than just the academic performance. Most teachers also base grades on class work and homework being completed, even if it's completed wrong. They get the credit for at least doing it.

Is that really fair? What should a teacher do with a very bright but lazy student? What if the student doesn't do any of the homework or class work, but gets "As" on his tests? Does he get the "C" or "D" that might be reflected in the grade book? Or does he get the "A" because he had demonstrated he is fluent in the material? I think he deserves the "A".

Here is how my district report card defines our grades:

  "A" Outstanding Achievement
  "B" Above Average Achievement
  "C" Satisfactory Achievement
  "D" Limited Achievement
  "F" Little or No Achievement

So let's get this straight. A student who is lucky enough to understand the material without needing to do the homework and gets an "A" on the test, gets a "D" or "F" for limited or no achievement. That doesn't make sense to me.

I had a student in my class who was considered a very "low" student. The student didn't qualify for special education services because there wasn't a large gap between what he was achieving and what he was capable of achieving. The conclusion was that he had a low ability, thus a low potential for academic success. This was a kid who came to school every day and turned in all of his work, even though it was all incorrect. Since he doesn't know the material, it makes sense that he gets the "D" or the "F". But he's getting the same grade as the student who passes the test? I have had several teachers try to explain this system to me, that homework or class work is a grade for responsibility. Schools are helping the students out by penalizing for not doing the work. I'm sorry, it still doesn't make sense to me, but this is the way most schools operate.

What are grades supposed to represent? Is it the overall performance in knowing the material? Or is the grade a compilation of not just how well he knows the material, but also how responsible the student is in turning in homework and class work? Personally, I think grades should represent how well the student knows the material, and is not also a place to penalize his or her work ethic. Isn't the reason students attend school to learn? One would argue they are also there to learn responsibility. Perhaps.

Maybe the problem is I'm taking this "grade" game much too seriously. The truth is grades are very subjective, and it all depends on the teacher's standard. Even though teachers may use the same grading scale, teachers differ dramatically in how they grade. Take my own example. I let my students retake tests, and replace a failing grade with a better grade. Isn't this going to mean that my students are going to have "artificially" higher grades? Is this fair to the other students in fifth grade at my school? Probably not. My point is that most grading systems are flawed and teachers do have the final say when it comes to grades.

The bottom line is teachers give grades based on a variety of criteria. In my school district, if a student is in Special Education and if it's indicated in his Individual Education Plan, we modify his grade according to what kind of progress he is making based on his ability. English Language Learners aren't always judged, and I think correctly so, using the same criteria used for fluent English speakers. Is it wrong for a teacher to add a few extra points to the grade of a student who has worked really hard but still only managed a "C" and not the "B-" the teacher put on the report card? I don't know. It's a mystery to me.

As a parent, I have developed a more tolerant attitude towards grades on a report card, thanks to my son Matthew, and the disastrous grades he received from the "zero tolerance on late work" teacher. He is smart enough to be a straight "A" student like his two very best friends, John and Joseph. But he isn't. Besides having very involved parents, John and Joseph are also very self-motivated students. Matthew is not. How important is it that he is like them? I would have loved it if he were more like them. Maybe I should have cracked the whip harder? But I didn't. The reality was, I did resent spending so much time thinking about his schoolwork when I had so much of my own and I was trying to finish my book. So whose fault is it then, Matthew's or mine? We did lecture, punish, and took away video games and time on the computer so that Matthew would put more effort into getting better grades, but he still didn't. He said he was happy with his grades.

Even though good grades were important to me, I had to be honest with myself and ask, "How important are grades in elementary school?" I came to the conclusion that elementary grades aren't important at all in the big scheme of life. When was the last time an employer asked what your math grade was in fifth grade? Maybe good grades in elementary school do set up a student for success later on in life. However, I'm not that convinced that grades are the sole precursor on how successful a child will become as an adult. (Don't you love how I can rationalize his poor grades?)

In high school grades do play a more important role because they are the criteria used in determining what college a student will be accepted into. Even colleges understand that grades aren't everything because they also look at extracurricular activities and whether the student did more with his or her life besides studying.

As for Matthew's elementary grades, I decided to just release it and thought back to my "Serenity Prayer." I needed the wisdom to know whether this was something important enough to change. I decided, as long as he is learning, I needed to accept "Cs," and, yes, he even had a "D" on his report card. (I still can't believe I have a child who "earned" a "D". But so be it.)

I may regret my decision, when he is in high school, about not setting the standard now in elementary school, but I'm sure it won't be the only regret I will have as a parent. My advice to parents whose children are not getting the grades you know they can earn, you have to do your own soul-searching and decide how important grades are to you.

As a fifth grade teacher, I used to be amazed when I didn't hear from parents after sending out report cards. Some students received grades that did not reflect what they were capable of achieving. Thinking back, I have never had a parent complain about their child's report card. I couldn't understand why they didn't call asking why their child wasn't getting "As" and "Bs". Isn't this what all "good" parents want for their child?

I now understand why those phone calls never came. They already knew what I just learned. Yes, better grades would be nice, but they aren't everything. We are so quick to label students by how they do in school. "She is a straight 'A' student." "He's a 'C' student." I decided Matthew's grades were not who is. Not only grades, but test scores, do not define who any child is. They also aren't the precursor to a child's happiness or his success. There are many great success stories out there from people who did poorly in school.

Everyone should try to be the best they can be. Often though, it doesn't happen in school. If you are a parent who is unhappy with your child's grades, don't think all is lost for that child. There's nothing wrong with being average.

Even "average" people accomplish great things.

Mystery #72: Why do school officials put so much value into school textbooks?

The new buzz words for our district this year is "core curriculum." It is replacing the former buzz words, "state standards," which had been the number one words for at least six of my last seven years of teaching. Why did "state standards" lose out to "core curriculum"? I really don't know. I really liked focusing on "state standards" but as it goes in education, nothing lasts forever.

What is "core curriculum"? This represents the state-adopted textbooks school districts buy and that teachers are supposed to use and teach with. What's wrong with that or why wouldn't teachers want to use these textbooks? It's not that teachers don't want to use the textbooks, it's sometimes a teacher wants to supplement material from good outside sources that are still aligned with our state standards. They don't want us to do that anymore.

Why not? I don't know. I guess they are afraid that we might use something inappropriate, which isn't aligned with the standards. Or maybe they are tired of spending millions of dollars on textbooks only to find out the teachers aren't using them. They decided they are going to put a stop that practice immediately!!! They bought the textbooks, now damn it, we're going to use them!

Let me explain to you about textbooks. When going through my credential program in college, we seldom used a textbook from start to finish. As a student this was very frustrating since college textbooks are very expensive. Why don't professors use them from start to finish? Because often they don't contain all of the information they need to explain things. In addition, many textbooks are pretty dry and boring.

As for textbooks and public schools, for the most part, teachers really rely on textbooks to move through the curriculum. I could be wrong, but I don't think most public school textbooks are written by teachers from that grade level. They are written by a team of educators, most of whom probably have a PhD. I know schools "test pilot" programs that include textbooks, but I don't know if the publishers of textbooks give them to a classroom of students to see how effective they are. My guess is, they probably don't.

Despite a publisher's best intentions to make a kid-friendly text and a school district's careful examination prior to deciding and purchasing textbooks, it's hard to really catch the flaws in textbooks until you use them. For example, take my fifth grade math book. On the state test, our students are tested on multiplying integers, or positive and negative numbers, but I cannot find a lesson in our textbook that teaches that.

A bigger problem with the math textbook is that it breaks down the lessons into so many parts that it's almost impossible to finish the whole thing, lesson by lesson, in the time required. This is because it has too many lessons on things that aren't really necessary for them to know. I pride myself on always finishing the main points of the textbook, not by the end of the school year, but before the state testing. That means I finish it six weeks prior to the end of the year. Believe me, it's not an easy task.

Also, our math book is organized so that it doesn't give students much review of prior skills taught. Usually, we teach, then go onto the next skill. As you know, if you don't use it, you lose it, especially if you're only ten years old. There is a program out there called Excel Math. It is this gigantic legal-size worksheet of math problems. Every day is a new lesson and it constantly reviews the previously lessons. It is a great way to teach math.

The problem is, Excel Math is not approved by the state as adopted curriculum, so even though it's a great tool to reinforce math skills, in reality, we aren't supposed to use it even though it is aligned with the state's math standards.

There are flaws in our language arts textbook as well. It too is designed so it is hard to cover some very important language arts skills prior to testing. Also, it too gives very little practice to skills students need to be working on all year long.

There is even a problem with our fairly new science book. On our California state science test, fifth graders are tested on concepts like "first level consumers," "food webs," and my favorite, the "Mohs Scale of Hardness," yet NONE of these things are found in our science book. But it will be the teacher who is blamed for the low scores in science. Remember, as teachers, we do not have access to or are privileged to see the state assessment tests. They don't want us to know what's on it because that would be cheating. Well, how can we teach something if it isn't in our science book and we don't know it's going to be on the test?

Oh, well. A teacher's job is not to second-guess its administration and their push for "core curriculum." A teacher's job is to do just what you are told. If test scores are low, at least the teacher can say, "But I used the core curriculum." Besides, why am I even worried about teaching science? It's not really as important as language arts anyway.

Mystery #73: Why do they think smaller classes in lower elementary grades have helped students when in reality there is no evidence to prove it?

I am very grateful for class-size reduction, mainly because it is a reason I became a teacher. So in that regard, I am glad most

California school districts reduced the size of classrooms from 32 students to 20 students in grades kindergarten through third.

When I was teaching my class of twenty kindergarteners, I used to look in horror at those fourth and fifth grade classes of 33 students and wonder, "Why would anyone teach those grades? What fools those teachers are." And then I actually became one of those fools. Who would have ever guessed? That taught me a lesson didn't it? I shouldn't have been so judgmental.

I must confess, now that I am actually teaching 33 students in fifth grade, I do find it's manageable. There are so many students in the class that you definitely get a variety of personalities.

However, as I have mentioned much too often, it's the huge workload and the fact you have too many students and too much to teach in too little time that makes working with so many students difficult. I would say the best benefit of class size reduction is it makes teachers happy and less stressed.

Many people believe that reducing class size allows teachers to provide more individualized instruction, thereby improving student achievement. However, has it increased student achievement?

A sixth grade teacher I know recently made this observation about how effective class size reduction has been in our school district. She commented, "Where are those kids who were supposed to benefit so greatly from being in classes of 20? How come the caliber of sixth grade students is exactly the same as when students were in first and second grade classes of 32?"

Hmm. Interesting questions, aren't they? She felt class-size reduction has been a huge waste of money. Pacific Research Institute, a free-market think tank providing practical solutions on issues that impact the daily lives of individuals, agrees with her. They feel, "Class-size reduction in California has not been shown to improve student achievement significantly, and has caused numerous problems such as funding distortions." They even go as far as saying, "Class-size reduction should be eliminated and the funds re-directed to areas/programs that have a better track record of improving student achievement."

I see another problem associated with class-size reduction that is seldom brought up. Many good, elementary school teachers choose to teach in first through third grades just so they only have to teach twenty students. I often think about "moving down" just to get a break from the work load as a fifth grade teacher. However, I know it won't happen. I think fifth graders are the best and I like the curriculum despite all of the hard work.

Thus, it did make me ponder. Is there a grade level where class-size reduction really would benefit students? Maybe it should be in middle school writing or math classes. Or maybe even in high school algebra or literature classes. Which classes should be the ones that have the least amount of students in them and would be the ones where we do get the most bang for our buck?

I don't know the answer to any of those questions. I do agree with the Pacific Research Institute. Instead of just giving certain grades the luxury of fewer students, shouldn't the money be put to better use? Why not give all classrooms a maximum of 25 students?

I know that eight less students in my fifth grade class would mean more time I could spend with those students who need the extra help. It also just seems to me that divvying up students equally is not only more equitable, but would really benefit students the most in the long run.

Of course, then again, nobody said life, or public schools, was fair.

Mystery #74: Should students be expected to pass a state test in order to pass on to the next grade?

Before I became a teacher, I was in shock when I heard that students were graduating from high school with very minimal English and math skills. How could they do this? Didn't they have to pass tests and get at least a "C" or "D" in the class before they could get credit? How could teachers live with themselves knowing students graduated or passed a grade without really fulfilling the necessary requirements?

Many state governments agree that students need to prove that they learned what is taught in one grade before moving on. It is becoming more and more popular around the country that students are required to pass a state test in order to go on to the next grade. In some states, they only have to pass it at major intervals like fifth, eighth, and twelfth grades. So I must agree with this idea? If I weren't a teacher, I probably would. However, I have seen the reality of students and their abilities firsthand. My conviction against passing tests in order to advance was further cemented by what I heard, by chance, of a radio talk show.

One day, I had the misfortune, (at least I thought at the time) to use my lunch hour to go to my daughter's school to give her a field trip permission slip that she had to have that day. On my way to her school, the nationally syndicated Rush Limbaugh show was on the radio. From the moment I was in my car, he was discussing a show CNN had aired about testing and No Child Left Behind. When I heard the following story, it just cemented my belief that this anti-social promotion stance has gotten out of control.

Rush played a sound clip from this CNN show about a boy in Florida who had failed to pass his fourth grade state assessment test for the third time. In Florida, they must pass in order to promote to the next grade level.

This twelve-year-old black child was going to repeat fourth grade for the fourth time! For the record, most fourth graders are between 9 and 10 years old.

Rush thought this was great? He thinks this is why NCLB is great? Why? Obviously this student just doesn't have what it takes to pass this test. He must not be getting the help he needs because, the way I see it, here is a child being left behind in fourth grade for the fourth time. The sad thing is, I believe Florida uses a norm-referenced test for it's state assessment. I go more into different types of test in Chapter 8. What this means is, instead of using a criterion-based test which only tests the information he was actually taught, his ability is being compared to a "norm," based upon a typical group of students.

This may come as a shock to many bright individuals, but not everyone is born with the same intelligence capability. Sadly, there are kids with really low I.Q.s who just aren't going to get what we teach in schools. How do I know? Because I have had them in my class; I have met them firsthand. Maybe this boy is one of them.

What are they, the state of Florida, proving by having him repeat fourth grade one more time? Contrary to what many of you who disagree with me think, I couldn't care less about hurting his ego. He needs to move on because after three strikes of taking the state test, he should be out of the fourth grade ballgame. Even if he miraculously passes this year, do you think that's going to make him better prepared for fifth grade? I doubt it. Fifth grade is a completely differently animal than fourth grade. It is a very tough grade for many students who don't have learning problems. So what? He'll have to do four years in fifth grade as well?

It's so absurd I find it difficult to believe it is true. But sadly it is true. Again, let's ask ourselves, how much of the information that we learned in fourth grade is the stuff we rely on to get us through our daily lives? If we were honest, not much. Yes, we should know how to speak well and be able to construct sentences with subjects and verbs, but that's about it. Even the bank tells us how much money we have left in our accounts, so you don't need math for that.

I am not advocating a nation of stupid people. Lord knows, there's enough around without my help, and many have high school and college diplomas. I'm just suggesting that we know when to cut our losses, and that's the right thing to do in this case. I hope they follow this child throughout his education because I would love to know how old he is when he finally graduates. Or should I say if he graduates?

Mystery #75: Why is social promotion considered a bad thing?

I will never let my schooling
interfere with my education.

— Mark Twain

Contrary to what the government thinks, there is a time to leave a child behind, at least behind in the same grade level they have just finished. That is when they are in kindergarten, or maybe any of the lower elementary grades, and they are really struggling with the work. In the case of retaining kindergartners, with the insane late admission date in California, oftentimes it is a maturity issue. So for the record, I am not totally against retaining students or holding a child back.

However, as students get older, teachers also see kids who really just don't have the desire to pass, like my student Albert. He was retained because he didn't learn it the first time in fifth grade. As I told you, he didn't learn it a second time with me. It wasn't because he was stupid, it wasn't because we teachers didn't try, it was because he didn't care. Technically, he should still be in fifth grade if we were true to the "no social promotion" goal. Would yet another year in fifth grade finally bring home the point he needed to work hard to move on? Absolutely not.

There are other students who just don't want to deal with all the pressure of test scores and achievement because they don't see the relevance of algebra, geometry, and world history. A fellow teacher knew of students who were retained because they didn't do their homework. How absurd is that? These students haven't bought into our social agenda that knowing these subjects or doing things like homework will help them be more successful.

What happens to these students? They usually drop out. Is that what we want? By socially promoting our academic "failures" and having them stay in school, maybe they will find that one class, that one teacher who will give their education meaning. Isn't that a more preferable choice? Once those kids drop out, that's it. We don't get a second or third chance to help them. In addition, our current public school system doesn't offer an alternative to students who just don't want the type of education our high schools offer. Sure we have continuation schools, or alternative schools, but these just offer more of the same except in a less strict environment.

Why does the government make such a big deal of the number of students who drop out of high school? Isn't that the student's right? If they don't want to do the work, why should they waste a teacher's time and energy? If a student fails and drops out, does that mean that the school failed also?

I don't know. Isn't it the job of public schools to educate students, not rescue them? Or are we expected to do both? The truth be told, yes we are supposed to rescue them.

However, the public school system can only do so much for these kids who do not want to learn. Maybe we have to cut our losses and let them move on. As my husband says, there are lots of low-paying jobs that need to be filled by all the unmotivated Alberts of the world.

What is so wrong about social promotion? Instead of saying they "passed" the seventh grade, let's just admit what many students did. They attended the seventh grade. As I explained earlier, teachers are so connected with education because they can't imagine their life without it. However, these are our values, not the values of the kids who don't see it our way.

So a student couldn't pass geometry or algebra or doesn't know ancient history? How is that really hurting them? How is that hurting society?

In the end, students who drop out will find out firsthand what their lack of education will mean. But then again, maybe not. What if they possess the skills of a great entrepreneur? There have been many great successes in the world who did poorly in school.

There are many ways to a happy life and maybe for a few it doesn't have to include the knowledge a public education gives them. It is, after all, their life. Maybe it is not our job to rescue them and bestow upon them our values of what we think is important.

Mystery #76: Why do we expect students to get excited about learning when some of the things we expect them to learn seem pretty irrelevant to their lives?

Never mistake knowledge for wisdom.
One helps you make a living;
the other helps you make a life.

— *Sandra Carey*

"Mom, when am I ever going to use this?" my daughter asked me sincerely as I was trying to explain to her how to use a slope to graph linear equations, a lesson she got a "D" on in her 7th grade pre-algebra class. All I could do is tell her was that I was sure there was a reason why some people needed to know it, but all I knew was that I had never been called upon to have this knowledge.

I'm sure I'm not the first parent who has had to justify a subject or lesson that seems pretty useless to a child. Many times students don't see the big picture in learning subjects like social studies or math, but often there is a valid reason for learning them. Other times, as this instance, I don't know myself.

Why do we put so much emphasis on learning such skills as trigonometry or physics if a child knows they have no plans to enter a scientific or medical field? I know they might need them to get into college, but why? Passing classes like these definitely shows you're smart. In addition, I guess the more we use our brain for higher level thinking, the smarter we'll become in other areas of life? That's the best I could come up with. (Obviously, I didn't do very well in classes like physics or trigonometry.)

It's really no wonder that so many students get bored with school or even frustrated in a subject they really can't get. Why should they? Many students don't want to learn something just so they can feel smarter. Yet we make them learn it anyway.

We have friends who home-school their children. They find subjects that their children really have a curiosity about and explore them in great depth. How wonderful is that? Then learning isn't something you have to do, but is something you can't wait to do. It's just too bad we can't incorporate this type of thinking into public schools.

Mystery #77: Does the public understand that teachers' unions advertising may not reflect the opinion of all teachers?

I touched upon this mystery in Chapter 5 when I discussed money and schools. Yes, God bless teachers' unions. Really. They do mean well. Yet it does disturb when I hear the constant barrage of advertising on the radio station I listen to every day. Maybe it wouldn't bother me as much if I agreed with their point-of-view, but many times I don't.

I also wish teachers unions would rally so strongly behind causes other than money. Why don't they insist that state assessments tests only be given the last two weeks of school? Why don't they tell the public how detrimental it is for the child to be enrolled in kindergarten if they are only four-years-old? Instead, the public only hears the cries about "we need more money."

I just hope the people who aren't teachers and hear these ads realize that the teachers' union ads might not reflect the opinion of all teachers.

Mystery #78: If there are so many experts on education, especially in the media, why haven't they "fixed" our public schools yet?

The function of the expert is not to be more right than other people, but to be wrong for more sophisticated reasons.

— David Butler

Obviously, I'm the first to admit that public schools are far from perfect. Yet despite what some people, public schools are doing a good job of educating our children.

Yet it drives me nuts when I listen to my talk radio station out of Los Angeles, and I hear two very well-known syndicated radio talk show hosts blast teachers and our public school system. I've already shared a story about one of them. The other one goes so far as to tell her listeners she would never put a child into a public school. (Isn't that a benevolent attitude?)

Again, why is it necessary to lump all public schools together? For her information, public schools are where 55 million students obtain their education from the ages of 5 to 18. Out of those 55 million, public schools have produced the majority of workers, white-collar and blue-collar, in our country. We must be doing something right to have a country that is thriving and prosperous.

I just wish she would keep her comments to herself or recognize that public schools have produced a lot of fine citizens. (And I don't even hold it against them that they listen to her program.)

I also hate it when I read columnists who criticize teachers and public schools. They often use low test scores as their ammunition and, I think, truly believe we are purposely leaving minority students or children from low socio-economics households behind.

Yet while these self-appointed experts seem to have all the answers on how to improve schools and endorse legislation like the

No Child Left Behind Act, in actuality they don't have a clue what it's like to teach kids who don't want to learn or those students who actually come in with low abilities. I think there should be a law that anyone who criticizes public schools should be required to teach in a classroom at an underperforming school and see what kind of job they can do. Let's see how easy it is for them to make all students successful. I do have one fear now that I have written this book. I am afraid I will become one of "them." Do you know who I'm talking about? I'm afraid I'll become one of those self-anointed experts who because they have written a book, now think they know it all. For the record, I may know lots of things about being a teacher, but I do not know what will really fix our educational system.

**The only thing worse than an expert,
is someone who thinks he's an expert.**

—Aly A. Colon

There are other "experts" on education who aren't the media, but use the media to champion their views and opinions. (Sort of like me.) These are the self-proclaimed experts, usually someone in education, who go around pontificating on what is wrong with public schools and how we need to fix them.

I heard one of these "experts" on a radio talk show who was espousing his steps for fixing public schools. They were all really lame at best.

I didn't have to listen further than his very first point to know he didn't know what he was talking about. His first recommendation, "Hold schools accountable to ensure that students at all levels are attaining grade-level proficiency in reading, writing, and mathematics as measured by the California Standards Test—not just achieving 'growth' in meeting standards."

What kind of idiotic thought is this? He is this "big expert" and yet he thinks just because the government is using "growth" as measurement that that's what teachers are doing? I would like to remind him of a little piece of legislation called the No Child Left Behind Act. We aren't told just to get our students to achieve a certain percentage. NO!! All students are expected to leave the grade at grade level. He "recommends" that the state identify "grade level performance" as meeting "proficiency." Hello? They already do!!!! The interesting thing about this expert, he hadn't written a book but I imagine was using the radio as a platform to get more consulting work from school districts.

Our district also paid lots of money to a man who did write a book about "what great teachers do." He gave us an "inspirational" speech. He himself had only been a classroom teacher for two or three years, then I think he became an administrator. It's amazing how much knowledge he acquired about "great teachers" in that time frame. I will admit, he wasn't any dummy. His six-inch by nine-inch paperback book sold for $29.95.

Schools are so desperate for answers or things that will make students attain proficiency levels that I think they'll try about anything or follow the advice of anyone who acts like they even know a little bit about public schools. You know, maybe I will find a career in education outside of teaching.

Mystery #79: Why aren't classroom teachers the ones who determine educational policies instead of so-called "experts" who have never stepped inside a classroom?

What is the obvious way to make our schools better? I know, let's form a committee. And are we going to put lots of classroom teachers on this committee to share what they know about public education and to see if we can come up with solutions? Of course not. Why would we put teachers on a committee to revamp the public education system? Besides, aren't they part of the problem?

I think our governor truly has the best interests for most Californians in mind when making decisions about policies. This doesn't mean I agree with all of his decisions when it comes to public schools. To his credit he is really trying to make California's public schools better. What is one way he is doing this? He (or his team of advisor's) created a 15-member committee whose job it is to overhaul the state's public school system.

Now, on this committee is a former movie studio head, a couple of school superintendents and, of course, a lawyer for the American Civil Liberties Union. They also included the executive director of Ed Trust-West, a group, as they web site states, "who works for the high academic achievement of all students at all levels, kindergarten through college."

It continues to add, "While we know that all schools and colleges could better serve their students, we concentrate on the institutions most often left behind—those serving low-income, Latino, African American or Native American students. We are squarely and relentlessly focused on California's most serious problem: the huge achievement gaps separating poor students and students of color from other young Californians." Who can argue against that admirable goal? Okay, they can be on this committee.

Also on this committee are the regional director of Industrial Areas Foundations, a chief executive of Fiscal Crisis Management and Assessment Team and, what the heck, they even threw in one elementary school teacher. (What harm could one teacher do to this committee?)

Why is this committee comprised of the above people? Do they have some vast knowledge dealing with the schools? Do they have the secret to motivate students? Do they know the public school system so well that they will advise the governor on what works and what won't work? Maybe, but I don't think they have this knowledge. Maybe the governor is using people outside of education to come up with some fresh ideas about looking at an old situation.

And if one committee is good, wouldn't two be even better for our educational system? Not long after this committee was formed, our state schools chief, Jack O'Connell, decided we needed another one aimed at improving California's struggling public educational system.

Isn't this what the first one is doing? No, no, no. This one is different. It has 16 members on it. They call it "The P16 Council." Isn't that clever? So they have brand new people on this committee? No. I'm sorry. Despite my thinking that there are lots of educational experts out there, they will have to use a couple of members from the governor's committee. Is one of them the elementary school teacher? Of course not, silly. They are going use the former movie studio executive and the couple of superintendents.

Also, the governor's committee is replacing the Quality Education Commission created in 2002. It was designed to analyze the state's school finance system. No wonder they're getting rid of that one; they probably couldn't find anyone who wanted to be on that committee.

Maybe people outside of education will have fresh ideas and a different perspective on what can help public schools. Maybe because educators are so entrenched in the system, they have lost the ability to see things in a new light. Nevertheless, who knows schools better than someone who has worked in one for years?

It's okay to have "fresh blood," but that should be in addition to a committee of classroom teachers from all areas of the state representing rich and poor schools. Aren't the teachers the ones who know what the problems are and maybe could come up with some solutions? But look at these committees. They don't even have the decency to put teachers on them. Or is it they don't think we college-educated workers on the front line are up to the task. I just don't get it.

If the powers that be are not going to put teachers in positions where they can be heard and give their input, then how do they expect real results to happen? My only hope is that these non-teacher committees don't screw things up for us even more than they already are.

8

No Child Left Behind Act, No Child Left Untested

My mother used to tell me that "if I don't have something nice to say about someone then I shouldn't say anything."

Okay, let me think about that. I can say that the No Child Left Behind Act had its heart or intentions in the right place. I also truly believe the creators of this education-altering legislation really thought they were doing the right thing. And boy, are teachers and schools busting their buns to get students to succeed. I think I did pretty well. I actually came up with three positive things about the No Child Left Behind Act. But forget what my mother told me. There are more pressing things at hand than being polite, or politically correct. I feel someone has to speak out against the absurdities and injustices of this inane piece of legislation.

Mystery #80: What is the "No Child Left Behind" Act?

Even if you don't have school-age children, it's hard to escape the attention that the No Child Left Behind (NCLB) Act has created. I think most people, maybe even teachers, do not really understand the real impact or consequences that NCLB brings to public education.

So to get myself educated, I went to the "No Child Left Behind" website (http://www.nclb.gov) in hope of making sense of this law, which the government calls a "landmark in education reform designed to improve student achievement and close achievement gaps." They go on to remind readers that this legislation was "passed with overwhelming bipartisan support from Congress." President George W. Bush signed the law on Jan. 8, 2002, and it has been creating havoc with teaching ever since. (Oh, sorry, that's my opinion, not from their web site.)

This isn't really a "new" law, but an amended old one, the Elementary and Secondary Education Act of 1965. What's the difference between the old and the new?

"The new law represents a sweeping overhaul of federal efforts to support elementary and secondary education in the United States. It is built on four common-sense pillars: accountability for results, an emphasis on doing what works based on scientific research, expanded parental options, and expanded local control and flexibility."

How ironic. I hate the No Child Left Behind Act on four common-sense pillars: accountability for results, an emphasis on doing what works based on scientific research, expanded parental options, and expanded local control and flexibility.

Actually, I'm okay with expanded parental options. So in its place I will substitute the biggest problem, and I mean biggest problem with the No Child Left Behind Act is it puts no responsibility on the student or the parents. But more about that later.

Mystery #81: Why does the government think that children are being left behind?

Once upon a time there was a government agency whose job it was to analyze data on student achievement. They liked making charts and decided to take their data and make charts showing the differences in student achievement based on ethnicity and income level. What did they find out?

Surprise!!! They found out all sorts of startling information. For example, they discovered that Caucasian children in fourth grade were scoring dramatically higher than African-American and Native American students. Their charts showed that white children were also scoring higher than Hispanic students. Their conclusion: That we teachers are only teaching to the white children. We must not care about African-American or Native American or Hispanic children because … look at the statistics. We are purposely leaving children behind!

They got us, didn't they? How did they know that teachers all of these years only have been teaching to white children? I confess, it hasn't been an easy job teaching only to white children due to the fact the African-American, Hispanic, Asian, and American Indian students have to sit in the classroom while we teach. Somehow, we all do it!!!! (Sorry, this is my attempt at sarcasm.)

So this is why the No Child Left Behind Act insists that schools break down test scores into "subgroups." Schools need to break down their data to show that all students, regardless of ethnicity, are learning. We wouldn't want a school to pass because they had a high percentage of smart Caucasian or Asian students who scored very well, thereby offsetting the fact that the small group of Hispanic students actually failed.

Mystery #82: Will a school be designated "underperforming" even if all the subgroups have made progress except for one?

"Every state has developed benchmarks to measure progress and make sure every child is learning. States are required to separate or disaggregate student achievement data, holding schools accountable for subgroups of students, so that no child falls through the cracks."

— Quote from the No Child Left Behind website

Let's say your child is the only Pacific Islander at his school. Does that mean he or she is a "subgroup" of one?

That's silly. Of course not. The government says you have to have a certain number of students to qualify for being a "subgroup."

For example, a couple of years ago, at the school where I teach, our Caucasian students were a "subgroup" that wasn't measuring up to the NCLB standard; they weren't making adequate growth. This year, it doesn't matter because we have fewer than 100 white students out of a total student population of one thousand students. They are no longer classified as a "subgroup". So now we don't have to care if they reach their goal. (Thank goodness, because it's been a drag teaching white kids all of these years! Again, this is sarcasm.) I also guess the government isn't concerned now what happens to these kids that are a really small minority at the school.

As I pointed out, even though the bill is called "No Child Left Behind," in reality, the government doesn't care about subgroups that make up less than 10% of the school's population. I guess that's why they didn't call the bill No Subgroup Left Behind.

What if a school has all of their children showing growth except maybe a subgroup of English Language Learners? Does the whole school still fail? Absolutely! Remember it's called *No Child Left Behind* (except those in a really small subgroup of less than 10%.)

This story is from the September 2004 issue of the *California Educator*. This particular issue is devoted to how schools are being set up to fail by the NCLB. One of the articles profiles Southwest High School located near San Diego, not far from the Mexican border. Here in part is their story:

"Who says this isn't a good school?"

By Sherry Posnick-Goodwin

Southwest was named one of the top 300 schools in the country by Newsweek for "its many AP(Academic Performance) classes and its AP results. The school's AVID (Advancement Via Individual Determination) college-prep program is used as a national model. Not surprisingly, a high percentage of Southwest graduates attend college.

The school has more than met its growth target on the state's

Academic Performance Index; test scores have risen 117 points since 2000, with Southwest making the second-greatest gains of all high schools in the district.

Despite these achievements, Southwest High School has been branded a "failing" school under federal standards and could ultimately be taken over by the state, closed down or turned over to a private company. It is just one of thousands of schools throughout the United States that fall into the "failing" category under NCLB, which growing numbers of people now recognize as a mandate with impossible requirements that deliberately sets up schools for failure.

How could a good school like Southwest be labeled as failing?

Under NCLB, students in all "subgroups" must achieve a certain level of proficiency, even those who can't speak English or are enrolled in Special Education classes. Because ELL and low socioeconomic students at Southwest failed to score high enough on the English Language Arts test, the entire school did not meet Adequate Yearly Progress (AYP) requirements, was put into Program Improvement (PI) and is facing sanctions.

So their test scores rose 117 points since 2000 and they are considered an "underperforming" school? That makes sense, doesn't it? The No Child Left Behind Act was revised to allow more flexibility for ELL students, but the changes are not retroactive.

Mystery #83: Why isn't there just one standard test that all states take to determine student achievement?

Our federal politicians went to great lengths to create this worthy program of accountability so that schools in all states show yearly progress. However, did they tell the states they all had to use the same test on which to base this progress? No, that would make too much sense.

California's State Superintendent of Public Instruction Jack

O'Connell offered this great quote about what No Child Left Behind is really doing: "The federal government uses a status bar, which is arbitrary, like having a high jump all students must jump over or the entire school fails." One state might let a student pass if they only have to high jump twenty-four inches. Another state wants to have higher standards and expects all students to jump 48 inches. According to NCLB, as long as each state is making progress towards reaching their goals, then they are succeeding.

This is so absurd. Here's another sports analogy. It's like judging people on how many baskets they can shoot into a hoop, but letting some people shoot from the free throw line, while others only shoot from mid-court. Which ones will get the most baskets? By letting states dictate their own goals, this equates to how NCLB is judging schools.

This "comparing apples with oranges" is what actually happens with No Child Left Behind. Because of differences in the kinds of tests and expectations that are used in the United States, some states look like they have glowing successes, while others look like dismal failures.

Case in Point:
My own lovely state of California

Why do states use different tests? My guess is that the federal government wimped-out and told the states they could decide their own assessment standards because it felt guilty about this demanding legislation and was hoping the state governments would "buy into" it better if they were given some control. So it said, "We will tell you what results we want; you get to decide what tests you use."

That does sound like a very noble gesture, allowing each state to set its own definition of proficiency. If a state was "smart," they would set very low expectations, therefore assuring all students could achieve that "proficient" level. That sounds a bit harsh, let me rephrase it. If a state was smart, they would use realistic criteria and establish goals reasonable for most children to achieve.

However, in the wonderful state that I live in, California, officials got caught up in their own egos. Prior to the NCLB being enacted, California approved a set of standards that was the highest in the nation. The goal was that "all students would meet University of California requirements." Excuse me, what was that? Did this mean they wanted every student to be able to qualify for admittance to the state university system?

What were they thinking? Obviously, that idea didn't come from a public school teacher who knows that not everyone is college material. I'm not saying that they couldn't be if they wanted to be, but why should everybody need or want to go to college?

What is wrong with admitting that not everyone has to go to college? Why do we think that college is the cure for society in the first place? Maybe it made me a better supermarket cashier because I had attended college. I doubt it, but is this the line of thinking they are going on?

Back to our story. So when California needed to set criteria for success in schools for the No Child Left Behind Act, did officials do the smart thing and now lower their standards, so that they were more realistically in tune with our society? No, they wanted to play the martyr and keep these high standards. Consequently, guess which state has more schools in Program Improvement than any other state? That's right, California.

In the article from *California Educator* that I quoted earlier it said, "Currently, 1200 California schools are in Program Improvement, the precursor to more severe sanctions if test scores don't rise." It also gives the grim prediction that "By 2014, nearly all of California's schools are likely to be labeled as 'failing' under the federal No Child Left Behind Act."

How could this be? I think it is because 2014 is when 100% of the students are supposed to be "proficient." You don't need to be a psychic to know that no way, no how, are all of the students in our state going to be at that proficient level.

I don't know about you, but I can't think of anything that we can judge 100% of the people on except for the fact that they are all breathing.

In fact, it is mathematically and statistically impossible for all students to reach some artificial academic goal. Yet, this is the very premise that No Child Left Behind is based on.

Maybe I shouldn't be so mad at NCLB, but at California and its poor judgment. It's very commendable that California wants to have high expectations for all, but what were they thinking? Do they not know who their students are? Do they not know that the wave of illegal immigration is bringing a group of students who might not speak our language? Do they not understand that by setting such unrealistically high goals, they only set themselves up for this failure? In a way, like most of the problems in California, the powers that be have no one to blame but themselves.

If the federal government wants states to have their own goals and assessments, that's fine, but then they need to determine success by a different measurement. Mr. O'Connell says, "The more accurate model is the growth model, because all students don't come to school equally prepared." The growth model he is talking about would measure individual student's growth in learning. An example would be a "C minus" student would be expected to move up to a "C" while maybe the "B minus" student would be expected to move up to a "B". If both students did this, then the goal has been achieved.

It would be great if both of those students would become "A" students, but we aren't a world filled with "A" students. I have a friend, Linda Moore, who is a second grade teacher at the same school I work at. In discussing students we both have had, she made the observation that a child's ability is pretty consistent regardless of the teacher they have. Those "A" students always tend to be "A" students as they move upward; "C" children often stay "C" children. That is so true.

One would argue that's because teachers' expectations are low for students, but that's not the case. I tell my students that if they work hard, they can achieve more. I also never look at my cumulative folder before starting a new school year because I don't want to prejudge a child's ability by their last year's report card.

The fact is, it's not that students are being labeled, it's just that some students don't have the motivation and the wherewithal to do better and this is something that the No Child Left Behind Act never even remotely considers!

Mystery #84: Why does the government feel it is necessary to label schools as failures?

What's in a name?
That which we call a rose
By any other word would smell as sweet.

— William Shakespeare

I must be fair. The NCLB website is emphatic that they do not label schools as "failures." And I quote:

A school or school district that does not meet the state's definition of "adequate yearly progress" (AYP) for two straight years (school-wide or in any subgroup) is considered to be "in need of improvement". No Child Left Behind does not label schools as "failing." Instead, schools are identified as "in need of improvement," and they are given assistance to improve by doing such things as instituting a school improvement plan or increasing professional development for teachers.

They also try to dispel the myth that "in need of improvement" schools lose federal funding. They answer these charges by saying,

Federal funds have steadily increased to support schools in need of improvement. These schools have increased funds targeted for the professional development, and are specifically required to work with parents, school staff, district and outside experts to develop an improvement plan.

Or by any other name, or phrase like "in need of improvement," doesn't it still mean a school is failing? I think so. It is true that the government on this website never does identify a school as failing. Maybe I'm just too sensitive, but I say actions speak louder than words.

If it is not failing, then why notify parents whose children attend these "in need of improvement" schools that they have the option of going to a more successful school? Doesn't this stigmatize schools that do need help and then, to add insult to injury, make the school inform the parent of its unworthiness and their option to transfer? You know which students will transfer don't you? That's right, the good ones. Don't bad schools need good students too?

If I'm a parent who was told that my child's school was an "in need of improvement" school and they were required to notify me of this, I know I might think of changing schools to one that is a higher performing school.

As Pam Kingsley, chair of California Teachers Association's Assessment and Testing Committee, said in the *California Educator*, "Once people hear something bad about a school, it takes a lot of extra things to get it on track again."

At one Santa Barbara middle school in her district that has been labeled as failing, "parents are opting out of sending their children there because they think there is something wrong with the school," she says. "How does that help an underperforming school? There's a stigma that comes when a school gets labeled. But it's understandable; if you heard bad news about a Ford would you go out and buy a Ford? No, you'd probably wait until it improves."

I guess I should be happy that a letter going home is all that happens. I'm waiting for the day when a politician suggests teachers at underperforming schools wear a giant "L" for loser.

The article goes on to state that one school went up 86 points one year and down two points the following year and was labeled as "underperforming."

"Is that fair?" she asks.

As for the part about schools not losing money when they are labeled "underperforming," it might be true that they don't lose money directly. But schools will have less money to work with if they have fewer students who are attending because they have chosen to go somewhere else. Money also is required to be used for corrective actions that include using up to 20 percent of Title I funds to transport students to "non-failing" public schools, and to pay for tutoring by outside providers, including faith-based organizations, if requested by parents.

Harvard University's Civil Rights Project in its report, "Inspiring Vision, Disappointing Results," comments that "Money taken away from general Title I funds and redirected to such services concentrates resources meant for many children on only a few."

Mystery #85: Why does the government think it's fair to compare one group of students from one year with a completely different set of students, and then expect better results?

This is the most absurd concept that drives me nuts about this mania over testing and No Child Left Behind. Why does the government think that it is fair to compare completely different sets of students? Are they insinuating that all students come into the classroom from one year with the exact same kind of background, the same biological make-up as the class from the previous year? Do they really think children are like robots void of personalities or histories that might accentuate or hinder their learning abilities? Well, I have news for them, it doesn't work that way with adults, and it definitely doesn't work that way with children.

I will promise you that the class from my second year of teaching will do poorer on their state tests than the class from my first year of teaching fifth grade. I can say this despite the fact that I have a year's experience under my belt, I am a better teacher of many of the subjects because I know them better, and I learned from the mistakes I made last year. So how can I be so confident they will be worse?

It is because the group of students I had my second year were a nice group of students with average to low-average ability. During my first year of teaching fifth grade, I had about eight to nine students who were brainiacs or "A" and "B" students. That's almost a third of my class. They were motivated to learn and they worked very hard. They also picked up on ideas very quickly.

That doesn't mean the fifth graders from my second year of teaching won't be successful, it just means they had to work much harder for either the same results, or lower results.

How could I have classes of such diverse abilities from one year to the next? Ask any teacher and they will tell you that it just happens. In my case, a lot of the students with the stronger academic ability in our fourth grade classes were channeled into a newly created fifth grade Gift and Talented (GATE) class instead of staying in a regular fifth grade class like the one I teach.

Yet, my teaching will be judged on how well my second year class's test scores compare with those of my first year's class. What will it look like when the test results come out? I wish someone would explain to me why this is considered fair to compare two groups of completely different students.

An introduction to "norm-referenced" tests

An even more important reason why it is so wrong to base so much on test scores is that many states use norm-referenced tests (NRT). According to the website Fairtest.org (http://wwwfairtest .org) these types of tests compare a person's score against the scores of a group of people who have already taken the same exam, called the "norming" group.

Norm-referenced tests are designed to compare and rank test-takers. By definition, they are constructed so that 50 percent of the test takers will be in the top 50 percent and 50 percent will be in the bottom 50 percent, so that 25 percent will be in the top 25 percent and 25 percent will be in the bottom 25 percent. If a norm-referenced test does not do that, the test makers change the questions until it does. This doesn't make sense to me but this is how they explained it.

"In education, when test makers construct norm-referenced tests, they select which questions to include in the test or exclude from the test according to how many students can answer them correctly, not necessarily according to whether the questions are over content that has been taught," reported EdResearch.info on their website http://www.edresearch.info.

This is ridiculous that we make students take tests on questions that aren't based on what they have been taught. No wonder I feel my students are so screwed when they take the California Science Standards test.

Fairtest.org also states that, *"One more question right or wrong can cause a big change in the student's score. In some cases, having one more correct answer can cause a student's reported percentile score to jump more than ten points. It is very important to know how much difference in the percentile rank would be caused by getting one or two more questions right."*

"In making an NRT, it is often more important to choose questions that sort people along the curve than it is to make sure that the content covered by the test is adequate. The tests sometimes emphasize small and meaningless differences among test takers. Since the tests are made to sort students, most of the things everyone knows are not tested. Questions may be obscure or tricky, in order to help rank order the test takers."

"Tests can be biased. Some questions may favor one kind of student or another for reasons that have nothing to do with the subject area being tested. Non-school knowledge that is more commonly learned by middle or upper class children is often included in tests. To help make the bell curve, test makers usually eliminate questions that students with low overall scores might get right but those with high overall scores get wrong. Thus, most questions which favor minority groups are eliminated." I found this information to be almost unbelievable.

EdResearch also comments about the myth of reading at grade

level. They stated that *"It is mathematically impossible for all children to read at grade level. When below-average readers read better, the average changes. It is also mathematically impossible, long-term, for all children to read at or above the 50th percentile or higher on norm-referenced tests (e.g., the SAT 9). Norm-referenced tests are, by definition, constructed so that 50 percent of the test-takers will always be in the bottom 50 percent. When this changes, the test questions are changed so that once again 50 percent of the test-takers will be in the bottom 50 percent."*

In fairness, not all states use a norm-referenced test. Texas's Texas Assessment of Academic Skills (TAAS) is a criterion-referenced test. Criterion-referenced tests, such as a driver's license test, measure how well a person has learned a specific body of knowledge. Everyone correctly answering a pre-determined number of questions passes. This sounds like the most logical type of test to give students, yet teachers in Texas are often criticized for "teaching only to the test."

If you want more information on norm-referenced based tests, I highly recommend the easy-to-read websites I've cited. I understand that whenever researching a subject, it is easy to find biased opinions. However, I didn't find anything positive about norm-reference based testing, but only that it is not the appropriate way to determine a child's success in school.

Mystery #86: Why are Special Education students held to the same goals as students without disabilities?

The goal of NCLB is having *"every* child make the grade on state-defined education standards by the end of the year 2013–14. Does that mean every child regardless of what language they speak? Does that mean every child even if they miss 68 days of school? Does that mean every child who has an identifiable learning disability that hinders their reading skills? Does that mean every child who couldn't care less about education, especially their test scores?

Yes. The government wants *"every"* child to make the grade regardless of mental capacity, physical ability, socio-economic background, or motivation. After all, this is why they called it "No Child Left Behind." Even Special Education students are required to take the tests and show growth. This is totally absurd and ridiculous. Special Education students aren't going to be able to meet the same standards because they are not coming in with the same ability. I'm not being judgmental when I say this, just truthful.

It would be very nice if they said, "Well, okay, some of the kids can be left behind if you have a good reason." But you know why they can't do that? They know how we teachers are. Instead of teaching, we would probably be spending all of our time finding excuses why our students couldn't achieve. (I'm being sarcastic here.)

As long as they think everyone in life is born with the same ability to achieve the exact same educational standards, regardless of their life's circumstances, why is the government stopping there? Why don't they create the "No Adult Left Behind Act" and say it is mandatory that every adult in the United is capable of earning $50,000 a year. Imagine all of the problems that would solve in our society.

Mystery #87: Why does the government say a school can't make its progress goal just because less than 95% of its students take the test?

The absurdity about No Child Left Behind is that even high-scoring schools in affluent areas have been declared "failing" if the school tests fewer than the mandated 95% of all students in each subgroup. They require this 95% participation because they probably think schools would tell their low achieving students to stay home on the day of testing. Schools wouldn't do that, would they?

In the article in *California Educator* it gave an example of a high school in Palo Alto, California. Many juniors opted to skip the California Standards Test so they could study for the Advanced Placement exams. "Even the district's testing director said he couldn't fault the students for choosing to skip a test that would not have much impact on their future in favor of preparing for a test that could help them get into college." If the college-bound students are not inspired to take state assessments, why would regular high students be expected to be interested, let alone care about the results?

I guess the government forgot to legislate the part about requiring that all students must care about taking the state mandated testing.

Mystery #88: With so much emphasis on testing and a school year already too short, why do some states like California test their students four to six weeks before the last day of school?

I asked people around my school if they knew why we needed to test so early. Someone guessed that maybe it was because education officials think students "check out" at the end of the year, so it would be better not to wait so long. Perhaps. But I think students and teachers check out after state testing has ended. That means four weeks of wasted education time. The last two weeks of the school year are pretty wasted time academically, so it would make the most sense that this is when testing should be conducted.

My best guess is that we test early because it has something to do with placating the adults who have to total the results. They probably need final tallies by some certain deadline and the only way to get it done is at the sacrifice of student academic time. Maybe since it's a norm-reference based test, the adults might figure that an extra six weeks of academics isn't going to make that much difference in the results anyway.

Mystery #89: If the government has all of this "scientifically based research" on how to make schools successful, why then are there still "underperforming" schools?

"No Child Left Behind focuses on teaching methods that have been proven to work. There will be no more experimenting on children with educational fads."

One should never spoil a good theory by explaining it.

— *Peter McArthur*

For the benefit of those of you not in education, this whole concept of "scientific research" was born out of the response to the late '80s–'90s teaching strategy of "whole language" in teaching reading. Generally speaking, the idea of "whole language" instruction was based on the idea that children would learn how to read if they were immersed in a print-rich environment and nurtured into loving books so much that it would motivate them to read.

However, the reality is, "whole language" was probably created by someone who based it on "scientifically based research." In fact, my theory is that everything in education, good and bad, is probably based on "scientifically based research." A person could probably find a research paper arguing or supporting any idea used in teaching.

What I think is absurd is the arrogance associated with that statement. If "scientifically based research" exists that will actually help students succeed, then why hasn't anyone shared it with my school? Why did I still have a class of fifth graders who could only achieve at a "basic" level and not at "proficient?" Why are many schools still struggling?

Why did I have to waste my time in all those credential programs learning their theories, which I thought were also based on "scientifically based research," if they weren't going to help my students succeed?

More importantly, where can I find out now about this scientifically based research that applies to federal education programs? This is it what I read on the Department of Education's website.

No Child Left Behind sets forth rigorous requirements to ensure that research is scientifically based. It moves the testing of educational practices toward the medical model used by scientists to assess the effectiveness of medications, therapies and the like. Studies that test random samples of the population and that involve a control group are scientifically controlled. To gain scientifically based research about a particular educational program or practice, it must be the subject of such a study. Going back to the example of reading: No Child Left Behind requires that reading first support those programs that teach children five skills (phonemic awareness, phonics, fluency, vocabulary and comprehension). These skills have been shown to be critical to early reading success through years of scientifically based research on the practice of reading instruction.

I get the idea that phonics is a much better way to teach reading than whole language. In fact, this is how all of the teachers at my school teach reading. So why then are we "an underperforming school." Is this the best they could come up with?

The information goes onto to state that, *"in 2002, the Department of Education's Institute of Education Sciences established the 'What Works Clearinghouse' to provide a central, independent, and trusted source of scientific evidence on what works in education for parents, educators, policymakers and anyone else who is interested."*

Why can't they just admit it? Schools can have all of the "scientifically based research" curriculum they want, but the truth is there is no magic formula that will help all students be successful in school. Besides, if there were, we wouldn't need No Child Left Behind at all. It's easier just to blame the teachers.

Mystery #90: Why are schools with poorer students not making the same kind of progress as students coming from families with higher incomes?

I hate to sound like a broken record, but this is another mystery I wish I could understand. I can tell you which school districts are succeeding and which ones are failing in not only my county of Riverside, but our neighboring county of San Bernardino, without even looking at test scores. All I need to do is know the average price homes are selling for in the cities that are in the school districts. Is it just a coincidence that the school districts that are doing well are those districts that have a higher per capita income than the ones who are failing, like my own school district? No, it is not.

Most experts attribute this to the idea that the parents with higher incomes are more "involved" with their child's education. But is it really that simple a reason? You already know I discount any theory that it has to do with the quality of the teachers. But are our lower test scores simply because our parents are perceived as not caring and being involved? There are some low socio-economic schools that are succeeding. Is that because the parents of those students have now gotten "involved" with their child's education? I just can't help but thinking there has to be more to it than that. Doesn't it make more sense that parents in a lower socio-economic community would encourage their children even more to do better in school so that they could have a better life when they grow up? Or is life to them, not all about money?

I guess this is why I call the book "The 111 Mysteries of Public Education."

Mystery #91: Why doesn't No Child Left Behind put <u>any</u> responsibility for learning in school on either the child or the parents?

I will admit I have not exactly read every word of the No Child Left Behind Act, nor have I read all of the propaganda on the internet that the Department of Education has released for the purpose of helping parents understand better the elements of NCLB. I have read lots of it though, and nowhere did I read that for a child to learn that child has to want to learn.

Nowhere does it tell the parents the importance of a hot breakfast for your child, or attending school events, or reading information from the school, or helping your child with homework. Nowhere does it say that if your child is a brat and chooses not to learn, there isn't much his or her teacher can do to help. Why doesn't it explain these things to parents?

I must admit I started to get excited about the "No Child Left Behind Parents' Guide" when I thought I was going to find something relating to this matter. In the listing under Appendixes it has listed, "Appendix C: Key Sections of Title I—Improving the Academic Achievement of the Disadvantaged, Pertaining to Parent Involvement." Finally, was my wish going to be granted? Were they really going to tell parents what they needed to hear so they could really help their child?"

No, of course not! My dream had been shattered. What they did print was from the Title I rules saying that if a local educational agency was going to receive funds to implement programs and activities that they needed to get "meaningful consultation with parents of participating children." (It goes on to say other stuff, which I interpreted as "when it comes right down to it, it's the school's responsibility to get the parents involved." No, we wouldn't want them to think of the idea on their own.)

Mystery #92: Why does the No Child Left Behind Act assume that, given the parameters of public schools, every child is capable of achieving "proficiency" status?

I mentioned this subject when discussing Special Education students. I am not mean, I am not being negative. Despite wanting to have us all feel good about each other, the fact is all children are not born with the same health, with the same parents, and under the same circumstances. If people do not know this, then I'm sorry I had to be the one to tell them this. How do I know? Because I have met these children and I have taught these children.

When our forefathers said, "All men are created equal," they didn't mean that literally. We all know some people are born with physical problems like blindness, or are very short or very tall, or that some have a skin color that others resent, and others will have parents who don't care about them. This is hardly being "created equal."

What they meant is that all men and women, despite how they come into this world or what skin color they have or their parentage, are all equal in deserving life, liberty and the pursuit of happiness.

Yes, it's great that the government wants all students to reach this artificial level of success, but the reality is they won't. But to admit this now, is to admit they were wrong. What politician, especially the President of the United States, wants to admit their much heralded program is wrong? And this is my biggest concern with NCLB. Even though they have made minor changes with NCLB, I can't see anyone admitting the major inconsistencies and problems with the program, then either rectifying them or, my preference, eliminating NCLB altogether.

Mystery #93: Is standardized testing bad for schools and should it be discontinued?

Believe it or not, I think the idea of a cumulative test at the end of the year is good. How else does a teacher find out whether or not what she taught was actually learned by the students? But the operative words there are "what the teacher taught." What is the point of taking a test, like our California Science standards test, which has questions not even covered in the state adopted science textbook? I really don't understand why that happens. How absurd is that?

I think schools should use some type of criterion-based test where there is no guessing what your students need to know. Yet even using a test based on a given list of objectives, I will never think we should compare test scores from one year's class to another. I really don't see how that proves anything at all.

Mystery #94: Why is the government putting so much importance on all students achieving an artificial and arbitrary level of excellence?

I'd rather be a failure at something I enjoy than be a success at something I hate.

— *George Burns*

I often wonder, does the government really believe that students who do not reach this magical level of success are thus doomed to a life of failure and unhappiness?

Again, it's not that I hate teaching (mom, please read that), it's just that it's a very hard job and with No Child Left Behind I feel it is an impossible job. Why would anyone go into a field where you are set up for failure? Please don't think that I am pessimistic about our children, because I'm not. In fact I would argue I have more confidence in children than in the government.

By the government putting so much importance on No Child Left Behind, and insisting that ALL children must reach this *artificial and arbitrary* level of excellence, I feel they are insinuating that only then will they be able to succeed in school and probably in life.

I, however, have more faith in children than that. These are just state assessment tests and, in the big scheme of life, don't mean, or aren't worth, what's the old expression, "a pile of beans." The truth of the matter is, whether or not students attain this level of "proficiency" will not determine their success or their happiness in life. It will not even determine whether or not they make it into college or how well they will do in college. I guarantee you that.

What will be the bigger factor? How motivated that student is. Though we try our best to inspire everyone towards higher education, as I have said before, not everyone will end up in college. And that's okay too!

Mystery #95: Is the purpose of the No Child Left Behind Act really to put public schools out of business and implement a national voucher system?

I admit, I love a good conspiracy theory. One of the reasons it's so easy for me to get up at 4:00 in the morning to exercise is because I set my clock radio to the station that carries the talk show, "Coast to Coast AM with George Noory." It's a great show that airs a variety of topics not always considered mainstream. Often guests come on sharing their research that indicates everything isn't as it appears on the surface. I haven't heard this particular conspiracy theory on this show. However, I know it exists.

Will No Child Left Behind really put public schools out of business, starting with low-income districts? I don't think so. However, one must not ignore the fact that even if they paid vouchers to parents who would get to decide which school their child would attend, look how much money the government would save if it didn't have to support education and it was somehow privatized. There would be no more teachers' unions and kids would be taught in schools operating under a free-market system.

Personally, this is one conspiracy I have a hard time believing, but then again, do I have a better explanation for the creation of this insane and flawed legislation?

Mystery #96: Does anyone have anything good to say about the No Child Left Behind Act?

Absolutely. There is columnist Armstrong Williams. He only had good things to say about the No Child Left Behind Act. But wait. I forgot. The government paid him $240,000 to say good things about it. Maybe I too would have good things to say about it if I were paid $240,000. Nah, I still wouldn't. In fairness, I think Mr. Armstrong claims he was confused about why the government paid this money to him.

Besides paying for good comments, I don't think there's any other way the government could get journalists to say something positive about that "wonderful" piece of legislation. Wait, that's not completely true. Rush Limbaugh loves it and he doesn't get paid by the government.

Most of the editorials I have read recognize that it's good that schools have some accountability for student success. It's hard for me to admit this, but even I think many students have benefited from schools and teachers taking their lessons more seriously and understanding they can't teach the same way they have for twenty years. More importantly, teachers and schools do have to be accountable for doing the job they are paid to do.

However, there are just too many flaws in No Child Left Behind for it to carry as much weight as it does and have the ability to instill fear into school districts all across America. It is wrong to compare schools on a norm-referenced test, especially since each state also uses its own test. As a Los Angeles Times editorial said: *"Wouldn't it make more sense, and say more about what children are learning, to measure success based on students' improvement from one year to the next?"*

Yes it would make more sense. But then again, sometimes I think "good sense" is in short supply in the educational and political fields.

Mystery #97: Is the government finally seeing the light when it comes to NCLB?

When it comes to changing the No Child Left Behind Act, any change, no matter how small, that will allow states more flexibility and allow additional alternatives is a good sign. This is what the government claims is going to happen. Secretary of Education Margaret Spellings announced new guidelines in April 2005, called *Raising Achievement: A New Path for No Child Left Behind.*

Even though she declares that such things as annual testing to determine student achievement, reporting results by student subgroups and highly qualified teachers are areas not up for negotiations, the government is giving states "new tools" to help them meet the law's goals of getting every child to grade level by 2013–14.

Of course there is a "catch." The schools have to abide by the four basic premises of No Child Left Behind. They are 1) Ensure students are learning by raising overall achievement and closing achievement gaps. 2) Make certain that all students are included in the state's accountability system and the data is broken down in subgroups. 3) Ensuring information is accessible and parental options are available. 4) Improve the quality of teachers. (Of course, I'm sure this is the most important one.)

If these principles are met by a state, then the Department of Education will consider approving additional flexibility under the law. What kind of flexibility are they talking about? This is from a press release I found on the No Child Left Behind's website.

> *"One example of this new flexibility Secretary Spellings outlined is how students with disabilities are tested. No Child Left Behind already allows students with significant cognitive disabilities, which is about 1 percent of all students, to take alternate assessments. Under this new policy, students with persistent academic disabilities—approximately 2 percent of all students—will have the opportunity to take tests that are specifically geared toward their abilities, as long as states continue their commitment to improving special education instruction and assessment," notes Secretary Spellings.*
>
> *"This new approach recognizes that not all children have the same needs," said Secretary Spellings. "New scientific research has shown that some students with persistent academic disabilities can make substantial progress toward grade-level achievement given the right instruction and assessments along with more time... Of course, we must be careful to balance this new flexibility with safeguards to ensure that all of our students, including those with disabilities, receive the best education possible. That's why we'll continue to ensure these students count in accountability decisions."*

Imagine that. They are actually recognizing that some Special Education students might need a different assessment based on their disability? This is progress. Could "making parents and students accountable for their education" be far behind? Nah. That is never going happen.

Mystery #98: What can be done to help No Child Left Behind stay on the path of positive reforms and rein in some of the insanity associated with this well-meaning, but flawed legislation?

1. Write your representatives in Congress about your concerns and the flaws in the No Child Left Behind legislation.

This is my fantasy, that parents get involved and let their representatives and senators know that they are unhappy with the No Child Left Behind Act.

Tell them you don't think it's realistic to expect all children to reach this artificial standard of success, especially when it's based on testing that is flawed. You can tell them you think it's unfair that some states have easier criteria for success than other states. You feel it is disgusting how they portray the results of the test as some sort of barometer on whether or not a child is successful in school. Finally, let them know that you are angered that they put no responsibility on the students and parents, the two most important factors in the success of a child's education. (Sure, you'll do that, right?)

Well, at least this is what I would write. You see, I understand how hard it is to be proactive, even when something bothers you. I want to, but I just never get around to it. If you're like that I understand and you are forgiven if you don't write to Congress.

But if you are proactive and want your "employees", the representatives and senators who represent you, to know how you feel, then please write. If you do not know the names of your senators and U.S. representatives, just log onto http://Congress.org, a great website where you enter your zip code and they will tell you who represents you in Congress.

I will be eternally grateful for your time and effort.

2. When you read or hear the results of your school's "report card," don't worry about it. Don't send your child to another school when you get that letter in the mail telling you your

school is not performing. (Unless of course they really do have a "bad" school, then you can do it with my blessing.)

Are you confused? Does this seem contradictory to the above suggestion? It might be a little bit. My point here is, don't play their game and get caught up in fretting over your child's schools' AYP (Academic Yearly Progress) score, unless of course you want to. Remember, a school can be considered "underperforming" if not all of the subcategories have met their goal or if they didn't get 95% of their students to take the test. The most important score that counts is your child's and even then, the results are open to interpretation.

3. Judge your child's school by the environment and their involvement with improving the school's curriculum and not by not by your school's AYP score! Furthermore, go to the school and look at the school's campus. Is trash picked up, and do things look well-maintained? Or does it look run-down with graffiti on lockers and broken fences or windows? Even old schools can have a presentable appearance if there has been a consistent effort in keeping up on repairs.

As for the curriculum, if you have a high school student, does it offer a lot of Advance Placement programs or programs like AVID, a "fifth- through twelfth-grade program to prepare students in the academic middle for four-year college eligibility. It has a proven track record in bringing out the best in students, and in closing the achievement gap."

My stepson graduated high school from the oldest school in our city. It has the reputation of being a pretty rough school, as in fights not academics, and many students weren't really motivated to learn. In fact, it is currently among the schools in the No Child Left Behind program that are at risk of being severely punished because of their lack of growth in the AYP.

However, that night at his graduation there were lots of students who not only received scholarships, but had been accepted by some very well-known universities. In other words, motivated students can excel at what some would consider "a bad school." Moral of our story: Regardless of what level, be it elementary, middle or high school, those students who are determined to succeed will succeed regardless of the reputation of the school.

4. Judge your child's teacher by comments from fellow parents, what your child tells you, and by speaking with that teacher. Does the teacher still teach the way he/she has for fifteen years, or has he/she been open to new ideas? Is he/she fair about expectations and classroom rules? Is he/she a nice person who seems conscientious about doing a good job?

You don't necessarily have to "like" the person but you should respect his or her ability to teach and get the job done. Look at your children's work. Do they understand the work or are they struggling because the teacher is moving on too quickly? Know what your state standards are and whether the teacher is teaching to them.

Each teacher has a teaching style that is unique. Be open-minded and realize that as your child moves up through the educational system, there are going to be teachers you love, those you hate, and those you have no particularly strong feelings about one way or the other. Just remember that your child's current teacher isn't like a past teacher your child might have loved. Still, you must give the new teacher a chance. In time, the current teacher might turn out to be better than you thought.

9

TIME
It's all about time

Mystery #99: Why do experts expect so much from schools when in reality a child spends only 13% of their waking lives in the classroom?

Love and time—those are the only two things
in all the world and all of life that cannot
be bought, but only spent.

— *Gary Jennings*

Vilfrado Prado, an Italian economist, noticed that 20% of the people own 80% of the wealth and that meant that 80% of the people own 20% of the wealth. I've also heard that in a group, 20% of the people do 80% of the work. This is called the Prado Principle or is more commonly known as the 20/80 Rule.

This principle applies in education as well except for one huge difference. According to the *Time* magazine article, "What Teachers Hate About Parents": "By the time children turn 18, they have spent only 13% of their waking lives in the classroom." I know most children feel like they are always in school, but can you believe it is only 13% of their time?

If I were asked what would be the one thing that could make schools better I wouldn't say that it's "teachers need more training," or "we need lessons using scientifically-based research," or that "schools need more money." I wouldn't even say that "teachers need to be paid more" even though it would be nice and probably boost morale.

If there were a magic bullet to fix schools I think it would have to do with giving teachers more time. Time to thoroughly teach a subject before moving on. Time to help children who are struggling. Time to teach all subjects well. Time to teach lessons that help the student think about the world instead of just regurgitating facts. Time for busy parents to get involved in their child's education.

The way it is now, there's not enough time to spend helping each student. There's not enough time to teach social studies and science. There's not enough time to make certain every student understands a concept before moving on. There's not enough time to give students an hour to read in class and still get through all the lessons that need to be taught. There's not enough time to teach P.E. every day.

Remember that old game show "Beat the Clock," where contestants had only a minute to complete complex tasks? That is my life. That is the teacher's life. Every day I feel like I am playing "Beat the Clock" and my complex task is teaching 33 students 20 pages of state standards. My game isn't just played on a daily basis, it's played on a monthly and yearly basis.

Worst of all, our year is actually shorter than our mandatory 180 day school year. As I have mentioned several times, we take the state assessments test six weeks before the end of the school year. A student should have technically received the bulk of the education by the time state testing starts.

It's funny because when I taught kindergarten, I thought it was only kindergarten that didn't have enough time because our students are in class for only three and-a-half hours a day. Then, when I moved up to fifth grade, instead of feeling like I had more than enough time, ironically, I felt like I had even less time because my curriculum more than doubled.

I was at an in-service writing class and there was a teacher who taught seventh and eighth grade English. She didn't know me or my feelings about teachers' lack of time issue. As we were talking about writing strategies, she sort of sat shaking her head in disbelief. She didn't understand how she was supposed to fit this into her already crowded lesson plans.

This teacher, with over fifteen years experience, lamented how impossible it is to teach her students not only writing, but reading comprehension, spelling, and vocabulary in one daily 55 minute time period. She felt so overwhelmed and frustrated. With such limited time and a class of 35 students, the odds are stacked against those kids learning anything well. Yet politicians will sit back and wonder, "Gee, why aren't kids learning?"

Even though I had mentioned the idea of becoming a sixth grade teacher, I had never thought about what it would be like to teach in the grades above fifth grade. All of a sudden, I got a very abrupt awakening at what teachers deal with when they teach a single subject each time period.

I mentioned earlier that some districts like mine want their elementary schools to spend at least two-and-a-half hours on language arts. Then when they move up to sixth grade, or seventh grade if your child's elementary school has kindergarten through sixth grades, it decreases to 55 minutes? It doesn't make sense. But it does make sense why high school teachers get students who can't read and write.

Mystery #100: Why do today's kids still need three months off during the summer like students did when they used the time off to work on the family farm?

How you spend your time is more important
than how you spend your money.
Money mistakes can be corrected,
but time is gone forever.

—David B. Norris

In fact, one of the arguments for more parental involvement is that "a child is only in school for a short time of the day." Well, maybe then students should be in school longer where a teacher can help them with their studies. Besides, how many parents are finished with work by the time the child comes home from school? I bet not many. I'm a teacher, with teacher's hours, but do my kids see me when they get home at 2:30? No, they are lucky to see me at 4:30.

Why aren't school days longer to accommodate their learning needs? I think we would all be better teachers, and students would learn more, if there were more time in the school day.

Of course the problem with increasing the school day is the question of burnout, not just for the teacher, but for students. I don't know if my students could handle an extra hour or more of school. Come 2:20 p.m. they have mentally checked out. But then again, maybe I'm just making excuses for them. They could probably do it and the results might even surprise us.

Remember, in my "Homework" chapter, I mentioned meeting parents whose children were attending a charter school where they went to school until 4 p.m. They loved it. Even though the school year wasn't over, those kids didn't seem to be "burned out." I think kids would do quite well with a longer school day. Instead of worrying about after-school programs, if we extended the academic day they would not only stay out of trouble, but put that time to good use.

Maybe the answer isn't a longer day, but more days in the school year. Do you realize our traditional school year calendar was set up when children were given the summer months off so they could help with the family farm? But how many students in the 21st century need to help with the family farm? I wonder how many children do what my own son used to do before we saw he had so much missing school work: come home and play video games.

There is a research professor in education and psychology at the University of Illinois who has looked into what schools need to succeed. After reviewing 130 research studies, he came to the not-so-surprising conclusion, "the more you study, the more you learn." In other words, the more time kids spend on their studies, the smarter they are going to be.

He recommends longer school days, longer school years, or more graded homework. Obviously, I don't think graded homework is the answer, but I wonder how much better kids would do if they spent more time in school?

Mystery #101: What do European and Asian countries know about academic success that the United States doesn't?

It is a well-known fact that when the United States is compared to countries around the world in respect to academic achievement, we fall woefully behind most countries. Is the reason for other countries' successes that parents in other countries spend more time helping students with homework? I don't think so.

What we do know is that countries whose students do better than us academically have their students spend a lot more time in school. Students in the United State spend an average of 180 days in school. Out of those 180 days, there are probably a couple of "minimum days" provided for things like parent-teacher conferences or getting out of school early because it's the end of the quarter or before a vacation. Then there a few days which are used up for mandatory state testing. In elementary schools, there are days used for classroom parties, field trips, and other events.

As I brought up in an earlier chapter, why then are state assessment tests given six weeks before the end of the school year, leaving 30 fewer days to teach the standards which they are being tested on? That means students are only receiving an average 145 days of real "academic" days. And teachers wonder why we don't feel we have enough time?

In Europe, the average school year runs from 195–210 days.

In Japan, which we all think as a nation of well-educated people, they go to school 240 days a year. By far the country that has the right idea when comes to keeping students in school is Korea. Their school year is 260 days long! That is 80 more days than average for American schools.

Once my stepson came home from the Navy to visit us and he had a friend with him from Italy. His friend told me that in Italy students go to school even on Saturday. He said he couldn't believe it when he moved here from Italy that we didn't do the same thing.

Can you imagine students in the United States going to school on Saturdays? Often Saturday school is only used as a punishment for students who misbehave in class or if it has really been a bad winter, with missed days due to weather.

Earlier I said that more money wasn't necessarily part of the solution. That's not exactly true. The only way you could get teachers to work longer hours or more days is by increasing their salaries.

Who am I kidding? We can spend billions of dollars in Iraq destroying, then rebuilding their nation, but when it comes to our own children, guess who is really leaving all children behind? Our federal government, which has the nerve to criticize teachers and schools and claim we are the ones leaving children behind. Our government is not only leaving children behind without the best education, all children will be left behind with the bill for Iraq and a trillion dollar deficit.

So if the federal government doesn't have the money to give to the states, what are the odds that state governments will do it on their own?

I know I can't wear my rose-colored glasses when it comes to state governments because I live in California, a state that doesn't have the best record when it comes to finances. Even though Governor Schwarzenegger is trying to rectify that problem, education already takes half of our state budget. Is it fair to ask for even more? Are other state governments in a better position financially so that they could afford to send even more salary to teachers to have them work a longer school year? I doubt it

So here we come to the paradox of our educational system: One of the things that could help public schools the most doesn't have anything to do with how smart teachers are or how well they teach: That is more time in a day.

The federal government has the audacity to think that ALL students should be able to read at a proficient level by the year 2014.

I have news for them. Time is not on the side of education and their impossible request. I can only hope that maybe in time, they will finally understand that.

Mystery #102: Why won't a longer school year ever be a reality?

A longer school year is a solution parents might like. Even though teachers would benefit by having more instructional time, I think they would be the group that would have the greatest resistance to increasing the school year or day. Why? Because the job is already so demanding, I can't imagine adding another eighty days to our calendar. At the end of the school year, I, and most of my colleagues are totally wiped out. What a sad commentary about teaching that most people can only do it for 180 days.

Even if teachers received more money to compensate them for the extra time in the classroom, I don't know how many would look forward to making the school day or the school year longer. I know I personally would hate it and probably would leave the profession, I'm sure like many others.

It is true, many teachers complain about the relatively low pay they receive for the amount of education we are required to have, but having summers off is a very nice fringe benefit of teaching that many teachers aren't willing to give up. That's why I don't think the prospects are good for doing the one thing that could help students the most: time in the classroom.

Mystery #103: If we don't want to extend the school year or school day, what is the easiest way to solve this "time" dilemma?

There is a very simple solution that will help teachers and students get more time in the academic year. All the government has to do is mandate that all state testing takes place the last week or two weeks of school. As I pointed out, teachers and students tend to "check-out" after testing anyway. Why have them "check-out" when there are still 30 academic days left? Besides, nothing happens the last week of school anyway. It makes perfect sense that's when the state testing should be done.

I do not know if most states are like California and test so early before the end of the year but I imagine, because of the government wanting all of this "testing data," that California is not alone in this absurd practice. (But then again, who knows, maybe this is just another California phenomenon.) At least this is the only explanation I have been able to come up with. As I have noted, even my colleagues don't know why we test so early. It is indeed a mystery.

10

The Educational "Bill of Rights"

Helping your child, Helping our public schools

Mystery #104: What can parents do to help their child get the best education from a public school?

> A school system without parents
> at its foundation is just like a bucket
> with a hole in it.
>
> — *Jesse Jackson*

When we become parents, whether you're the mom or the dad, there is an unwritten rule that once you bring a child into this world, you must leave your self-centeredness in the maternity ward. No longer is it about what *I* want, but what is best for my child.

Yet who is the most important person in my child's life? That's right, *I* am, and *I* must never forget that. There also some other important *"I"*s that parents need to remember that can help not only the child but the public schools. I call them the Twelve *"I"*s that parents should remember to help their child and public education.

1. Be at least minimally involved

- "I agree that teachers work hard and deserve to be paid appropriately for it, but why do they get all of that time off?"
- "Why do teachers rely on parents to do their job!"
- "Parents already work hard. Why do teachers expect us to morph into tutors by night?"
- "Why do educators always nag parents about getting involved with their child's education?"

These are common complaints when it comes to our schools. As I look at my son's "D" in math on his report card, I can honestly feel other parents' pain if they get frustrated with their child's school or teacher. Why do I now have to spend my time off getting my son to know fifth grade math? What was his teacher doing all year?

Why do educators always nag parents about "You have to get involved with your child's education?" As this book has explained, because it is true. Unless you have been blessed to have a naturally motivated and bright student, for children to be successful at school they need both a teacher and a parent to be involved. Children can't do it on their own. As explained in my "Open Letter to Parents," the way our public schools are set up and with so much to teach in a set amount of time, teachers can't do it alone either.

"Being involved" doesn't mean you have to become PTA president and volunteer in classrooms. All teachers want is a parent who will commit to being just "minimally involved."

What is a "minimally involved" parent?

1. Monitor your student's work daily, if possible. It's not so much the grade you should care about, but what your child does not understand or needs help on.
2. Help your child as much as you can in understanding concepts he or she doesn't get. (I guess I am asking you to "morph into a tutor" at night.)
3. Make the kids go to bed at a decent time and try to feed them in the morning. Find a way to provide for them the clothing and school supplies they need.
4. Don't let them rule the roost at home because then they will try

to rule it at school as well. Teach them to respect teachers as well as other students.

5. Speak positively and often about the benefits of an education. Make them come to school every day unless they are sick.

2. Be Inquisitive, then Inquire

Be curious about things at school. For instance, do you know how your child's teacher deals with completed homework? Does he or she grade homework or just check it off? This information can be helpful in case of a bad grade on a test. If you know your child had done the homework on it, then why the poor test result? If the homework wasn't corrected, maybe your child didn't know he was doing something wrong. If the students don't go over the work in class and the teacher doesn't check it, doesn't it make you wonder how they are supposed to know if they are doing the work correctly?

Speaking of homework, wouldn't you find it strange if your child, who has always had homework, suddenly is telling you he is getting it done at school? Check things out. I had a parent who wondered if it was true that her son was taking Accelerated Reader quizzes in my class. No, it wasn't true. He hadn't taken even one test. When in doubt, ask the teacher.

Being inquisitive also extends beyond just the academic area. How are things at recess? Even if your child isn't being bullied, are other children? I had a parent whose son told her this story about a "sexual harassment" complaint that was against one of the students in my class. She wanted to question me on the story and the facts. I welcomed her phone call and was happy to explain the real version of the story her son had told her. I'd much rather parents hear things from me. I think one of the most important things a parent can do is ask their child lots of questions about what's going on at school. By this, I mean, beyond the usual, "So how was school today?" which is usually answered, "Boring." And of course we are all very familiar with the "What did you learn today?" question. Response: "Nothing."

I try to ask questions that will make me feel better about myself as a teacher. For instance, "How many times did your teacher yell at your class today?" (Only kidding.) But I do try to ask a different question about school every day, even it's something as simple as, "What did you and your friends play at recess today?" There are some questions you should ask your child every day like, "Are there any papers I need to sign or read?" Or "Do I need to know about any events coming up, or any projects that are due?"

It's important that you just don't ask, "Did you finish your homework?" Have them show it to you. If they said they did it at school, tell them you still need to see it. Most teachers don't accept homework early; they want it on the day it is due. Yes, they could have left it in their desk, but tell them they need to bring it home and show you. Of course, these are tips I know not from being a teacher, but being a parent.

Also inquire about any projects that are coming up or that are due. This advice comes from my history as a supermarket cashier. I can't tell you how many times customers came in late at night looking for supplies for a project that was due the next day that they just found out about that night.

3. Be Interested

Be genuinely interested in what is going on at school. Ask every day. Don't just accept the answer, "fine" or "boring." Find out one specific thing every day.

If your child starts to talk about school, just don't listen half-heartedly while you're also thinking about what to make for dinner. Really listen and hear what your child is telling you.

Be interested in events at school as well. If the school is having a fundraiser, as I have explained before, every little bit helps. If your child has an event at night, find ways to get off work early and attend. We all have busy days and there are nights I just don't want to go to another "Harvest Festival," but I do and end up having a good time, speaking with parents I only see at these events. It's another way to find out what's happening at the school.

4. Improvement

Straight "As" or good grades are great, but they aren't the only things a child can be praised for. Sometimes a little praise goes a long way. If your child shows improvement in academics, or getting along with kids, or behaving in the classroom, or even for remembering to bring his library book to school on library day, say an encouraging word about it. It's easy as parents to focus on the negative and forget the positive. We never know what will be the catalyst that will motivate the child to continue on the path to improvement. More often than not, it's just the self-confidence one attains when they see they are capable of changing for the better.

Besides just praising your child for improvement, there's something else parents need to take an interest in to improve it. That is the public school your child goes to. Don't be afraid to become proactive if there is something at your school that doesn't seem right or needs changing. The squeaky wheel gets the grease and the parents who complain the loudest and most often can get positive changes to happen at a school.

5. Be Informed, not just about your child's school, but about what's going on in your community.

In this case, I'm not talking informed just about school, but also being informed about what's going on in your community. Do you know who your school board members are? Do you know what they stand for? Every household that has children should be subscribing to at least the local newspaper.

I know so many parents who think of themselves as very good parents because they put their kids in activities, and they help out at school, and they attend all of the school events. Yet, when I would ask, "What do you think of the school district's plan to redo the boundaries?" They would reply, "They are redrawing the boundaries? Where did you hear that?" How sad, she didn't feel it necessary to subscribe to the local newspaper.

The local newspaper is the best source of information about your child's school and school district. Don't just subscribe to it, read it, or at least glance at the headlines. It doesn't take a lot of time. And look at the good example you are setting for your child.

Vote for issues that will make your child's school and school district a better place. Last year, the citizens of my city approved a $50 million bond issue. As I have told you, because of this, all of the schools replaced their terribly worn and tattered carpeting that has been in place for probably 15 years. Of course, other big things are also planned for the money, but none of it would have been possible without the approval of this bond measure.

Also vote for libraries! What better way to invest in our children's education, and our country's future success, than by having a place where books and even computers are accessible to all. While I'm proud that my city did vote for the bond issue, I am still very disappointed that years earlier they had defeated a measure that would have financed a new library.

Our library is housed in a small building built decades ago when the population was probably 30,000 people. Now we have 165,000 people and the same library. I congratulate how well our library staff has made it work.

My school district is on the watch list of districts that need to improve their test scores according to No Child Left Behind. Is there a correlation between our low test scores and the fact that the community didn't see the need for a new library? Do they not put an importance on books, reading, and education? Or did they just not want the expense of a library? I don't know. I just know we have the same library as we did before the city incorporated over twenty-five years ago.

6–11. Important, Inspire, Independent, Individual Intellect, Integrity. In other words, it's important to inspire your child to be an independent thinking individual with intellect and integrity.

In the same issue of the *California Educator* that I referred to earlier in this book, there is this great quote from Steven Warva, a biology teacher at Southwest High School. He said,

"It is absolutely absurd that the federal government has insti-tuted such a punitive and degrading system of school evaluation that relies totally on a continually changing set of standardized tests and omits positive achievements of a school and its students. Sometimes a number just can't be used to accurately rate the qual-ity of a school and its associated community."

Amen. If I have done nothing more than to impress this fact on just a few parents out there, then I will have succeeded beyond my wildest dreams. When it comes to being successful in life it doesn't have to do with what your standardized test score is. It doesn't even matter whether you graduate from college or just get a high school diploma.

What matters is that we raise a generation of adults who exer-cise their own will or judgment without the guidance or control of others. An independent person is also one who is self-reliant and can take care of him or herself and doesn't sit around and ask what others or the government can do for him.

Intellect distinguishes men from brutes.

— unknown

As for intellect, you might be surprised to know that the dic-tionary doesn't refer to intellect as being "smart." A person with intellect is one who has the power of perception or higher thinking powers.

Intellect allows us to have a greater understanding of the laws of the universe. Things like the concept of cause and effect, or right from wrong. It's the kind of knowledge that is best learned from parents who not only set the example, but positively influence chil-dren to seek the higher road. That's what it means to inspire.

Of course, integrity means to have an uprightness of character. People with integrity do the right thing not because they have to but because they want to.

There is a group of individuals out there whose parents must have done a good job in raising them because they represent the kind of person I'm speaking about. They aren't necessarily the ones with college degrees, but the young men and women who voluntarily enlist in the armed services. There is no greater show of integrity than those individuals who risk their lives for not only our country's freedom, but for those who reside in other countries.

These are the kind of unselfish and determined people our country was founded by and these are the ones that will keep our country great. If only we could really teach this in schools and have students understand this concept, then our public school systems would truly be successful.

The "Educational" Bill of Rights

One of the unexpected joys in moving up to teaching fifth grade is getting to teach 10- and 11-year-olds social studies and the story of how our great country was founded. This is brand new information to them. I am glad I am the one to emphasize how we have so much today because of the efforts of so many people hundreds of years ago who didn't want to lose the one thing money couldn't buy: freedom.

I am the lucky one who gets to introduce them to the brilliant words of the Declaration of Independence and the magnificent blueprint of our country, the Constitution of the United States. I also get to explain that despite the greatness of these two documents, some leaders complained that the Constitution did not contain a "bill of rights" or rights that were listed in the Declaration of Independence.

As our social studies textbook, "A New Nation," (McGraw Hill, 2000) states, "A bill of rights is a document that describes the basic rights of the government." In 1791, the first ten amendments to the Constitution were ratified ensuring basic freedoms. These, of course are known as our "Bill of Rights." They delineate rights that the government cannot take away.

What a great concept. So I thought maybe this is what education needs. Teachers and parents should know exactly what their rights are when it comes to helping our children getting the best education. Unfortunately, I wasn't able to come up with ten rights. Another problem with my "Educational Bill of Rights" is these "rights" depend on the action of the other party for them to be actualized. You'll see what I mean when you read them.

My theory for these educational bills of rights is, if parents do everything that they are expected to do and teachers do everything they are expected to do, maybe we wouldn't need to rely on standardized tests in knowing our children are being properly educated. If only this were a perfect world.

Mystery #105: What are the "Parents' Bill of Rights"?

1. The parent has the right to expect the teacher to be teaching the subject/grade they are hired to and putting in a reasonable amount of effort into teaching that subject. Playing "Hangman" in an Honors English class just doesn't cut it.
2. The parent has the right to know on a timely basis and with frequency how well the student is doing in class and whether he or she is missing work.
3. The parent has the right to know if a student is failing, what they, the parent, can do to help. Parents do not have the right to expect teachers to provide after-school tutoring to all failing children.
4. The parent has the right to expect all students are treated equally, despite what may be personality conflicts between the student and teacher.
5. A parent has a right to expect good communication from the teacher. Most teachers have only a small window of opportunity to return parents' calls during the day. However, this does not give teachers a "pass" from returning those calls. It amazes me how many times I have heard stories from friends, many who are teachers, complain about all the messages they have left for a teacher or counselor, yet never get a response. To help solve

the problem of messages that are never returned or even "phone tag," when possible email should be a source of communication that is not only encouraged, but recommended.

6. A parent has the right to question or challenge the practices and policies that take place in a classroom. However, they must also realize that just because they don't like the way a particular teacher does things, the teacher is not obligated to change his/her policy.

7. Parents have the right to expect the teacher to behave in a professional manner.

8. Parents have the right to expect the teacher will have positive expectations for student success and will present lessons that help accomplish this goal. (Thank you, Harry Wong.)

Mystery #106: What are the "Teachers' Bill of Rights"?

A teacher should expect the following minimal involvement from parents.

1. Teachers have the right to expect all children to come to school adequately prepared. This means they are fed, clothed properly for the weather conditions, and come to school with supplies.

2. Teachers have the right to expect parents to help solve classroom discipline problems that the teacher may be having with their child. Making excuses for the child's behavior or denying it even exists because "the teacher doesn't like my child" doesn't help rectify the situation at all.

3. Teachers have the right to expect children to come to school daily and on time. Doctor appointments, if possible, should be done after school, and vacations taken during breaks.

4. Teachers have the right to expect that if children are having problems academically, the parents, once informed, will provide help at home or find tutoring from someone who is able to help the child. Remember, yes, our tax money is paying for

your child to get a "free" education, however the reality is, there isn't enough time in the day for teachers to individually help all children who do need the extra help.

5. Teachers have the right to expect good communication from the parent. If the teacher sends home notes, parents should be responded to them in a prompt manner.

6. Teachers have the right to expect that parents not only say they stress the importance of a child's education, but show it by participating in school functions and monitoring work that comes home.

7. Teachers have the right to expect that parents take their role and responsibility as parents seriously despite many other stressful factors in a parent's life. A child's education should not be a low priority, but a high priority.

8. Teachers have the right to have all students treat them respectfully.

11

Are our public schools really that bad?:

How would I fix the schools?

Mystery #107: Are our public schools really as bad as the media and government portray them as being?

Bill Gates, multi-billionaire and founder of Microsoft, thinks our high schools today are obsolete. In a speech to the nation's governors in 2005 he stated, "American high schools are obsolete. By obsolete, I don't just mean that our high schools are broken, flawed and under-funded. By obsolete, I mean that our high schools—even when they are working exactly as designed—cannot teach our kids what they need to know today."

Ouch! He goes on to say, "Training the work force of tomorrow with the high school students of today is like trying to teach kids about today's computers on a 50-year-old mainframe. Our high schools were designed 50 years ago to meet the needs of another age. Until we design them to meet the needs of the 21st century, we will keep limiting—even ruining—lives of millions of Americans every year."

I do agree with him. But the improvements can begin even before high school. In this day and age of technology, I think its absurd that at my son's middle school they offer the computer class to only one track. It is the most sought-after class but only a few students get to take it every year. This doesn't make sense. In fact, it would probably be a great idea that every middle or junior high school student be required to take keyboarding. Most kids already have a built-in interest in computers. Our schools need to take advantage of this enthusiasm and provide meaningful technology lessons that will make them better prepared to face a future filled with computers.

What kind of school would Bill Gates like to see? He points to a public school district in Kansas City, Kansas, where 79% of the students are minorities and 74% live below the poverty line. They adopted a school-reform model, which, "among many other steps," required all students to take college-prep courses. Now that district's graduation rate has climbed more than 30%.

This is truly amazing. If they have been so successful, why aren't all high schools adopting the same policies? Some high schools in Oakland, Chicago, and New York are following their steps. They are even considering the idea for Los Angles high schools.

And all it took was requiring students to take college prep courses? Not exactly. He cited the challenging curriculum, along with courses that clearly relate to their lives and goals, and that they "are surrounded by adults who push them to achieve." I see, they were surrounded by "involved parents and teachers!" What a novel idea!

Even though I find this approach contradictory to what I would have expected, who am I to criticize something that is working.

However, I do take offense with his comments that "If we keep the system as it is, millions of children will never get a chance to fulfill their promise because of their ZIP Code, their skin color or their parents' income. That is offensive to our values." He even wants data broken down by race and income to prove all children are learning. (Excuse me Mr. Gates, but President Bush already beat you to the punch on that one. It is called the "No Child Left Behind" Act.)

Here we go again. Is he insinuating that teachers are leaving poorer, minority children behind, just like our government? This is offensive to my values. Teachers just can't win, can we? I definitely have my work cut out for me.

But are our public schools, especially the high schools, as bad as Bill Gates says they are? Are we at risk of becoming a new kind of third-world nation because a country like China has six times the number of college graduates in engineering? Is there a shortage of engineers, doctors, and business people because our students are so unmotivated towards academic success? He bemoans the fact that our 12th graders are near the bottom in math and science when compared to countries like China. But remember, we test all, or at least nearly all, of our high school seniors while many other countries, such as China, do not.

Personally, I think the death of our economy and society due to an upcoming generation of underachieving non-college graduates is being greatly exaggerated. Despite soaring costs of college, most aren't lacking students to fill them. So why are we, or why is Bill Gates, so worried? Is he predicting a calamity of epic proportions if we don't change the ways our public high schools operate?

Despite all of our problems with public schools, whether it be at the elementary, junior high, or high school level, we must be doing something right because our nation still is thriving.

While Mr. Gates thinks it will benefit our populace to have more citizens as college graduates, doesn't the higher level income they expect with their degrees put them at an economic disadvantage compared to college gradates of countries like India and China who will do the same work for less? Does Microsoft not participate in a popular business practice called "outsourcing," where college-educated foreign citizens do the jobs for less money than the Americans who used to hold those same jobs?

Personally, I do think our schools have much room for improvement. Nevertheless, we must still give credit where credit is due. Despite schools' shortcomings, they haven't done such a bad job for our country thus far.

Mystery #108: How would I fix public schools?

Even though I don't profess to know the answers, these are some of the things I would do to fix public schools. Some people might think some of my ideas are fanciful and farfetched. However, I'm just trying to find solutions to those things about public education that need to be changed.

1. **Fix the "time shortage" issue.** If there is a crisis in public schools it is because there just isn't enough time in the day. While we can't do much about increasing the number of hours in the day from 24 to 36, there are things we can do to make the most of the hours we are given. I have four possible solutions to this "time crunch" public schools face.

    Plan A: We would get over the concept in education that everything has to be done on an equal basis. I would only make the children who need more time for academics go to school longer. It doesn't seem quite right to make all kids attend school longer if some are able to "accomplish" their learning within the parameters of a school year. Some would also balk at having just the "underperforming" schools have a longer school year. Besides, even paying them more money, I doubt that many teachers would want to work longer days with struggling days. I like the idea that Japan has. Children who need more help must attend a school after school for at least two hours to get them caught up.

    Plan B: Make the school day longer. Why do students need to be out of school at 2:10, or 2:20, or even 3:00 p.m.? Students should be in school at least until 3:30 or 4:00 p.m. Also the earliest time schools would start would be between 8:00-8:30.

    Plan C: Make the school year longer by adding a couple of more weeks of vacation during the year and limiting summer vacation to about 6 weeks.

    Plan D: Adopt a "less is more" attitude. Streamline state standards teaching only those which are really important

to the success of the student. Maybe it's not about not enough time, but we have too much to teach. Let's examine and define what all kids, not just college-bound students, should know. I would prioritize those academic skills that are the most important, and give students time to master a few things instead of allowing them to learn nothing very well.

2. **Mandate all state testing takes place the last two weeks of school.**

3. **Eliminate homework.** This would happen only if schools were in session longer. Actually, "homework" doesn't need to be eliminated, for the most part; it should be done at school.

4. **High schools students would be tracked into trade/technical programs or college preparatory programs.** Despite what Bill Gates thinks, not all students want or need to be "college material." Similar to European countries, students would get to decide which route they want to take, and, as Bill Gates suggested, take courses that are relevant to their lives.

5. **Eliminate class-size reduction in all grades except kindergarten and first grade.** All other grades/classes, including those in middle school and high school, would be limited to no more than 25 students. If financially this is impossible, than class size reduction should be used only at underperforming schools and eliminated elsewhere.

6. **Make a partnership between colleges and public schools to expand Work-Study programs to help schools with tutoring students and provide clerical help for teachers.** All teachers should have their planning period built into their workday so when the students are done, so are the teachers. We also need to find a way to help them with paperwork so nights and weekends can be spent grading papers.

7. **Adopt a strong discipline plan.**

    Plan A: Give students with behavior problems only three chances and then they are out of public schools. What do we do with them? This is a tough one. I would either demand that the parent home-school their child for a minimum of three months before they could return to public schools or they would get a voucher to go to a private school. (Sorry private schools out there.) They also have to do some kind of community service as part of their academic day.

    Plan B: Bring back some form of corporal punishment.

8. **Eliminate No Child Left Behind and have the accountability for a child's educational success placed on the parents' and students' shoulders, as well as the teachers'.** The truth is, we're all in this together. Parents will also be evaluated on a yearly basis on such parenting skills as student attendance, bringing students to school and picking them up on time, giving them adequate supplies, and being involved with their education.

9. **Adopt a "No Rescue" policy.** Any student not wishing to try, who doesn't want to learn and makes no effort at school will not be forced to learn. Those students who choose not to learn would still be expected to attend school and when moved to the next grade level will have a notation on their permanent record that they had "attended" the grade or class, and not that they had "passed" the grade.

10. **Make certain that an equal number of classroom teachers and non-educators are on any kind of executive board that makes decisions about public schools.**

11. **Use financial rewards as incentives for parents and high school students.** I would give some kind of tax credit to parents whose children attend school regularly and whose children

actively turn in assignments. Note: This financial incentive would not be based on grades or test scores since I recognize that all students come to school with different intellectual abilities. I would also find some kind of financial incentive for high school students who attend school, are not behavior problems, and are productive.

12. **Require that all schools be retrofitted with solar panels to eliminate the expense of electricity.** (Hey, at least if we're going to spend money, let's do on something that will in the long run save us money. I would probably have this financed through, what else, bond measures.) Recently, my husband and I installed solar panels for our home. Do you know how great it is to go from a $300 electric bill to a $30 bill? That's what happened after we installed solar panels on our roof. Solar panels should be looked at as an investment, not an expense. In the long run, they are going to save the school districts so much money.

As you can tell, I probably won't be getting any invitations to be a member on either of the governor's educational committees any time soon. Although some of my "ideas" may seem "tongue-in-cheek" or that I'm not taking the issue of public schools seriously, nothing could be farther from the truth. If we could find a way to implement any of these ideas, I think we would help schools get results far beyond what the government's own "brainchild," the No Child Left Behind Act, ever will achieve.

12

Could I be wrong?

Could it really be "all about the teachers"?

For the record, I don't know what teaching is like for other teachers out there. However, I would imagine many teachers can relate to many things in this book. I also acknowledge that not everyone is going to identify or agree with things I wrote in this book. Who knows, there might be a teacher out there who is a big supporter of the No Child Left Behind Act and a parent who wishes their child had even more homework.

"There are eight million stories in the Naked City; this has been just one of them."

— *"The Naked City" television show*

This book is like an episode of that old television series, "The Naked City," which first aired in 1958. (A very good year I might add.) According to a website about it, it states that,

"Every episode was intended to be a look into the lives of real human beings. In the words of the tagline, originally used in the feature film, 'There are eight million stories in the Naked City... this has been one of them'."

To paraphrase their information,

"This book was intended to be a look into the life of one real human being, who happens to be a public school teacher. There are probably eight million stories out there about public school teachers ... and this has been one of them."

Not too long ago at the gym, I ran into a fellow teacher turned-middle-school-librarian who used to work out at 4:30 in the morning before school like I do. We used to talk about education and about what was happening at our schools.

We hadn't seen each other in a few months, so we had some catching up to do. In the course of our conversation, No Child Left Behind, or as he called it "No Child Left Untested," was brought up. He didn't know I was writing this book. He agreed with me that a major problem with NCLB is that it doesn't consider the unmotivated kids, or the really-try-hard kids who despite their best effort seem to have a hard time in school, or the Special Education kids who have all sorts of issues to deal with including just struggling with basic life skills. How are teachers supposed to get these students up to the level the government wants? How can the government be so unrealistic about their righteous goal and why is there so much pressure on teachers to do the impossible?

But then again, if one teacher, like Ron Clark, can get impoverished and unmotivated students to succeed, shouldn't I think all of us can?

That would be great, but even if our politicians think that all children are created equally, the truth of the matter is, all teachers aren't created equally. Some of us don't have the right stuff it takes to be so dedicated and unselfish. Even if we did, I still believe there are students out there who even Ron Clark couldn't get to a "proficient" level within the parameters of one school year. I don't think of myself as being negative, just realistic. But am I being totally honest with myself?

As I was doing my final revisions for this book, I had a phone conversation that uncovered yet one more mystery. This time it not only involved just a mystery with teaching or schools, but one also about me. It challenged not only who I am as a person, but who I am as a teacher. Despite devoting over two hundred pages of questions and reflections in writing this book, could I actually be wrong on the one thing I was so convinced of? Could teachers, could I, really be the reason my students aren't succeeding?

Mystery #109: Might teachers, like myself, who work at low socio-economic schools be to blame for at least some of their students' low test scores because we unconsciously have lower expectations for our students?

High expectations are the key to everything.

— *Sam Walton, founder of Wal-Mart*

This is the one "mystery" that I am most uncomfortable with because I don't want the answer to be "yes." However, in a phone conversation with a fellow teacher from my school she brought up this theory that got me thinking about something I had never considered. In her opinion, she thinks many teachers at poorer schools don't do as much as they can because they assume the students won't do well or, worse yet, aren't capable of doing well. She thinks teachers have lower expectations for their students at poor, minority schools. We know these kids are from disadvantaged backgrounds where parents themselves don't have much of an education. We work with them day after day, and we see what kind of results we get.

However, do we defeat ourselves because we play the labeling game?

At first I thought this was absurd. It's not about the teachers; it is about the students and their parents. Of course I have high expectations for my class, why wouldn't I? I don't label my students either. Remember, I don't even look at old report cards because I don't want to label them by what they did in previous classes. I don't look at old test scores, because I don't want to assume that this is all they can do.

But then I thought about it. The truth is, I don't need to do any of this. I already know who my students are. They are students living in a "low socio-economic area" and their school is considered "underperforming." Every day I teach, I "label" them just because of who they are and where they go to school. Could it be true? Are my students not succeeding because, unconsciously, I don't think they can succeed?

Let's go back to Ron Clark, our "Teacher of the Year." He went to Harlem and taught a group of students who were considered "un-teachable." Yet do you know what he accomplished? He tells this great story about how twelve of them were accepted into one of the most prestigious middle schools in New York City. How did he do it? Obviously it took lots of work and commitment, not only by him but by his students.

But if you were to ask him the one thing that made the difference, would he say it was the curriculum or the teaching strategies that he used? Not at all. It would be the one thing that he "preached" (and I mean that in a nice way) to the teachers in my school district when he spoke to us one Saturday morning. His message was, teachers have to learn to uplift their students, all students, and make them think they can achieve. It's not only the students who must believe that they can succeed, but their teacher as well.

Are the teachers at poor, minority schools not "uplifting their students" into succeeding? Is this the "missing ingredient" that politicians and educators have been looking for this whole time? Is this the solution to the "mystery" I have been trying to solve? Have we been wasting our time looking at "scientifically based research" for the perfect way to teach when success has nothing to do with teaching but inspiration?

To get children to succeed, to get adults to succeed, they have to believe it will happen. The truth be told, I don't think my students at my low socio-economic school can succeed. I make up all sorts of excuses for them. Their parents aren't involved. They aren't motivated. They don't have the biological make-up. They don't …. Well, you can fill in that blank.

Why don't I believe in them? Why don't I think they can achieve? I finally realized what really is the worst part of the No Child Left Behind act.

Mystery #110: Is the real problem with No Child Left Behind that, by putting so much emphasis on test scores, instead of becoming a motivating tool for teachers to succeed, it becomes a demoralizing way of proving that some students can't succeed?

Being defeated is often a temporary condition. Giving up is what makes it permanent.

— *Marilyn Vos Savant*

I was finishing my book in March. It would be the last March I get off because many of our schools, including my own, are going back to a traditional calendar. It was only five days before I returned to teaching and I was just dreading it. Why? Do I hate teaching that much? While it is true I much prefer writing all day, that's not the reason I didn't want to go back to school. I knew when I returned it would be a short five weeks before our standardized testing begins. Five weeks, and I have so much to cover. Five weeks. My students have so much to learn. How will I do it?

That was the sad thing. Despite my best intentions, I did not feel I could possibly get them ready for that test. It wouldn't be their fault. It would be my fault. Once again, I would probably fail them.

The worst part is that in six months there will proof that I was either right or wrong. But I know I will be proven right. They aren't going to be at that "proficient" level even though I think I worked harder this year than last year.

How can I be so negative? Because last year, I thought I did a great job teaching and still the majority of my fifth grade students only reached the "basic" level of achievement. This year's class wasn't as "sharp," so why would I expect better results?

The problem with No Child Left Behind, and testing and test scores and "making growth," is that it defeats and demoralizes you as a teacher. Sure, if you make growth, it can have a positive effect. You get to do the old "I knew we could do it!" cheer.

However, if you don't make the goals year after year, it can beat up a teacher's self-confidence pretty thoroughly. How can you inspire students to "Do your best! You can reach the top!" when a teacher doesn't believe it herself because she has those blasted test scores showing that they can't? You and your school become so identified with being "underperforming" or "not good enough," it not only becomes a stigma hard to break, it becomes a self-fulfilling prophecy.

Mystery #111: "Is that all there is to teaching, worrying about test scores?"

Wise are those who learn that the bottom line, doesn't always have to be their top priority.

— *William Arthur Ward*

Wait!

To paraphrase Peggy Lee's song, "Is that all there is to teaching, worrying about test scores?" Why should I dread teaching because I'm afraid my students aren't going to do well on a state assessment test? Why I do I live in fear that I will be labeled a bad teacher even though I have taught my heart out to students who have fallen short of the proficiency goal? Sure, I'm probably not as inspirational as I could be, but I am a very nice teacher and I really like my students, well at least most of them.

Robert Fulgham got it wrong. Everything you need to know about life you learn in fifth grade. Despite not reaching the desired level of "proficiency," my students are exiting the school year much smarter than they entered. Some of the most important things I taught them won't be found on any state assessment test.

Yes, they now know how to add, subtract, divide and multiply fractions and decimals. They know how to find the area of a triangle and parallelogram and what a scalene triangle is. They learned how to read graphs and find coordinate points. Sure they might get 50% wrong on a test, but that also means they got 50% right. What's wrong with being a 50% person? These are all skills they didn't have before entering fifth grade. Isn't that still progress?

My fifth graders' days weren't just filled with math lessons. For the first time, most were taught science lessons. They learned about the systems in their body and how one isn't more important than the other. Whether it's the circulatory, respiratory, or the endocrine system, they all need to work together in order for us to live, just like all the people in a society need to work together to live.

They have learned about atoms, electrons, and protons. They know that everything is made up of matter. I hope they also learned that what matters most in life is how we treat each other.

However, my greatest accomplish this year was opening their eyes to the great country they live in and the people who sacrificed so much so we could have it all. They now know George Washington is no longer is just the face on the dollar bill they want to spend. We read that despite his great leadership, he too sometimes felt discouraged and wondered if this dream of independence for the colonies would become a reality. It didn't look good in the winter of 1777 for Washington and his men at Valley Forge who "could have tracked the army…by the blood of their feet" upon the snow because one out of three soldiers did not have any shoes. Yet not only did they survive that winter, under the guidance of a

German soldier named Friedrich von Steuben, they trained hard and became a better army. I hope they learned that sometimes when we're faced with what seems great adversity, all is not hopeless as long as you hang in there, work at making yourself better, and do not give up.

My fifth graders were taught how to write a multi-paragraph essay. But what I'm more proud of is how they learned about the power of the written word by reading the story of Thomas Paine and his *Common Sense* pamphlet, which made the colonists realize they "owe no loyalty to an unjust ruler." They also not only learned the commanding words of the Preamble of our Constitution, but they all are able to recite it from memory.

Throughout the school year, my students read stories in their language arts book about earthquakes, animals, and students their age. However none of those stories will have the significance in their lives more than a document they read in social studies written by a 33-year-old Thomas Jefferson over 240 years ago.

"We hold these truths to be self-evident, that all men are created equal, that they are endowed by their Creator with certain unalienable Rights that among these are Life, Liberty, and the Pursuit of Happiness."

Even though I doubt that any of my fifth graders will remember these exact words a year from now, I do hope the words "Declaration of Independence" will continue to have meaning for these ten- and eleven-year-olds. Most importantly, when they celebrate the Fourth of July, at least they now know it's a holiday not just about picnics and fireworks, but about a document that, as one President put it, gave "hope to the world, for all future time."

Being American is not a matter of birth.
We must practice it every day, lest we become something else.

— *Malcolm Wallop*

And teachers don't have time to teach American history because they need to devote more time to language arts to improve test scores? Many students are missing out on these important lessons about our country, including my own son whose fifth grade teacher also didn't have "time" to teach social studies. This is the bigger tragedy in our schools, not the fact test scores aren't rising!!

It is insane that teaching has become all about test scores in the first place. Yes, we all want children to do their best, however in the big scheme of life, it's not about taking an end-of- the-year test and what your test score is. It's not even about "showing growth."

What do these "results" really mean anyway? Things like the "Annual Yearly Progress" score that No Child Left Behind uses don't even compare similar children. They are comparing one group of students with another completely different group. So how scientific is that?

Each year when I get my new class of thirty-three new students, I have thirty-three new faces with unique personalities, completely different from the previous year. Since my students don't come in with the same faces as my previous year's students, why does the government assume they are coming in with the same abilities and backgrounds as my previous year's class? It is wrong to compare them to anyone, especially with a completely different class.

Do not let what you cannot do interfere with what you can do.

— *John Wooden*

So what if my class doesn't make their "growth" compared to last year's class. What does that really mean? Does this mean they won't be able to handle sixth grade? Does this mean they might not be "college material" or, better yet, good citizens? Absolutely not! All it means is they didn't do particularly well on that particular test. That's it! That is all it means!

And you know what? There's nothing to be ashamed of, if they gave it their best but came up short. Life will go on and there will be other opportunities for success, if we want to call achieving "proficiency" being successful. Everyone has something that they are good at or has a talent for and it's okay if that something isn't state assessment tests.

Why not go out on a limb?
Isn't that where the fruit is?

— Frank Scully

It isn't a mystery why I was so inspired to write this book. Though I am not in the league of Thomas Paine, I feel someone must be the voice of reason against the propaganda machine that maligns teachers and public schools under the guise of the No Child Left Behind Act. I must tame this beast by explaining to people, particularly parents who have children in public schools, the shortcomings of this well-meaning, but flawed legislation. Teachers shouldn't be demoralized. Students shouldn't be labeled. Public schools can get better, but they aren't failing us or our children either. There are millions of teachers out there who are making sure of that.

Our forefathers were poor and many lacked any formal education, let alone a so-called "good" one. By today's standards, they might even test out at a "below basic" level. But did their lack of education stop them from creating the greatest country on this planet? No.

Granted these are much different times than when 56 brave patriots signed a document proclaiming their independence from a country an ocean away. Or are they? Thomas Paine wrote in 1776, "These are the times that try men's souls." With the threat of terrorism looming at our door, an economy dependent on a non-renewable resource like oil, an influx of people entering the country illegally, and of course with our country being stuck in what often seems a hopeless situation in Iraq, who is to say that we too aren't in times that "try men's souls?"

**Knowledge cannot make us all leaders,
But it can help us decide which leader
to follow.**

— Management Digest

Our schools aren't failing children, but maybe our government is. The bigger tragedy in life is not "leaving children behind" based on some artificial and arbitrary academic achievement goal that in the big scheme of things has absolutely no relevance to the potential for success or happiness of a child. Instead, the bigger tragedy in life is "Leaving Behind to Our Children" a trillion dollar deficit and a world which requires them to fix the mistakes of the generation that was supposed to be comprised of "smarter" people than they were. Now that's a reason to want higher academic standards. Our nation can't afford to have leaders or citizenry who make poorer decisions than the ones they grew up with. We need people like those who founded our country.

While I have presented 111 mysteries about public schools, in reality, there is no mystery to what makes a good public school. It takes dedicated people, teachers and parents alike, who are committed, as Cicero said thousands of years ago, to teaching that "rising generation."

I really hope this book can help public schools be better, even if it's only in some small way. I hope it motivates you to get even a little bit more involved with your child's education and understand what teachers are up against: A clock that waits for no one and a government program that wants the impossible.

I want to think that maybe one teacher, one author, could make some small difference in helping students and parents feel better about the education they are getting at public schools.

Never forget that your child is not about what his or her test scores are on a yearly state assessment test. No matter how many years they go to school and how much knowledge they obtain, in the end, his or her success will not be determined by the number of "As" on a report card or even how much money is earned in a year.

After all is said and done, there is no mystery about what is important in life. As that old saying goes, "Teaching children to count is not as important as teaching them what counts."

What counts is teaching children that life isn't just about what we learn in school, or what our test scores are, but what we do with our lives after we leave school. That means living life to the fullest as our creator intended, cherishing friends and family, rejoicing in laughter and tears, and believing in dreams and goals. Most importantly, it means leaving behind the world a better place than we found it.

About the author

Debra Craig is a resident of Moreno Valley, California, but grew up on a farm in northern Colorado. She received a Bachelor of Arts degree from Colorado Women's College where she majored in Organizational Communications. Debra has been a teacher for the Moreno Valley School District for seven years, after a successful 13-year career as a supermarket cashier for Ralphs Grocery Chain. Debra also worked 12-years for American Multi-Cinema and two years for the Riverside Press-Enterprise.

Even though her passion for writing lied dormant for many years, it came alive while she was working the express lane at Ralphs. Even back then, Debra had a "wondering" mind. She couldn't figure out many peculiarities about supermarkets. Why was the express lane the slowest lane when it was designed to be the quickest? Why do people like to pay in the express lane with loose coin only found at the bottom of a deep, dark purse? Which tastes better, store brand corn flakes or Kelloggs' corn flakes? What does the recipe on the back of the Shake 'N Bake box taste like?

Not wanting to waste the talent of her inquiring mind, Debra contemplated a career with *The National Enquirer* or writing a monthly newsletter called, *The Supermarket Checker*. Because she didn't like the humid Florida weather, Debra launched her newsletter which became an almost instant success with supermarket shoppers all across America. *The Supermarket Checker* was mentioned in *USA Today*, the *LA Times*, the *Riverside Press-Enterprise, St. Louis Post-Dispatch* to name a few of the fine newspapers who spread the news about her newsletter with their readers. Debra also made television appearances on two nationally-syndicated morning shows, The Home Show and the Mike & Maty Show. (Yes, those were real shows.)

But that was then, this is now. Debra is married to husband Gary, a Los Angeles City firefighter/paramedic, and has two children, Jenna and Matthew. She also has a stepson, Jonathan, whom she is very proud of. He is currently serving in the United States Navy.

Once she obtained her life long dream of becoming a supermarket checker and teacher, Debra realized the sky is the limit in the goals and dreams she can accomplish. Besides becoming a full time writer and public speaker, Debra's other lofty ambitions include finally getting her desk organized, watching every Lifetime movie made, and appearing on The Daily Show with Jon Stewart, The View, and maybe Oprah Winfrey to promote her book.

Debra can be reached at Debracraig@hotmail.com
or via the mail at
P.O. Box 1226
Moreno Valley, CA 92556